THE ESSENTIAL COLLEGE SURVIVAL HANDBOOK

THE ESSENTIAL COLLEGE SURVIVAL HANDBOOK

An Insider's Guide to Making College Work for You

RALPH AND VALERIE CARNES

Playboy Press

Copyright © 1981 by Ralph and Valerie Carnes.

All rights reserved. No part of this book may be reproduced, stored in a retrieval system or transmitted in any form by an electronic, mechanical, photocopying, recording means or otherwise, without prior written permission of the author.

Manufactured in the United States of America
FIRST EDITION

Library of Congress Cataloging in Publication Data
Carnes, Ralph L.
   The essential college survival handbook.
    1. College student orientation—Handbooks, manuals, etc. 2. College, choice of—Handbooks, manuals, etc. I. Carnes, Valerie. II. Title.
LB2343.3.C36   1981   378'.198   80-84881
ISBN 0-87223-684-6   AACR2

Playboy Press/A division of PEI Books, Inc.

This book is dedicated to Roosevelt University, Chicago, Illinois.

Twenty years before it was popular to do so, President James Sparling and the founders of Roosevelt University had the courage to make a commitment to the ideas of liberal education, to provide upward mobility to a diverse urban population, regardless of race, color, creed, or national origin.

Under the leadership of President Rolf A. Weil, Roosevelt has had the fortitude to remain faithful to that commitment, and to make it a day-to-day reality for its students and faculty.

The entire educational community owes Roosevelt University a debt of gratitude. It was the national pioneer that led the way for everybody else.

Contents

ACKNOWLEDGMENTS ix
PREFACE xi
INTRODUCTION xiii

PART ONE
CHOOSING A COLLEGE

1. *Starting Off the Right Way*   3
2. *Narrowing the Choices*   31
3. *Long-Range Planning:*
   A Few Preliminary Notes   51
4. *How to Get into the College You Choose*   56

PART TWO
GETTING READY TO GO

5. *What to Do When You're Accepted*   91
6. *Putting Your Pad Together*   117
7. *Putting Your Wardrobe Together*   133
8. *What to Do if You're a Special Case*   151
9. *For Women Only*   176

PART THREE
DIGGING IN FOR THE DURATION

10.	Sources of Information	191
11.	Planning a Program	203
12.	Learning How to Study Effectively	235
13.	A Few Political Considerations	266

SOURCES AND RESOURCES   307

Acknowledgments

SPECIAL THANKS are due to:

The administration, faculty, staff, and students of Roosevelt University, particularly Art Eckberg, Lily Rose, Dave Steere, Chuck Simmons, Mary Kevlin, Edith Nicholas, Phil Stevens, Elaine Davis, Robert Franklin, Phyllis Stroup, Randall Jackson, and Curt Clemmer, for the information and technical expertise they shared with us.

Roosevelt president, Rolf A. Weil, and all the members of the Administrative Council, who provided us with many years of wise counsel, stimulating debate, and priceless insights into the realities of maintaining a fine university on a day-to-day, year-by-year basis.

The faculty of Roosevelt University, including dear friends, friends, and friendly enemies, whether Saints, Enlightened Nobility, Corrupt Cardinals, Scholastics, Defenders of the Faith, Young Priests, or Heretics, False Prophets, and Other Sinners. It is easily the most dedicated group of people we've ever known, and we can't praise them too highly, however exasperating or inspiring they might be at one time or the other.

Annie Coleman—dear Annie, whom we love—for being our friend and sister.

Dominick Abel, for more reasons than we could list on this page.

Preface

THE MESSAGE of this book is simple and direct; it is a practical, no-nonsense guide that gives the inside details not only of survival in college but of success there as well.

This kind of information is hard to come by. College recruitment pamphlets are self-serving; high school counselors often get kickbacks for steering students toward certain campuses; preference tests and career profiles are sometimes superficial and unreliable. Even with all the pre-college counseling, most students take potluck when they get there.

The grubby details of going to college are seldom covered by either advisers or recruiters. Most of the time, prospective students won't really know which questions to ask. This book tells them what they need to know before they make a choice, and what they need to do once they arrive on campus.

So if you are trying to decide where to go, or if you're already in college and you want to make the most of it, or if you're getting ready to transfer to another school and you want to do it right this time, this is the book for you. Whatever your situation, you'll do better in college if you read this book.

Introduction

A FEW horror stories, just to let you know how serious all this is:

· Joe Glitch, a high school junior, was unable to get a lead on a summertime job, so he dropped by the counseling office in his high school. He had been told that the office kept files on jobs.

Unfortunately, the counselor Joe saw had just finished a refresher course in testing. By the time Joe left, he didn't have a lead on a job; instead he had been set up for a "forestry preparatory sequence." He didn't want to be a forester, but the preference tests indicated that he was ideally suited to sit in lookouts scanning the woods for fires.

What Joe really liked to do was read and write, and he wanted to be alone when he did it. He liked to go fishing in the forest, since it was one of the ways he could find the solitude he needed to read and write. The counselor never dug deeply enough to find out what Joe really wanted to do, and settled on a mistaken interpretation of the testing data.

It took Joe two years to argue his way out of forestry school. He was a great disappointment to his high school counselor.

· Gertie Schlemiel knew little of the ways of college. She did pretty well there, considering the fact that she had been out of high school five years before she started. In the second semester of her sophomore year, she heard about the Graduate Record Exams (GREs).

Since she wanted to go to graduate school, she dropped by the philosophy department office to get some advice: What are the Graduate Record Exams, where do I take them, and when does all this happen?

The chairman of the department, lost as usual in his own research, didn't pay very close attention. He told Gertie that she would have to take the exams two weeks hence in order to get the data into the record in time to be considered for graduate admission.

Gertie studied hard, took the exams, and performed fairly well, considering the fact that she had had only two philosophy courses.

The catch, of course, was that she was two years premature in taking the exams. The department chairman assumed that Gertie was a senior. Gertie assumed that the chairman knew what he was talking about. She carried those scores around her neck like an albatross for the next five years, since once she had taken the exams they were "on the record." Had she taken them as a senior, she would have turned in a great set of exams. As it was, she did what a second-quarter sophomore could be expected to do.

The fact that Gertie got the wrong advice from an indifferent chairman made no difference at all to the admissions committee. She got into graduate school, but on the strength of her course work.

· Norman Schlimazl didn't study the college catalog when he started as a freshman. Instead, he went to the undergraduate associate dean and let him do the interpreting for him. Unfortunately for poor Norman, that was the year that Crawling Ivy was trying to beef up the enrollment in its flagging classics department, in order to justify hiring more professors. By the time Norman got away from the associate dean, he was committed to a year of Greek.

He didn't need it for his major.

He didn't have the languages background for the course.

Twenty-eight other students took Greek that fall quarter. By the beginning of the winter quarter, eighteen were left.

Introduction

By the end of the spring quarter, only Norman and four other people were left.

Norman has never read any Greek since then, and he has never had occasion to use the Greek he learned, since none of the waiters in the Greek restaurants speak Ionic or Attic Greek of the first millennium B.C.

Better he had read the catalog!

· And then there was Al Glitch, Joe's brother. He put off taking certain courses until his senior year. Surprise! The courses, requirements for graduation, weren't offered during his senior year. As it turned out, it wasn't his senior year after all. He had to wait until the following year to graduate.

· Last but not least there was Josephine Snafu, who made straight A's in English at Chicken Lick Community College. When she transferred to the big state university, she thought she would be a whiz at English. Unfortunately, the gap between the standards of Chicken Lick and those of the state university was so great that Josephine spent the first nine months of her junior year trying to learn how to write a clear, clean sentence. Back at Chicken Lick, everybody had been friends, but nobody had really tried to teach anybody anything. They didn't want to force their structure on other human beings. Get the picture?

Farfetched? Afraid not. All of these stories are about real people we've known at different points in our careers. If you are planning to go to college, what you do for the next few years will have a profound effect on your life. We want to help you make sure that you do the right things. We'll tell you how to avoid being a schlemiel and a schlimazl, and perhaps we can steer you away from some glitches.

We'll also give you some laughs along the way.

PART ONE

CHOOSING A COLLEGE

1

Starting Off the Right Way

SO YOU'RE THINKING of going to college? Good! Let's start with the basics first—the GPA, class rank, extracurricular activities—all the things that count toward making you desirable "college material," as admissions committees like to put it.

You're probably in high school—a junior, we hope, but more likely a senior who has waited until the very last minute to start thinking about where you're going and how to get in. Or maybe you're a less-than-recent graduate who has been out of school for a few years, has decided that the big world out there is pretty bleak without a degree, and now would like to crawl back behind the ivy for a while. Maybe you're a veteran who would like to make good use of those VA benefits. Or a person who has decided that he or she must have some college credits to advance one step higher in the company.

Whatever your situation, this chapter is for you, to help make the whole decision-making process a bit easier. For, given the tight economic market and the number of want ads that list the B.A. or B.S. as a prerequisite, college is becoming more a necessity than a luxury these days. True, a degree—even the much-touted M.B.A.—is no longer a guarantee of money or success. But it's still the minimal set of credentials, the necessary "union card" that's required for credibility in the job market.

It's been said many times before but we'll say it again: The choice of a college is important—in fact, it's probably among the two or three most important decisions you'll make in your entire life. Whether you intend to stop at the bachelor's level, go on to the M.A., M.S., or M.B.A., or get graduate or professional training, these four years of undergraduate training are extremely significant. They determine the kind of job you'll be able to command, how much you'll be paid, the kind of further training you'll require—and also the friends you'll make, the clubs you'll belong to, the books you'll read, and what you'll do with the rest of your time. Quite possibly, they'll even determine your choice of marriage partner; many people still *do* meet on campuses. In a very real sense, then, these four years determine—or help to determine—the direction of the rest of your life.

So make your decision with care. Don't feel that you have to decide on a college within a few weeks or even months. Give yourself plenty of time to read, shop around, think, plan, talk, and consider all the alternatives. Talk with friends, relatives, neighbors, and strangers. If possible, start visiting college campuses in your area as early as sophomore year in high school. Try to spend a weekend with a friend or relative who is a student somewhere. (If you don't know someone, and ask ahead of time, often the college you're visiting will arrange for you to spend a night in an empty dorm room.) Spend at least a day walking around the campus, lunching in the Student Union or cafeteria, sitting in the coffee shop, browsing in the library, and generally looking over the facilities. Visit some labs and sit in on a class in your favorite subject if at all possible; take a look around the field house or gym; and drop by a fraternity house if you've any interest in the Greeks. By all means, eat at least one meal on campus. And talk to as many students, faculty members, counselors, and administrators as you can. The more you know, the better equipped you'll be to make the right choice when the time comes.

Other sources of information: college catalogs (become a collector!), your local newspaper's College Guides (start saving back issues), your high school career or placement counselor, the public library, popular magazines. Men and women alike might plan to look at the August issues of such magazines as *Seventeen* and *Glamour*; although they're targeted specifically for women, they have some very informative articles about various colleges and college survival strategies. Recently, too, their College Advisory Boards have included a healthy sprinkling of not-so-token males. And of course, there's *Playboy*'s annual college issue, which has current info and ratings of major campuses across the nation.

OK, so you're in the process of gathering information. What else can you do to get yourself started on the right track?

GPA, CLASS RANK, AND EXTRACURRICULAR ACTIVITIES

Our first advice is to tackle the hardest part first: raise your grade-point average, or GPA, as it's called in academese. While it's no longer true that the GPA solely determines who will be admitted and who gets turned away, those numbers are still very important. No matter how high your test scores, how prestigious your family or social connections, or how articulate you prove to be in the final admissions interview, the GPA can still be the decisive factor. All other things being equal, a college admissions office will bet on the person with a high GPA. And *all* colleges, from the Ivy League on down to the lowliest local junior college, have certain minimum admissions standards—that is, they all have a certain GPA (usually in the C to C-plus range) below which you *cannot* fall and still be admitted. It is usually in the C range, but better check before you get ready to apply, not afterward.

How do you determine what your GPA is? The calculations actually are done by your high school registrar or by the principal's or headmaster's office. But it's helpful to know how the points are figured. Most schools have a system of assigning so many quality points to a letter grade: typically, $A = 4$, $B = 3$, $C = 2$, $D = 1$, and $F = 0$. For each "academic" course per semester (that is, a course that has academic content, such as English, math, or history, and is not simply a "credit/no-credit" course such as chorus, physical education, or shop) you get so many quality points, depending on your grade. Let's say you have a semester in which you earn three B's, one C, and one A. Your total average for the semester will be 3.0 (B). Your overall average for the four years of high school will be computed in the same way: a composite total of all your courses in all your terms (including summer) will be compiled for an *overall GPA*.

How to go about bettering your GPA? Well, like most things academic, it can't be done overnight. Slow and steady wins the race. *Don't*—we repeat, DON'T—wait until the final semester of your senior year and then go into a crash program the week before finals in the hopes of pulling six A's and raising that shaky C-minus average to a respectable C-plus. It just can't be done. Instead, start thinking total GPA early in your high school career. Freshman year is the best time, sophomore is next best, and junior year is a poor third. Senior year, alas, is almost too late. Unless you're pulling down strong grades by then, you might need to postpone or rethink your plans for immediate college entry.

As for raising the GPA, the most obvious strategy is to study harder, or at least more efficiently (see our tips for effective study later in this book). You'll have to raise your average by getting higher grades in your academic courses. If you're desperate and have little time to raise your average, try shopping for some "second-string" academic courses to raise the average: current events, political science, psychology, sociology, marriage and the family; some creative writing, art, or music courses. And certain health education and phys. ed. courses may be less demanding than trigonometry or plane geometry and thus can help you load your transcript with B's and A's. But be careful before you load up on Chorus, marriage and the family, business-letter writing, and driver education in the hopes of pulling a straight-A average. Most schools limit the number of such courses you can take as credit toward the diploma. Many high schools don't count phys. ed. courses at all in the total quality points needed for graduation. Check it all out before you make your move.

Don't assume, either, that all the nonacademic courses are automatically easy. Many are quite as demanding in their own way as world history or second-year French. You *can* flunk typing, home economics, shop, driver education, and even PE! A word to the wise: don't count on the automatic A or B unless you have some special facility in the course. Ye clumsy and uncoordinated—shy away from tennis and basketball! Likewise on typing: if you can't spell or are "all thumbs," forget the stenographic and typing route. You'll do better to stick with an academic area in which you have some real talent. If you're a whiz with numbers, skip English history in favor of more math courses and a whirl with data processing. Verbal people should go for the poetry, creative writing, literature, and journalism courses and take less of the numbers work. And so on.

What if you're already long out of school, a college dropout looking toward college again? And you're doing your looking with a slightly worried frown on your face, too, since that GPA is nothing to write home about. Sure, you should have studied, but then your freshman year turned out to be the Year of the Big Party. And what with the real essentials—dates, cars, movies, the job, the family—college got shunted to the bottom of your list of priorities, and your GPA is thus considerably less than a C. In that case, consider raising your average with CLEP testing (more of that later), a short hitch in a junior college, or a probationary period in the college of your choice where you take a part-time load and perhaps some remedial work until you've brought the average up to par.

Another factor that will undoubtedly have a bearing on

your admission is your class rank, or your place in the class based on GPA relative to the other students who graduate with you. The college admissions office, remember, deals with students from many different high schools, large and small, urban and rural. Some it knows by reputation; others it's never heard of. The admissions office may not know anything about your school's grading system, standards, level of difficulty, or general academic standing. Therefore, it doesn't mean much to say that you got an A in marriage and the family at dear old Ragweed High or even to say that your overall average was B-plus. What *is* significant to the admissions office is your class rank—the number that says you were eleventh in a class of 354 or forty-seventh in a class of 916. These figures are significant because they set you in relation with other students of your same age and locale. Also, tests and GPA aside, class rank is one of the more reliable predictors of success in college—and admissions officers traditionally like to bet on a sure thing.

Of course, class rank is very much dependent on school and class size and severity of standards. It may be easy for a student from a small suburban or rural high school to attain a high rank; much more difficult for the big-city student who has to compete against a thousand or more students. But class rank remains important and will continue to be so, as long as admissions officers tend as they do to "go by the book." The simplest solution? Raise your GPA, consider both your required and elective classes as opportunities to enhance your rank, be selective with extracurriculars, and study, study, study. That's the only sure means to college admissions after all!

What else goes on your high school record besides the GPA and class rank? Extracurricular activities—and the more the better, right?

Wrong! You may think that the more activities, clubs, sports, service organizations, committees, and publications you can list to your credit, the more favorably the admissions officer or committee will look on you. But more likely, this man or woman (or group of men and women) will look at all your whirlwind of furious activity and ask, "So when did that person ever study?"

The key is selectivity: finding activities that are really significant, interesting, and related in some way to your future interests, major subject area in college, or career/profession. Hence, if you're considering a literature or journalism major, by all means go all out for the school newspaper, annual, literary magazine, creative writing fraternity, writers' workshops, and theater productions. On the other hand, joining the Ragweed Boosters, the Ragweed cheering squad, and the Ragweed basketball team may just help to create the image of a less-than-serious student who is so involved in extracurricular "joining" that he or she neglects his or her studies.

The extracurricular activities you choose (two or three at most) should be significant ones—things with some "meat" in them, such as a serious sport, a publication, a theatrical or musical activity, a charitable or philanthropic cause. Most admissions officers agree that they'd much rather see a student do well—really well—with a few important activities than join everything in sight. Depth and selectivity are more important here than just numbers or names of clubs.

Obviously, schools being what they are, selecting an extracurricular activity in an area where your prospective college excels doesn't hurt at all. If your choice of alma mater is a school known for a super-good soccer or hockey team, your one sport might just be soccer or hockey. If running is the thing at old Crawling Ivy, then get into marathons before you apply. If the school is heavily into journalism or theater or political action or canoeing or tennis, then take your cue from that and try to present some activities that parallel these strengths. Athletic or arts scholarships aside, the similarity of interests will come out strongly on your application.

TESTS, TESTS, AND MORE TESTS

SAT! ATP! ETS! PSAT! NSMQT! ACT! The very names sound like a veritable alphabet soup calculated to strike terror into the hearts of even the bravest of souls. *Testing*: it's the one ordeal of college admissions that can bring bookworms and athletes, bespectacled scholars, and partygoers to their knees in sheer terror.

We've all heard the horror stories, of course: the straight-A student who blows one test and is forever banished from his rightful place in the ivy. And then there's the star athlete with a decent average, a scintillating personality, a moderately good track record of extracurriculars who lands the dream athletic scholarship—and suddenly the test scores come in, the verbal OK but the math way under par—and the scholarship disappears as mysteriously as it came. And we've all heard tell of the mediocre student who bumbles through his courses with just-passing grades and goes into a test unshaven and hung over, held together with No-Doz and black coffee, only to learn two months later that his scores were just short of the miraculous as he starts getting offers from all the big-league schools on the strength of that one day's performance.

Interesting stories, all of them, and fine for retelling on rainy nights in the frat house or dorm. Still, it's consoling that most of them are either untrue or so grossly distorted that even the principals would find them unrecognizable. The tests simply are neither that terrible nor that important.

Let's clear up a few common misconceptions. First, few, if any, contemporary universities or colleges make the standardized tests the sole basis for admission. And few weight them as heavily as they once did—for many complex reasons, some of which we'll treat later in this chapter. So dismiss the idea that you can make or break your college admission solely on the basis of one morning or afternoon of tests. It just doesn't happen, lunchroom scuttlebut to the contrary.

Second, remember that all colleges do not require all the tests for admission. Given the current economy and general patterns of declining enrollment, fewer and fewer colleges are as rigid in their test requirements as a decade ago. True, there was a time, when the "baby boom" children were first starting college, when every school, from Harvard and Yale down to Podunk U., made the entire roster of standardized tests a must. But now the attitude is much more relaxed. While most schools require—or at least "strongly recommend"—the tests, few will base an admission or rejection solely on test scores. If you have been a good-to-average high school student and happen to test poorly, the admissions officer will probably take a second look at your other credentials—class rank, GPA, extracurricular activities—and ask for a second opinion or supplementary materials. Remember that what admissions officers are looking for is a pattern to the data that will indicate what sort of college "risk" you are, that is, what the odds are of your probable success or failure. Great discrepancies between high school records and test scores (doing either much better or much worse on the tests than your records would seem to predict) usually invite not outright rejection, but further looks at your credentials.

Now let's take a quick look at some of the major tests that you'll be required to take, or at least know about. First, there's the SAT (Scholastic Aptitude Test), which is used along with your high school record and other information to assess your ability for college work. The test lasts for two and a half hours and is entirely multiple-choice in format. The verbal section tests reading comprehension and vocabulary range. The math portion covers arithmetic, algebra, and geometry.

There is also a thirty-minute supplement to the SAT called TSWE (Test of Standard Written English) which tests your ability to write standard (correct, grammatical, formal or informal) English. The TSWE score, if applicable to you, is used slightly differently by each college. Some schools use it to determine what level of freshman English you should enter; others use it to determine if you are eligible for exemption from freshman composition. If you take this supplement, check with your prospective college for further details on how it is to be used. Probably you'll need to take it only if you're a foreign student, have learned English as a second language, or have demonstrated marked difficulties with standard English.

The SAT is part of the entire ATP, or Admissions Testing Program, administered by the College Entrance Examination Board (CEEB) in conjunction with the Educational Testing Service (ETS) located in Princeton, N.J. The SAT differs from the Achievement Tests, also administered by the ATP, in one important respect: the SAT is intended to measure the general intellectual abilities you have developed over your lifetime, while the Achievement Tests measure proficiency in special subject areas. The SAT is administered nationwide six times during the school year: November, December, January, March, May, and June. A special October testing is sometimes arranged and given in special locations, but this is a limited, not a general, testing. The test is administered at literally hundreds of schools in the United States; your local college testing or placement office will have specific information on request.

Fifteen one-hour subject matter Achievement Tests are offered on the same test dates as the SAT and the Test of Standard Written English. These Achievement Tests measure the skills and knowledge that students have developed in certain well-defined subject areas. Remember that you can take either the SAT or three one-hour Achievement Tests in a single morning—but not both.

Students can select preferred subjects for the Achievement Tests. The range is wide: American history, social studies, biology, chemistry, English composition, European history and world cultures, French, German, Spanish, Russian, Hebrew, Latin, literature, mathematics (levels I and II), and physics.

The language proficiency tests measure only reading ability. There are reading/listening tests which are available individually through some schools, but these are no longer offered nationally. If you are interested in demonstrating speaking or listening ability in a foreign language, check with the school(s) of your choice to see if they offer additional testing.

For specific information on testing dates and a calendar of which Achievement Tests are given on which dates, consult your high school testing or counseling office or contact the CEEB for dates and a booklet describing the Achievement Tests.

There is also a battery of tests administered by the American College Testing Program (for information about the ACT Assessment Program, write to ACTP, P.O. Box 168, Iowa City, Iowa 52240). It consists of four tests: (1) the English Usage Test—75 items, 40 minutes; (2) the Mathematics Test—40 items, 50 minutes; (3) the Social Studies Reading Test—52 items, 35 minutes; and (4) the Natural Sciences Reading Test—52 items, 35 minutes. As in the SAT, the questions are all multiple-choice.

The ACT battery is scored test by test, with each possible score ranging from 1 to 35. The composite final score is an average of the four individual test scores. The maximum composite score is 35 and the average is about 20; most ACT test takers fall in the broad range between 15 and 25.

Several weeks after you take the ACT battery, your SPR, or Student Profile Report, is sent out to you, to the colleges or universities you list on your registration form, and to your high school counseling or placement office. The SPR will contain scores for the four academic tests, an average of the four scores, information on your experiences, interests, and goals (which is collected from information you supply on the ACT Interest Inventory and its Student Profile Section), and some information for you about the colleges receiving your SPR.

The tests are normally given on a Saturday morning and are scheduled five times a year: October, December, February, April, and June. Registration begins about ten weeks before the test date and closes about a month before. Get an ACT information/registration booklet from your high school counseling or placement office and follow the registration instructions given there. About three weeks after you've sent in your registration folder to ACTP, you should get a form admitting you to one of the local testing centers on a specified date.

The National Merit Scholarships are awarded each year by the National Merit Scholarship Corporation to about four thousand winners nationwide. The Corporation also sponsors an achievement program which tries to increase educational opportunities for minority students across the nation. The test (PSAT/NMSQT) is administered by the College Entrance Examination Board and the National Merit Scholarship Corporation (the scholarship-granting body) in conjunction with ETS (the Educational Testing Service). Taking the PSAT (Preliminary Scholastic Aptitude Test) qualifies you to compete in the National Merit Scholarship Program (if you request that scores be sent to the Corporation)—hence the test's other name, NMSQT. The test can be taken only once in a school year, at the time it is normally administered (October). High school counseling offices will have the exact date and location of the test, or you can write directly to the granting foundation: National Merit Scholarship Corporation, Educational Services Department, 1 American Plaza, Evanston, Ill. 60201, or to PSAT/NMSQT, Box 1025, Berkeley, California 94701.

The test itself measures verbal and mathematical ability and thus serves as a sort of preview of the SAT. It's an hour and forty minutes in length and is multiple-choice in format. The verbal section lasts fifty minutes and the mathematical fifty minutes. The verbal portion focuses on reading comprehension and vocabulary range; the mathematical portion includes problems drawn from arithmetic, algebra, and geometry.

The tests, you should remember, are *not* a substitute for the SAT. Admissions offices will not (generally) accept them in lieu of the SAT. However, aside from putting you in the running for National Merit Scholarships (which are certainly among the most prestigious of all scholarships available to high school students today), they may also serve a useful diagnostic function for you and your high school counselor or adviser. They give some indication of your abilities in two important areas (verbal and mathematical); also, they suggest how well or badly you test, where you place relative to other high school students nationally, and what areas of strength or weakness you have. Just remember that the tests serve these very specific functions, and don't expect them to function as replacements for the SAT.

Now for some practical specifics on the tests themselves. Let's answer some of the usual queries first: for example, the advisability of taking the tests several times; whether or not scores can be canceled; the desirability of guessing, and so on.

As far as taking the tests more than once is concerned, the answer is generally yes, you can. Most of the tests have rules governing how often and when you may be retested. The SAT, for example, can be taken more than once—in fact, it's not uncommon for students to be tested several times. But you should know that your ATP score reporting is cumulative—that is, your total report will include scores from up to five previous test dates. So it's not just your highest scores that will be scrutinized; it's a composite of *all* your scores.

The ACT assessment battery can be retaken, although the ATP doesn't recommend it. The ATP also states that if you retake this test battery, you must complete all four pages of the registration folder over again. PSAT/NMSQT can be retaken, but be aware that the test is given only once a year, in October, so plan your scheduled repetitions accordingly.

In regard to test score cancellations (when you ask that your test not be scored, even though you have taken it), ACT Assessment tests and PSAT scores can be cancelled only by notifying your test supervisor *before* you leave the examination room. SAT is a little more lenient: you can cancel on the day of the test only, by telling the testing center supervisor or by writing or telegraphing the College Board ATP. Then your score report will record your official cancellation, along with any completed test scores. Generally, however, you shouldn't cancel a test score if you have completed a sizeable portion of the test; instead, go ahead and receive the score, learn from it, and then take the test again.

And that brings us to the subject of preparing for the tests. All the "authorities," testing boards and agencies take the position that you need only a general understanding of test-taking strategies to get through a test; that subject matter review will help only in a limited sense—you either know the material or you don't. However, many test takers claim significant increases in test scores as a result of preparation. And since there are so many excellent guidebooks on the market, why not use one? If nothing else, it will give you a better sense of the test format and how to structure your time during the test. If you like to feel prepared, then by all means invest a few dollars in a guide to the particular test you're scheduled to take—Monarch, Barron, and Cliff's Notes all put out excellent ones. You need everything going for you that you can muster.

As for guessing, every test maker has its own advice on this strategy. ACT says openly that since there's no penalty for guessing on the ACT battery, it's to your advantage to try to answer every question. SAT and PSAT, however, are a different matter. If you can logically eliminate one or more of the answers offered for a multiple-choice question, then it's to your advantage to guess, since it's no longer a completely "wild guess." But these tests discourage totally wild guessing of the eeeny-meeny-miney-mo variety by subtracting a fraction of a point for every wrong answer. However, no points are subtracted if you leave the answer blank. Obviously you must make wise judgments about guessing if you are to score high. The test guides can be an invaluable help in training you to make educated guesses and thus increase your testing ability. Remember, test taking *is* a strategy, a game, and the better a player you are, the better your scores will be.

How do colleges rate these scores? Again, much depends on the college itself. Richard Moll, in a book called *Playing the Private College Admissions Game*, reports that Brandeis University weighs class rank about 45 percent, personal ratings (recommendations and admissions essay, etc.) about 30 percent, and SAT and Achievement Test scores about 25 percent. Obviously, other colleges may assign either more or less importance to the scores, depending on how high or low their professed (and actual) admission standards are, how desperate they are for students in a particular semester, and how good or bad your particular records, exclusive of the tests, may be. You may or may not know that there has been a very dramatic decline in SAT scores over the last fifteen years, which prompted a blue-ribbon committee commissioned by the CEEB to analyze the phenomenon. The 1977 report attributed the decline to "the reduction in required or core courses, less interest in and attention to the mastery of skills and knowledge in high school, the influence of television as opposed to reading, the general disruption of education in the sixties and seventies, and the diminution of 'learning motivation' in high-school-aged young people."

You may or may not agree with the committee's reasoning, but in a sense this decline in overall test scores nationwide is to your advantage. While you'll undoubtedly be competing against some strong, highly motivated test takers, chances are that the majority of people also applying for the spots in your college will be average or below average—and thus will have scores that are about on a par with, probably below, yours. Don't let this make you overconfident, but on the other hand, don't go into the tests already defeated. Often mediocre students with a C average or worse score surprisingly well on the tests—and this is exactly the kind of student the colleges are often looking for. So give it your best effort and you'll be happily surprised at the results.

Still not ready to test without a few more survival tips? Well, here goes:

· A word of warning first: don't let these reassurances lull you into total complacency! Don't go into the testing center with the idea that any answer will do, that the tests are just a hurdle and don't count toward your admission. They still do matter—despite the furor over cultural, racist, and sexist biases, and despite the difficulties you personally may have with dragging your poor, sleepy, hungover self out of bed on a cold Saturday morning to spend the day multiple-guessing with the ETS. Believe us: it *is* worth it to take the tests seriously and to try to do as well as humanly possible on them. Give the day your most careful attention. But also, try to maintain that delicate balance between taking the questions seriously (no "Mickey Mouse" answers, please) and becoming so uptight over the whole process that you're literally scared out of your wits. A little anxiety probably helps rather than hurts—a healthy dose of adrenalin makes for top performance; on the other hand, a bad case of nerves or the shakes can blow the whole day.

· Let's say you're really a poor tester and you know it. You freeze on every math quiz, shake like a leaf at the sight of answer sheets and Number 2 pencils, lose ten pounds during exam week, and agonize over every word in your term paper. Is there hope for you?

Yes, there really are such things as the classic "poor testers." Some of them are just extraordinarily nervous people; a few have neuromotor or nervous disorders that skew their test results; a few are just psychologically incapable of working through a test without a tremendous lot of anxiety. Others don't get particularly nervous; they just don't deal well with multiple-choice, true-false, and other typical question formats.

If you're one of the super-nervous types, it helps to know yourself. Prepare as adequately as possible as far in advance as you can. Get a good night's sleep before the test and eat a high-protein breakfast when you get up. A game of tennis or a short run (nothing too exhausting) the night before the test may help you unwind and sleep. So may the old reliable remedy: a glass of hot milk before bedtime. But beware of tranquilizers and alcohol; they can oversedate you so that you approach the test dragged-out and sleepy, not calm and alert.

· We've talked about test preparation already, but let's hit it again. There *is* such a thing as overpreparing, to the point where you feel nervous and uptight about testing "strategies," overcomplicate every answer and try to second-guess the test makers even on simple questions of fact. On the other hand, if you're totally unfamiliar with the format and general idea behind the tests, you may do less well although you know the material factually.

Much of your decision on whether or not to prepare depends on your own academic style. Do you like to wing it, or are you comfortable only when super-prepared? If the former, read through a testing guide once or twice to familiarize yourself with the types of questions, relax and watch the tube the night before, and then go at it with your usual style. Chances are you'll do fine. But if you don't like taking chances, then get the study guides, go through them carefully, and do all the sample questions not once but several times. Also, you can create your own study program: a review of your old trig, geometry, and algebra notes for the math portion; vocabulary guides, rhetoric, or English texts for the verbal. For the Achievement Tests, focus on basic texts or outline-series paperbacks in history, chemistry, biology, physics. Take out your old language cassettes or workbooks if a language is one of the areas you've opted for. Just make sure you spend the time studying for the tests, not worrying about them.

- Suppose your aim is really to ace the tests. What's a reasonable length of time for preparation? Should you really start back in freshman or sophomore year, as some test junkies will tell you? (Remember, Gertie Schlemiel started first term of her sophomore year on the SAT verbals and still made only the top tenth percentile). Or is a quickie review the weekend before going to be sufficient for you?

Again, it pays to know thyself—and to know the school you're planning to enter. If your aim is a topflight score that will clearly qualify you for the Ivy League, several months of fairly intensive work may not be too much time to spend. Get some good basic texts in addition to the test-preparation guides, budget a certain amount of time each week for the review (say an hour to two hours a day), and stick to your schedule.

If, on the other hand, you're concerned only with passing scores, and the college of your choice isn't too picky about the difference between a 730 and a 735, a few days of preparation may be all you'll need. A comprehensive test guide and your old class notes, skimmed a few days before the test, will get you through in fine form.

• Do consider joining a test-preparation course, class, or workshop if you're particularly anxious or ill-prepared. Many schools now offer some preparatory work. Or often students who plan to take the tests form informal study groups and work independently. Several may pool their funds and hire a tutor or instructor in subjects like math or science or other "high anxiety" areas. Consider joining such a group. You can learn both from instructors and fellow students, and you and your friends can keep one another psyched up for the big day.

• Try to go into the tests in top physical shape. *You* may think it's the height of bravado to take the ACT stoned, hung over, or woozy from lack of sleep. But the ATP and ETS won't even recognize the grand gesture. So try to resist the urge to hit the local opium den or watering-hole the night before the big day. Eat something substantial but light—no tacos or refried beans unless you *like* frequent breaks for popping another antacid tablet and listening to your rumbling innards during the test. Go to bed early and plan to get up a half-hour early. Get your head and body together for the test. Time for a shower and a leisurely cup of coffee can do wonders for your mental state—and your test scores!

- Sometimes the unexpected happens, however, and you have to face test day with a galloping case of flu, hay fever, Montezuma's revenge, or the scrapes and cuts from a minor accident or injury. In that case, postpone, if feasible. Investigate alternative dates and see what can be done toward changing to the next date. (Another advantage to starting the procedure early—you aren't chained to one test time.) If it's impossible to switch, get yourself feeling as good as is humanly possible. Plenty of aspirin, hot tea, and vitamin C can do wonders for a cold within twenty-four hours, so you may feel much better the actual day of the test. If you were seriously ill or injured when you were tested, have your physician make note of the specifics and how they might have affected your test performance. If the results are marginal, a note from your M.D. might just convince the admissions officer to allow for a retest or a second look at your results.
- While you're in the actual test, don't feel too intimidated to ask questions. Matters such as time limits, the way to mark answers properly, utilization of break times, going back to an unfinished part, and so on are proper questions to raise. Testers will sometimes answer questions as to whether or not to guess. Here, knowledge of the various tests is important but, if you forget, ask the test official. Don't feel you're asking something "dumb"—your fellow test takers will love you for asking. But be sure to bring these matters up before the test starts, not afterward.

And remember that a testing center official (often a student aide or assistant) can answer only certain types of questions: no factual stuff, no decisions between two possible answers, or comments on the frame of reference or the theory behind such-and-such a question. Confine yourself to questions about test *format* if you want to be answered.

• Check out time limits in advance. You'll do well to follow them closely, though not rigidly. Don't shortchange yourself by forgetting to doublecheck your answers—particularly crucial in math, foreign language, and English tests, where accuracy and attention to detail are important.

But don't try to give yourself extra time by skipping breaks or lunch. (In any case, that's usually not permissible, since the tests are timed to the minute.) The breaks are scheduled for a purpose, and usually no one is permitted to remain in the testing room at that time. Give yourself time for a cup of coffee, a soda, a light lunch or snack, and a breath of fresh air. Walk outside if possible. You'll perform better later and get a sort of intellectual "second wind" because of it.

• Considering cheating on the tests? Forget it! Questions of morality and academic integrity aside, it's risky simply because often several different forms of the test are distributed just in case anyone has designs on a neighbor's answer sheet. So don't do it! You can be expelled from the test and a failing report turned in if you succumb to this temptation. We repeat: it isn't worth the risk. Besides, if you're not adequately prepared for college, you do no one a service—yourself, your classmates, your instructors—if you get in under false pretenses. Better to take a semester off for some remedial work, enter a junior college for a year, and *then* take the test again and enter a university. Don't hope to squeeze by this time on your 20–20 vision.

• During the test, when you come upon facts and material that are confusing or unfamiliar, don't panic. Instead, stop and analyze the question. Often if you lack the specific data, you can still make a connection with some familiar facts and deduce the answer in this way. Or you can use simple logic, and reason to the right conclusion. Another favorite trick of seasoned test takers: if it's multiple-choice, try eliminating at least two or more of the alternatives. Working with two or three variables instead of four or five gives you a distinct advantage. Now try to eliminate one more answer. Eventually you are down to two and thus have a fifty-fifty chance of choosing the right one.

· If you hit a long run of unfamiliar material and time is running out, it may pay to skip to the rest of the test and return to the difficult part later if time permits. Again, bear in mind how the test is scored. Is there a penalty for guessing? Are you graded on a percentage of the answers attempted? Are blanks counted as incorrect? Is the total of right answers subtracted from the total wrong? Base your decision on the facts in order to maximize your score.

And watch for erasures and cross-outs; some tests are machine-graded and erasures or random marks can foul up the grading.

GETTING THE MOST OUT OF COLLEGE DAY

If you're a student in a high school of any size—urban, suburban, or rural—chances are you have on your schedule as a graduating senior a "College Day," "College Discovery," or "College Workshop." Some large cities have full-scale college "expositions" where literally hundreds of colleges, both local and out-of-town, can come with their representatives and materials for graduating seniors to get acquainted with.

Regardless of the size or elaborateness of the occasion,

Starting Off the Right Way

the College Day format is usually the same. Graduating seniors are given a day off from classes, usually in the late spring of their junior year or the early fall of their senior year, to meet with a variety of different representatives from colleges and universities. Reading materials are provided, sample application forms are distributed, and in some cases, some fairly serious interviewing takes place on both sides.

Like everything else, College Day *appears* simple but is actually rather complex. Here are a few tips and ideas to help you make the most of the occasion:

· Whatever you do, *don't* skip your school's College Day. You may denounce it as Mickey-Mouse stuff and affect a bored posture of laid-back *hauteur*, but we can tell you: that gets you nowhere. If the questions seem naïve and simpleminded, it's up to you to improve their caliber. And if you stay alert and sensitive to the proceedings, you might just learn something.

· Also, don't dismiss College Day out of hand if you aren't planning to go to college immediately. Go and listen anyway. You may learn solutions to your problems—academic, financial, family, whatever—that will allow you to go after all. And even if you don't go next year or the next, you can learn things that will benefit you if and when you do decide to go.

· Don't wear your scruffiest jeans, even if you're permitted to wear them to class every day. Spruce up a little. You don't have to go the whole three-piece pinstripe suit route, but pants and blazer for men, and a skirt, pants outfit, or knit dress for women, will make a more favorable impression on almost any interviewer. Try to look, at least, reasonably neat, healthy, and alert, and you'll be receiving much more positive responses in your mailbox.

· Don't try to play all the tricks gleaned from *Winning*

Through Intimidation and *Looking Out for No. 1* when you talk with the interviewers. Chances are they've read all the power hype too and can spot your efforts at gamesmanship a mile off. You don't have to be meek and mousy, but you should try to be pleasant, mannerly, and open to new information. Arguing with the interviewer is sure to get you nowhere; interested questioning will succeed.

· Go ahead and talk with a number of schools, including several in which you may have only a casual interest. What if you don't get into any one of your top three choices? Get all the info you can, including material on financial aid and scholarships. You never know what can happen before next September, and the school you reject as only a "possible" now may turn out to be at the top of your list in six months.

· When you talk with the schools, bear in mind that a good part of what you're hearing is factual. Universities and colleges are known to be honest in their advertising. But a part of it is, invariably, "hype"—in other words, a sales pitch. Universities, after all, are businesses that depend for their revenue at least in part on student enrollments. It's absolutely necessary that they keep the enrollments up in order to keep afloat financially. So don't assume that everything you hear at the College Day interview is gospel truth. Much is, but some is the usual inflated rhetoric of good advertising. It's up to you to separate out what's genuine from what's merely a sales pitch.

The best way to separate out the factual data from the sales pitch is, of course, to have firsthand knowledge of the campus. Check it out! If you can arrange an early visit, so much the better. Lacking that, a friend, relative, or employee on campus whom you know can often do a good job of helping you sort through the rhetoric. But if you have no personal contacts and a visit is impossible, look first at the significant things about the campus: the size and prestige, as well as the credentials, of its faculty; the size and breadth of the library; the scope of its extracurricular activities; the cultural opportunities in the surrounding neighborhood or city; the size and composition of the student body; the depth of the program offerings. And remember that often phrases like "a secluded rural campus" or "bustling urban environment" can be misleading; the former may refer to a tiny place huddled out in the proverbial sticks, far from civilization, while the latter may mean a streetcar college deep in the inner city and equally isolated from the city's real culture. It's up to you to pick out the wheat from the chaff.

· Also bear in mind that the person you're talking to on College Day is probably an admissions or recruitment officer—not a faculty member or administrator of the rank of dean, say, or vice-president. Thus this person may not always be informed about all aspects of the university. He or she probably doesn't know much about the program for psychology majors, the yearly film festival, the caliber of breakfasts in the cafeteria each morning, or the quality of the coeds in a certain dorm. File these questions away in your head and make it a point to check them out on your own.

In general, the questions that you *should* ask should deal with the basics: the faculty and its formal credentials (and certainly its willingness to work with students), the size and variety of academic programs offered, the quality of the library, the kind of housing and living arrangements offered, and so on. The more personal, idiosyncratic kind of concerns will probably have to wait until that long-delayed campus visit.

- Finally, pick up all the information you can carry away (you might take a tote or briefcase with you that day to hold all the goodies). Pick up all the freebies you can find: price schedules, admission blanks, dorm applications, scholarship information, catalogs, flyers about departmental programs, and so on. Later at home you can cull through the stack and throw away what you don't need. But if you're like most of us, you're likely to leave with your head buzzing with names, titles, building locations, and assorted other trivia. You should go home and review and reassess it all at your leisure—and put as much as you can remember down in writing. It will sharpen your memory later and help you to be a more thorough and careful applicant.

Now get set to go and enjoy your College Day! The next move is up to you.

2

Narrowing the Choices

VISIT ANY CAMPUS and you'll find students of all descriptions and persuasions, walking, studying, arguing, eating, drinking, and doing all the things that human beings do. Why did they choose to go to the particular campus where they're doing all these things? Probably for one or more of the following reasons:

It's the best school for the field they want to major in.
They wanted to go to a small liberal arts college.
They wanted to go to a big-city college.
They liked the ambience of the school.
The school has a terrific reputation for (check one) academic excellence, good-time girls and guys, easy courses, tough professors who are really tops in their fields, being easy to get a degree from, being so hard

it assures them of getting a good job when they graduate.
It's the school their family went to.
It's near home.
It's close to where they work.
It's the only one they could get into.
They could get a grant at Crawling Ivy, but nowhere else.
They have friends here.
Many people of their ethnic/social/economic/political/religious/professional persuasion attend here.

The best reason to go to any particular college is that it's the best college to help you do what you want to do with your life. If you want to be a topflight journalist for a major urban newspaper, don't waste your time vying for the editorship of the Chicken Lick school newspaper while taking courses from the kindly old prof who was once the editor of the *Chicken Lick Town Crier and Herald Tribune* (you know the type: with ads for feed and fertilizer along the bottom of the front page). Better to go to a solid, urban school, and get into a journalism department that has connections with the city newspapers.

This goes for anything you want to major in. Do your homework *before* you go to college. If you've decided on a major, check out the journals in the field you're interested in or check out the faculty roster in the universities you're considering. It's easy to tell which departments really contribute to the field and which don't. Further, if the school you're considering has F*A*M*O*U*S N*A*M*E*S in it, the odds are that it's a good school. Otherwise, the dean could never have justified the amount of money that it takes to get a F*A*M*O*U*S N*A*M*E.

Many people want to escape the hustle and bustle of the

Narrowing the Choices

big city for the bucolic setting of a liberal arts college in a small, small town. There's a lot to be said for such a school, although the possibility of making contacts that will be helpful in the world after graduation is remote. Unfortunately, many faculty members in colleges of this type are there because they can't get jobs anywhere else. Don't despair, however. There is a growing number of faculty members at these little colleges who are really superb teachers and scholars but who can't get jobs in posh urban or state universities because there are no jobs open in their field. The way you ferret them out is to look at the catalog and see where the junior faculty got their degrees. It's no longer unusual to find a flock of assistant and associate professors at places like Chicken Lick with degrees from Ivy League schools or all the top state universities. Remember: know your catalog!

There are also people who want to escape the stifling confines of Chicken Lick and get some action in the Big City. They have definite career goals and they've received good advice about where to go to get on the road to success. They are more interested in the cultural and economic milieu of the city than they are in the close ties and relaxed atmosphere of the small campus.

Some state universities are 'way off in the sticks. Some (such as Georgia Tech) are almost downtown. There's something for everybody, so you can pick the environment you want and go there (if you have the money or if the money is available in the form of scholarships, loans, grants in aid, etc.).

There is no definitive source of information about the ambience, the excellence, or the rottenness of particular schools. Years ago, Harvard was the only school for philosophy. Then Berkeley was the school for philosophy. Then others got this reputation, some deserving and some not. The situation changes every year, and there are vast differences of opinion. What was a good-time school last year may now be straightening up into a tough, professional operation. Last year's premier liberal arts college may, because of financial problems, be losing the faculty that made it great. There's no magic formula that will tell you which schools are the best. Consult all the sources: catalogs, alumni, the rosters of the top businesses in your city, the Rotary Club rosters, the Kiwanis Club membership lists, and so on. Weigh all the information you get and then make your decision.

There are other reasons why people choose one college over another. While some of them may not be the best reasons academically, they all have merit given the individual case. Let's look at some of the more common reasons for choices. Don't condemn them too quickly, else you may be embarrassed when you make a choice someday based on the following considerations.

For many students, the choice is made the day they're born. Of course they're going to Snob U. Members of their family have been getting "gentlemen's C's" at Snob U. for a century and a half. They don't expect to really get an education here, they simply have to have the credentials that the family requires.

That's a good reason? In a way, yes. Pragmatically, if specific educational goals are secondary to the social connections that the school provides, and if these social connections are part of being a success in your particular socioeconomic/family situation, then by all means go to the family's old alma mater. The wheels may be greased for you, and you may be able to enjoy a degree of freedom unavailable if you go to a place where nobody knows you and the administration could care less whether you pass or fail.

If this sounds terribly cynical and self-serving, it's because it is. Here, the goal is not education or upward mobility, but merely going through the motions of being a part of America's hidden aristocracy. But don't forget: you may be surprised. You may actually get a dynamite education at Snob U., and you may just broaden your horizons enough to break out of the programmed future your family has planned for you so you can create your own life instead of re-creating theirs.

In short, if the way is paved to go to Snob U., and the school is a legitimate institution of higher learning, go to it. But try to break out of the mold. Go to it to get an education, not merely to get the sheepskin. Remember, it's *your* life, not theirs, that you're creating.

Some choices are made for convenience's sake. Let's say that you aren't the umpteenth member of the Wycliffe-Gore family, and instead you're just a plain Joe with talent who wants to make the most of that talent. There's a streetcar college around the corner, or there's a good junior or community college a mile or two away from where you live. If you go there, you can save X number of dollars on tuition, cut down the number of part-time employment hours necessary for survival, and get a solid foundation for your last two years of senior college work. Do it.

Check the place out, read the catalog thoroughly in terms of what your ultimate goals are, apply for admission, apply for whatever money's available, and get ready to go in the fall, the spring, or whenever you can get in. Time's a-wasting, and the sooner you start, the sooner you'll have the credentials that will open up the job market for you.

The only caveat here is living at home. If you're unmarried and still living at home, especially if you're the first member of your family to go to college, look for interference on the part of your parents. They won't mean to make things hard for you. But they won't know what you're up against, and there is usually no way to tell them. If you can swing it, get a room near the campus. If you can't, try to impress them with your seriousness about getting an education. Tell them that you must have a certain amount of time alone so you can do the best job possible. Be positive about the time college will take away from your life with them. Don't expect them to be able to understand the pressures of midterms and finals. Do expect them to be impressed if you really hit the books in a methodical and businesslike way.

Sometimes it's possible to find a happy combination of college and the job you're presently holding. Businesses often have arrangements with local colleges and universities so that students can get college credit for the work they do on the job. Work-study programs have become increasingly popular during the last few years as enrollments have dropped in universities all around the country. They're usually called "co-op" programs, and the school coordinates your course work with your job activities. If you are participating in such a program and you work at a place close to the school, you may find it convenient to juggle your schedule both at school and on the job so you can get the most out of both. A word of advice: don't slack off on either obligation. Both the job and the school are important, and you'll be graded on how well you integrate the two activities.

What if there's only one school you can get into? Then your choice has been made for you, but this does not necessarily mean you are stuck with a poor school. There are many reasons why people are turned down by particular

Narrowing the Choices

schools. Poor grades, lackluster high school work, and inadequate preparation are only the obvious ones.

More subtle and insidious are the covert reasons why you sometimes get turned down. Here are a few:

No scholarship money available.
No state tuition funds available.
Hidden quotas for ethnic minorities.
Hidden quotas for students from the area.
Hidden quotas for men and/or women.
Overbooking for the coming semester.
Overbooking or inadequate staffing for the field you've chosen.

Stories abound about straight-A students who aren't accepted because the school is trying to build up its national prestige by admitting large numbers of students from other states. Or schools that hoard their scholarship or fellowship money for students they feel will lend prestige to particular departments. Or supposedly egalitarian schools that really would be happier with fewer women/blacks/atheists on the campus.

Of course, admissions committees and scholarship committees will go up in smoke if such accusations are made. But the stories keep coming up. During the last twenty years, we've heard them all, and a depressingly large number of them are true.

In a way, applying to college is like submitting a manuscript for publication. Joseph Heller's classic *Catch-22* was turned down by more than twenty publishers before it was finally sold. The rest is literary history. Keep trying. If you run into prejudice, go the other way. You don't want to go there anyhow.

But what if your grades really are bad, and you really are going to Boonie U. because you can't get in anywhere else? Not to worry. When Ralph started college, he had been out of high school for five years. Because of family squabbles, a divorce, and interrupted schooling due to illness and moves, his high school grades held little indication of what he could actually do. When he finally did start college, he went after an education as if it were the most important thing in his life. It *was* the most important thing, and the work he put into his college studies paid off down through the years. After a slow start in a little community college, he transferred to Emory University in Atlanta. The small college had given him the necessary momentum. Emory demanded work and he was willing to do it. The five-year hiatus receded quickly into the past, and he went all the way for a Ph.D. All this while holding a full-time job. He did it, and you can do it, too. Don't let anybody tell you that you can't.

Another reason for choosing a particular college is an important one. If you *do* have to work while you're going to college, make sure that you can do it without ruining both your education and your job. Many schools allow what used to be called "day students": students who do not live on campus, do not take part in campus social life, and do not fit the usual "Joe College" image. If you have to work, make sure that such activities are appreciated and not condemned by the college of your choice.

Another horror story should suffice to make the point. When Ralph was a senior in college, he was the president of the undergraduate philosophy club. A meeting with another club at another university was scheduled in another city. Because of the demands of his job, Ralph was unable to break loose for the three days needed for the trip. The acting chairman of the department was furious, and suggested that if Ralph could not take part fully in the department's extracurricular activities because he had to work, then perhaps he should drop out of college and work full-time.

Needless to say, Ralph's response was immediate, precipitate, and not very politic. The enmity generated lasted for years. A rule of thumb: play politics when you have to, but if they don't understand who you are and where you're coming from, don't expect sympathy. Unfortunately, many academics live far removed from the struggles of common folk like us. Don't let it get you down. The important thing is the education and the degree.

If you can get a scholarship at only one school, but nowhere else (and if you must have the money to go at all), take the money. If you can rack up a good record, you'll be in a better bargaining position later on in applying for money if you decide to transfer. All other things being equal, if a school wants to give you money, take it and use it to get the education you want and need.

You have friends at West Sasquatch State Teachers College? But is it a good school? Does it have the kind of programs you need? Is there money available? Can you get a job? And will they let you work? Is it near home? Can you find a parking space?

You'll make plenty of new friends at school. Unless you decide to live in the old neighborhood, you'll probably not stay in touch with your high school friends anyway. Don't make a choice of schools on the basis of the presence of friends. More often than not, they'll take up too much of your time with their own problems to leave you time to worry about your own.

Remember what you're in college for: to get an education, to prepare for the future, to move up in the world.

Your friends should be there for the same reasons. Keep your eye on the ball, and forget about the safety and comfort of having old friends around. They won't help you do what you need to do: learn new concepts, new ways of thinking, new ways of handling yourself.

All other things being equal, if you have friends at West Sasquatch, why not go there? OK. But hold them at arm's length. We're not advising you to abandon old friends. We're just giving you some good advice on how to use your time. Better to get together with them during spring holidays and compare notes while you guzzle beer. Guard your time carefully. If you don't, your friends will use all of it and leave none for you and your studies.

Almost all colleges now have facilities for handicapped people. There are Braille books and tapes available in school libraries, and people are sometimes available to read for you if you have a learning disability. We have a friend and former student who is a member of Mensa (the group made up of people whose IQs are in the top 5 percent in the nation), but whose dyslexia is so bad, a page of print is simply a jumble. She made it through college, graduate school, and law school. She now has her own successful business, and teaches accounting in her spare time.

We have seen other students who had to be strapped to a motorized wheelchair, who had multiple amputations, who were blind, who had multiple learning disabilities, or whose physical condition made study an ordeal. One of Ralph's classmates in graduate school had to be carried from classroom to classroom. He's now one of Atlanta's most successful lawyers. Ralph himself had a heart condition and one eye. They did it. You can do it. If your disability is severe, make sure that the school has the proper facilities. Also, if you have a chance, talk to other disabled students

Narrowing the Choices

on campus. Ask them how it is. Take their advice. They're the ones who know firsthand, beyond the hype the recruiter might give you.

You're Jewish or black or Latino or poor or hardshell Baptist or a doctor's son or your family has voted Whig for the last one hundred years. You want to go to a school where you can be comfortable? Forget it.

Go to the school where you can get the best education or professional training for the career you want. Don't limit yourself by staying in a friendly crowd. Take a chance. Learn to know the enemy. Don't be afraid of new ideas and different ways of looking at things. The purpose of education is to broaden your horizons, not merely to reinforce the things you learned from your peer group or your parents. Some schools, such as Roosevelt University, are a miniature United Nations, where people of all races and religious and political persuasions learn to live, work, and learn together. They're slices of the real world, not merely cloistered campuses.

Few people when graduating from high school have decided what they want to do with their life. There's no good reason why they should have decided at such an early date. Often, however, high school counselors try to steer you in certain directions early, so you can get a head start on preparing for a career. All well and good if you happen to have stopped changing by the time you get to your senior year. On the other hand, if you continue to learn and absorb new ways of thinking after you reach college, you may find that all that high school preparation headed you in a direction that you aren't really interested in.

A university should enhance your growth. Don't seal up your options by deciding too early what you want to do with your life. Give yourself a year or two to find out what's been going on in the world for the last two millennia before you decide that it's the doctor's/lawyer's/teacher's/businessman's/actor's life for you. At various times, Valerie thought she wanted to be (1) a journalist, (2) a writer, (3) a teacher, (4) a designer, (5) a scholarly researcher. Ralph wanted to be (1) a musician, (2) a teacher, (3) an artist, (4) a writer, (5) an architect, (6) a doctor. Along the way, we both did work in almost all of these fields, and both spent years in the academic world as professors and administrators before breaking out to become what we really wanted to be all along: writers.

Too soon old and too late smart!

By the time you reach your senior year in college, you will have finished all or most of your required courses, and you probably will have found the career that you want. It's not too late to transfer. And it's the perfect time to map out a comprehensive program that will lead you right into the business or professional school of your choice.

One of the purposes of a general education is to acquaint you with the options you have. Never restrict yourself in your undergraduate work to a few narrowly defined areas. Take as much work in as many fields as you can without diluting your work in your major. The more you know, the more informed your final choice will be.

What if you do have long-range career plans? Once you've determined the criteria that are important to you, make every effort to become an expert in colleges that are the best in the field you're going to pursue. How do you do this? Here are a few tips.

• Write to the *Chronicle of Higher Education* and ask which colleges are the best for specific areas. The *Chronicle* is a tabloid that tells the news about higher education. The staff has a tremendous amount of data on schools from every state. It's the official news source for any professional in the field of higher education. If the *Chronicle* doesn't know, probably nobody does.

· Write to the American Association for Higher Education. The AAHE distributes hundreds of pamphlets on schools, faculty, professional standards, areas of study, etc. It's the largest association of its kind in the world, and its informational resources are enormous.

· If you've already decided on your field, or if you're getting ready to put together a major that will lead to a specific field, then write to the professional association that represents that field. If you want to be a philosophy professor, write to the American Philosophical Association. If you're interested in English or foreign languages, write to the Modern Language Association. If you think you'll eventually want to go to business school, write to the American Association of Collegiate Schools of Business. These professional associations not only can tell you which school has the best reputation in the field of your choice, they can also rate schools in your immediate geographical area. They're much more reliable than college recruiters, since they're trying to maintain the level of excellence in the field, not recruit students for a particular university.

· Call or write to people in the field you've chosen. Tell them what you want to do and ask them their opinion. They'll probably be flattered that you called. They'll probably also try to push their own alma mater, but listen to their arguments and collate them with the other sources you have.

Hit both the formal sources and the informal sources. Ask the associations, and also ask real people. If you've heard that a certain campus is famous for its work in the area of Libyan devil sculptures, and that field is your heart's desire, walk around the campus and buttonhole people who are majoring in the field. Make an appointment with one of the top profs and see if he appears to know what he's talking about.

· Take a good long look at your professors, your doctor, your family lawyer, your father's accountant, the people in the various businesses and professions with whom you come in contact every day. Are they impressive? Do they really know what they're doing? Ask them about their university.

· Finally, consult the catalogs of the schools you're thinking about attending. How deep is the department in which you want to do your work? How deep are the other departments? Do they have two full professors, three part-time instructors, and no graduate program? Probably pretty lightweight. On the other hand, does it have a Ph.D. program in the field, with a professorial staff that does consulting for business, industry, and foreign and domestic governmental agencies? Good bet. It'll probably be hard as hell, but the contacts alone will be worth the trouble, not to mention the education you'll get.

If you want the best, go with the best. If you want to slide through and find a good safe minor position after you graduate, the choice is up to you. If you've got the talent, don't settle for second-best. That's your life you're creating, you know.

If you haven't really thought about college, or if you don't really know what you want to do, then get cracking. Although the job market for college graduates is not what it was ten years ago, it will *always* be the case that the best jobs, the most rewarding careers, the most enriched lives will go to the people who've taken advantage of the chance to go to college, who've poured their energies into broadening and deepening their knowledge of the world around them, and who've used their college years to take control of their own lives. Both the money and the satisfaction go to the people who know who they are and where they stand in relation to the rest of the world.

If you want to go to one of the big Ivy League schools, start your preparations early. These are the elite schools of the nation, and they don't have to go begging for students the way some of the rest of the schools do. The very names Harvard, Yale, Stanford, or University of Chicago tend to strike terror in the hearts and minds of potential students from more remote parts of the country.

In the first place, you'll need the required grade-point average. During the sixties and early seventies, it became popular to decry the importance of grades. Many colleges went to the "pass-fail" system, or broke their curriculum down into easy-to-pass "modules," so that any schmo who wanted to could get through. Not the biggies. Harvard University was one of the first to return to a semblance of the integrated, comprehensive undergraduate curriculum. The big schools are not as trendy as some of the smaller ones. They don't have to be, because their operating budget isn't at the mercy of student enrollment.

Regardless of what may be currently popular in education, there's no substitute for a solid foundation in history, literature, mathematics, social studies, philosophy, languages, and the other fields that make up a liberal arts degree. The old saw about enriching one's life through liberal education happens to be true. That's why Homer's *Iliad*, Shakespeare's plays, Descartes' *Meditations*, Milton's *Paradise Lost*, and all those Bach fugues have been around so long. There genuinely is such a thing as culture, no matter what you may have heard to the contrary, and people who go to Ivy League schools are expected to have more than a nodding acquaintance with the classics of Western civilization.

Is this an elitist attitude? You're damn right it is! But look at the alternatives. Many state schools, especially junior colleges, are charged by the state to provide a higher education for every citizen. We know of one state university whose charter ". . . guarantees every citizen a higher education regardless of his intellectual ability." What that means in plain language is this: because of political considerations, some state-supported schools must devise a curriculum that anybody can pass. That way, everybody can be a first-class citizen in a country where higher education is a must for first-class citizenship.

What this means for the exceptionally good student is the lack of opportunity for genuine growth. What this means for the poor student is a chance to enjoy upward social and economic mobility without having the mental equipment necessary to learn and understand the complexities that such upward mobility requires.

This is not to say that poorly prepared people should not be allowed to go to college. If that had been the case, many people would never get into school in the first place. It is to say that a watered-down curriculum cheats not only the good student but the poor one as well. The good student doesn't get the breadth and depth his intellect deserves, and the poor student is gulled into thinking that he can survive in the real world without knowing much.

Ask any person who went through one of the slapped-together "touchy-feely" courses that became popular in the sixties how relevant that course was when he or she got out into the world of corporate finance, direct sales, and cost-effective budget planning.

John Dewey saw education as a means to arm a person

for what life would require of that person for success. Through many misinterpretations, this fundamental concept became an excuse for allowing everything into the curriculum from basket weaving to how to click with the group. What Dewey was really after was teaching people how to think, how to solve the problems that the environment throws at us every day. To think requires discipline. It's not easy to move from premise to premise to conclusions. But the ability to think through arguments and solve problems is absolutely necessary, not only to survival but to continued success as well.

And to think at peak efficiency, to generate conclusions that are not only workable but are the result of informed reflection, requires that your knowledge extend beyond the bounds of your own personal experiences.

That's what higher education is all about. It takes you out of the context of your own personal world, and allows you to see the rest of the universe. And it teaches you to use that knowledge to create, to solve—to live life to the fullest. If the curriculum in the college you plan to attend doesn't give you the opportunity to explore the rest of the universe, write it off. Go to a school that has a real curriculum.

The Ivy League and other top-notch schools traditionally train the future leaders of the country. The best leaders are the ones who have some sense of perspective about who they are, where they're going, and where the world is going. The best way to get that kind of knowledge is through a university curriculum that gives you solid, firsthand knowledge of the world around you.

A university education without practical experience tends to be sterile and empty. Practical, personal experience without the rich texture of a university education is lethally limiting. A combination of the two is the best guarantee not only of success but of significant contribution as well.

What if you're poorly prepared? Suppose you're the first member of your family to get a college degree, your high school grades are nothing to write home about, and you haven't got the academic background to launch a college career.

You've got problems.

You should turn your problems into projects. Then you won't have any problems. You'll have projects, which can be defined, described, and worked on. The best thing to do is seek the advice of somebody with experience in the area of educational counseling. This may be your high school counselor, and it may be somebody in the admissions office of your local community college.

Often, your state will provide counseling and testing as a part of its employment services. They're paid for by your taxes, and they're worth their weight in gold. If you have any talent for college work, it's likely that you can secure both counseling and extensive testing free of charge from various state agencies.

If you have a disability, the local state vocational rehabilitation office can help you. That's how Ralph went to college. The heart murmur and injured left eye made it possible for the vocational rehab department to pay for his complete undergraduate tuition, plus a quarterly allowance for books.

An integral part of such counseling and testing is the diagnosis of educational weaknesses. If remedial work is indicated, there are probably ways to get it, without a great deal of expense on your part. The basics are reading and mathematical skills. If you're weak in either of these areas, there are courses you can take, books you can read, tapes you can hear, and people with whom you can talk and from whom you can learn.

Sometimes it helps to cite an extreme example. Many people have emigrated to the United States from other countries, barely able to speak English. The newspapers almost daily carry stories about people like them who have made fortunes within a decade of getting off the boat or plane.

What's their secret? Well, in the first place, there wasn't even the *opportunity* to get a higher education in the old country. Now, there is. The opportunity of a lifetime. And they make the most of it.

Otto Wirth was a refugee from Hitler's Germany during the thirties. He is not a big, strong man, but rather a short, genial man with a twinkle in his eye and a disarming smile that masks the strength that lies behind it.

Otto could barely speak the language. He had no money, and he had no education. But he saw America as a legendary land of opportunity. Although not physically suited for it, he went to work in a steel mill near Chicago, and sweated his way through years of grime and hard work. He went to school during his spare time, during the few hours he had left after work.

He never stopped working. He earned not only a bachelor's degree but a master's and a Ph.D. as well. He was the dean of faculties and the vice-president of academic affairs at Roosevelt University for years, and is remembered as not only a scholar but as a man who understands how to survive in the gritty world outside academia as well.

Otto is retired now, and spends his time writing his magnum opus on Thomas Mann. We see him occasionally, and we always marvel at this man whose gentle and jovial exterior belies the incredible inner strength that saw him through the horrors of Nazism, the heat and hard work of the steel mill, all the way to a university vice-presidency. And he is a man without affectation, without pomposity. He is beloved by all who know him.

Now. What do you mean, you don't have time to go to school? What do you mean, you don't have time to make up for the things you didn't learn in high school? What do you mean, you're too tired to make up for your poor preparation, too tired to work and go to school at the same time?

Otto would put his arm around you, lead you into his office, sit you down, and in his charming Viennese accent say, "Now. Here is what you must do."

So do it.

3

Long-Range Planning: A Few Preliminary Notes

CAREER PLANNING begins today in high school. Counselors and teachers have watchful eyes focused on their students, and they try to spot specific talents early, so that the students can receive the kind of guidance they need to succeed. Just make sure that you don't make your decision before you've investigated all the available alternatives.

We mentioned John Dewey in the last section. Early talent-watches are a natural outgrowth of his philosophy of education. If the mind is a problem-solving tool, and if everybody living in this competitive environment has to use whatever talents he has to make it through the night, then the teacher must do two things: teach problem solving early and spot talents early.

Not everybody has the same talent for problem solving, but everybody is thought to be talented at something. If each person is to realize his or her potential to the fullest, it is the task of the educator to discern what talents the student has, and how much. Then it is the duty of the educator to help the student develop those talents, with an emphasis on using them to solve problems.

Dewey's influence on American education cannot be overestimated. The conception of the mind as a problem-solving instrument is almost universally accepted. The notion that the mind can do things other than solve problems is sometimes met with laughter by professional educators, and with downright hostility by those joyless people who administer psychological tests in an attempt to classify you.

All this, of course, neglects some of the fundamental aspects of the human mind. Aesthetic sensibility, the feeling of love for someone, and the transcendence of the religious experience are three of the most obvious kinds of experiences that are definitely *not* problem-solving activities.

Moreover, if the educator is going to fasten onto a person's natural aptitudes as a means of finding out what the person should do with his life, a few fundamental considerations may be overlooked:

- First, what you have a natural talent for doing may not earn you a living. There are thousands of artists, really good ones, beating their brains out trying to make ends meet, and there are as many gifted musicians living on one-night gigs in bars and restaurants.
- Along the same lines, what you have a natural aptitude for may not be what you *ought* to do if you want to lead a truly satisfying life. Not every "born" musician will be happy playing every night, and not every "born" artist will consider his work either significant or satisfying.
- Also, natural aptitudes are multifaceted. A keen sense

for analysis could mean that you are a budding mathematician, logician, literary critic, architect, engineer, physicist, television technician, or astronaut. All of these vocations require a talent for analytical thinking.

· And most importantly, what you are on fire to do right now may skew your test results. You will encounter subjects in college that you never knew existed before. You may be on fire today to be a biologist. Next year, you may find that it is really the philosophy of science that you're interested in. Today you may want to be a theologian. Next semester's course in comparative religion may be enough to send you into anthropology for good.

With these considerations in mind, let's see if we can come up with a few guidelines. None of them are absolutes, but all of them can help in one way or the other.

· Don't choose a major while you're still in high school. Your major will lead you into your career. Don't make career choices with only a limited amount of data.

· When you choose your major or your career, make sure (if it's possible) that you will be happy with the choice on down the line. It's like getting married. You never know what the other person is like until you live with that person, so don't think you know all there is to know just because you've spent a few nights together.

· Take a good long look at people who've been in the field for a long time. Is this what you want to become?

· Be practical. If your natural aptitudes seem to indicate success in the field, and you think you would be happy in it, and you aren't too freaked out by the people who've been in it for a long time, *can you make a living at it?*

· While you're at it, take a good look into yourself. What kind of life are you used to living? What's your standard of living? If you've been used to the good life, with a steady supply of cash and few worries about status, count the cost of getting into a field that will never give you the money you're used to having.

• Don't think that when you get to college you can become merely a gadfly, flitting from one major to another, taking only the elementary courses in several fields. You'll have to plan your courses carefully, so that you maximize your options while at the same time building generally toward a definite goal. For example, if you know that you're going into one of the sciences, get the math that you'll need for all of them. If you're going into some aspect of literature or language, get all the courses you can that will give you insights into what literature and language are about.

• Check out the projections on the job market for the field you're interested in. Check them out for *four years from now*. That's when you'll graduate from college. For example, yesterday's news reported that there will be a surplus of physicians by 1990. If you start your freshman year this year, you'll finish college in four years, medical school in another four, your internship in a year or two, and your residency in two more. That's about eleven years. If you were a doctor now, you'd be in pretty good shape. In eleven years, who knows? Ten years ago, there was a shortage of lawyers. Now many law school graduates can't get placed in a decent firm. The time to check things out is before you commit yourself. Go to the placement office and ask the adviser. He or she will have the reference books and the bulletins that will tell you what you need to know.

• Whatever you do, take full advantage of the educational opportunities that are open to you. While you are a high school student, the sky's the limit. When you are a freshman, your options will be multitudinous. By the time you are a junior, you won't have so many. By the time

Long-Range Planning: A Few Preliminary Notes

you're a senior, you'll be on one track or another. By the time you're in graduate school, there won't be many choices at all. By the time you get your graduate degree, it may be too late to change without going back and starting, if not at square one, at least at square two or three.

· Remember that college may be your only chance to learn about the world as a whole. It may be your only chance to tap into the tremendous wealth of information and insight about the human condition that the libraries and the faculty provide. Prepare now, so you'll be able to make the most of it. Throw yourself into it completely.

· But don't become a drudge just because you're going to college. There's nothing written anywhere that says that education isn't painful. Most new ideas are painful to contemplate, especially when you're required to reexamine your most cherished beliefs. But college can also be a grand adventure. Besides, you'll meet others along the way, and you can enrich one another's lives immensely. There's plenty of opportunity for fun and games. Take advantage of them. It'll be an important part of your personal development. Fall in love. Take chances. Become the world's expert in the works of Woody Allen. Go to film festivals. Get laid. Stretch your mind. Read the complete works of Ambrose Bierce. Argue for the legitimacy of science fiction as literature. Embrace Eastern mysticism for at least a semester. Try to square the circle. Get into campus politics. Learn how to debate. Learn how to do logic. Read poetry. Go to concerts. Collect old Beatles records. Be the first one in your dorm to have the complete works of Buddy Holly. Start a library. Get away on weekends. Become an Existentialist. Dismay your parents. Ride motorcycles. Fall in love again.

4

How to Get into the College You Choose

THE APPLICATION

YOU'RE NOW a little past square one: that is, you've attended College Day, narrowed some choices, decided on at least several possible types of college that would be right for you. And now you're ready to go through the admissions process and win that final acceptance letter that means you're in college at last.

How to go about getting yourself admitted? It can be a long, involved process, but most colleges will work with you to simplify and expedite the procedure as much as possible. Meanwhile, here are a few tips to get you started:

· First, remember that few colleges are really as "selective" as they claim. Most of that much-vaunted selectivity exists purely on paper for the purpose of convincing alumni, donors, trustees, and distinguished full professors that their standards really haven't dropped at all. (Remember, the university is a business like any other and must survive economically; as our colleague Hermann Bowersox once remarked, "Students are tuition-bearing animals.") So try to read between the lines on statements such as "Crawling Ivy admits only one out of every six applicants." Unless Crawling Ivy is truly one of the most sought-after schools and can afford to be so selective, that's probably a carefully calculated overstatement.

· What to do if you really are applying for one of the big league schools? Not to worry: even these schools have certain academic quotas they'd like to fill. They can't get away with every student being incredibly rich, attractive, brilliant, and athletic. Richard Moll, in *Playing the Private College Admissions Game,* names five categories of students who will usually get admitted, provided they have decent records: the intellects (650 or higher on verbal and/or math sections of the SAT, and good high school grades); the special talents (the superb hockey or tennis players, the excellent musicians or actors); the family "legacies" (sons and daughters of distinguished alumni); the "All-American kids"; and the "social-conscience category" (students admitted to maintain an ethnic or even a geographic balance). The last category covers a multitude of possibilities —for example, an eastern school may *need* midwestern or southern applicants, while a prestigious West Coast school may be hungry for non-Californians. Don't rule yourself out because you think only people from a certain geographical area can get in. You may surprise yourself.

· Send off for the application materials *early.* The beginning of the winter or spring quarter before you plan to enter in the fall is too late. Better to send off for all the paperwork by the beginning of the fall term. That way you have the rest of that term, plus early next term, to decide which applications you plan actually to complete and to get them in the mail. Better early than late with this whole procedure. Deadlines for applications are usually set fairly early in the winter if you want to start with the rest of the freshman class in the fall. So get moving!

· What about multiple applications for admission? Everyone talks about it, but no one seems to come up with any clear-cut answer as to the convenience or the ethics of applying to several schools.

Let's clear up a few points right away. Many colleges, as we've already noted, really are super-selective. They can afford to be. You'd like to get in big Crawling Ivy, of course, but you're not sure you can make it. Just in case you don't, you also apply to Staghorn Fern College, a smaller private college, big Sprawling Juniper State U., and even a couple of small junior colleges, just in the event that nothing else comes through. That's five applications that you're going to file. Yet you're going to attend only one college—preferably one of your top choices. The other four schools may admit you, but all will receive "Dear John" letters from you saying that you regretfully decline their kind offer but you're going elsewhere.

Prior to the early sixties, there was a first-second-third choice rule which made high schools assume that you were going to apply only to three institutions simultaneously—and that you'd clearly indicate to the colleges you applied to which was top on the list, which second, and so on. Now everyone, or almost everyone, applies to a number of different schools. True, high schools often charge for the additional transcripts (if there are more than three), but the extra charge is worth it. It's insurance for you.

There's one interesting side-effect of the multiple admissions game. Colleges themselves are sometimes thrown off in their projections by the number of applications they receive. As *Lovejoy's College Guide* points out in its most recent edition, if a college wants to enroll 300 freshmen in September, it may need to accept 600 or even 700, putting some on provisional status or a waiting list, because each accepted candidate probably was also accepted by several other colleges. Sometimes everyone seems to be running late and will take the spring weeks up to the Candidates Reply Date Agreement (usually around May 1) to decide on a final choice. So the earlier you can narrow down your choices and let the other schools know, the better both for you and them.

· What do you include in the application for admission? Most applications are fairly simple and straightforward. They'll tell you exactly what to put in. There's usually a personal information form with data such as name, address, place and date of birth, father's occupation, permanent residence, a record of military service (if any), previous schools attended, and so on. Usually there's a request for appropriate test scores, transcripts from your high school, and letters of recommendation from instructors, the principal or headmaster, and counselors. Finally, there's usually a short essay portion that gives you a chance to explain some of your previous training, discuss your goals and interests, and generally describe "who you are." More on this very important essay portion later.

· In filling out the applications, type if at all possible. If you don't type, it's well worth the money to invest in having the forms professionally typed—or barter some service or possession with a friend or family member who can hit the keyboard for a couple of hours on your behalf.

Next best to typing is to print in large, legible block letters. Third down the list is neat, legible handwriting—*in ink*. You should *never* fill out a college application in pencil. And avoid garish orange, red, or purple magic markers or felt-tip pens. Only a fountain pen or ballpoint will do.

Be brief and concise when you fill out the application form itself. Condense information, if necessary, so that it fits into the space provided. If you need another page, attach an appendix or additional sheet. Don't turn in something the admissions office needs a road map to read.

• As soon as you start to file the admissions papers, go visit your high school placement officer or counselor (or registrar, if there is one). Ask him or her to send transcripts to *all* the schools on your list. Pay the extra $2 per transcript on the spot so that they will all arrive on time. Check to make sure that all your test scores are also on the way. Most colleges won't process your application form or essay until these necessary supporting documents have been filed.

• Considering faking transcripts or other credentials? Our advice is the same as with cheating on tests: forget it. If your records genuinely are beyond hope, far better to take a year's remedial work and prepare yourself adequately to get into a decent school. We repeat: don't do it. Most colleges have means for detecting faked credentials, anyway, and while a poor record won't get you permanently barred from old Crawling Ivy, a faked transcript will.

• Take time with the application and essay. Don't throw it together the night before it's due to go off in the morning's mail. If necessary, draft any portions that ask for extended essays and show them to a high school teacher, the principal or headmaster, or a counselor. Try them out on some college friends at Thanksgiving or Christmas. Get your sister, the spelling and grammar whiz, to read over the final version to catch typos and misspellings. If you're uncertain about a question, call the college admissions office and talk with an admissions counselor. They'll appreciate your concern for details.

• The letters of recommendation are an important part of every application. Usually there will be a request for three or four. At least one should be from a high school instructor, preferably one who knows your work and has taught you in several classes. The longer the acquaintance, the better; that way, the person can talk about your intellectual development and the changes you've evidenced over the past several years. The colleges don't want or expect perfection; they *are*, however, looking for someone who is growing intellectually, socially, and personally—who is changing for the better, and is achieving some degree of maturity.

At least one letter should probably be from your principal or headmaster, or perhaps from a person on the high school counseling staff. Check around to see who customarily writes these recommendations in your school. Often the headmaster's staff assistant will actually draft the letter for his signature. Just be sure you supply plenty of lead time (at least a month) for the letters to get typed and mailed.

If a "character" or "personal" reference is required, you have several options: a family friend, a local minister or youth leader, a coach or athletic director whom you know well, even a friend's father who is prominent in business or community affairs. Whomever you pick, it's important that he or she be able to write persuasively without being flowery or sentimental. Pick someone who can write a balanced, coherent, but positive letter and your chances of being admitted will be greatly enhanced.

• Suppose you don't trust your references to write good letters? People being what they are, some personality clashes are inevitable. No one gets along with *everyone*. And while it rarely happens, you may just cross swords with an influential faculty member, counselor, or even the principal. In such a case you *know* the recommendation will be a bad one. Maybe it's deserved, maybe it's undeserved. The point is, how do you deal with the possibility of a really damaging letter to the college you want so desperately to attend?

The best way to deal with the problem is to circumvent it. If you have a running feud with the principal but good rapport with the assistant principal, ask him or her to write in lieu of the boss. If your English teacher finds you undisciplined and disorganized but your art instructor praises you for being creative and open to new structures, it's obvious whom you should ask for a letter. And remember, when in doubt, ask, "Can you write me a favorable recommendation for Crawling Ivy?" Most teachers who honestly don't feel they can recommend you will say no, they'd prefer not to.

· If you have a choice of several people who would give you "good" recommendations, pick the one with the best reputation both inside and outside the area, the one with the most political sense, and the one who's the best writer (not necessarily the English teacher, either). The reason? Schools are used to hearing what's called "routine praise"—the kind of letter that assures us that Dudley is absolutely the best mind of the century, the most creative student the writer has ever taught, and so on. Pick someone who will avoid the clichés and talk about your specific talents instead. You'll fare better in the end for it.

· Once you've got transcripts, test scores, and letters lined up, settle back for a good long, hard look at the essay portion.

Your first reaction will probably be panic. Here, four

years after you started high school, you're being asked to fill this incredibly long blank space with words of wisdom on "what's important to me," "who I am," or "where I'd like to be in four years."

Yes, the topics are often ill-chosen and amorphous. Yes, they're hard to write on with any intelligence at all. And yes, the very vagueness of the topics probably does increase your anxiety a good 150 percent.

Still, you've got to give it your best. Often essays get people moved from the "in" to the "out" box—and vice-versa *if* the essay evidences thought, sophistication, analytical skill, or even simple writing ability.

Admissions officers to whom we've talked tell us that the essays are usually poorly written and full of clichés, and bear the distinct mark of "what I think a college admissions officer would like to hear." They are seldom a personal statement of any kind, emotional, intellectual, cultural.

The essay shouldn't be your version of what you *think* a college applicant should sound like. It should be you at your best, writing as clearly and simply and concisely as is humanly possible. The admissions committee, remember, isn't looking for *War and Peace*. It wants to be assured that you're a sentient being who can think, reason, put simple sentences together, deal with an unstructured ("free") essay assignment, and express some ideas of your own. That's all. No big mystery. But it's amazing how few applicants can do it.

· A few things to avoid in the essay: the "I want-to-be-me" paean to total selfhood (Tom Wolfe has already identified the Me Generation; you don't need to prove once again that you're part of it); the embarrassingly confessional essay (on your first date, first big party, first plane ride); the too revealingly intimate essay about your family life (if your father is a wife beater, better they shouldn't know; if you grew up in unbelievable poverty, save the details for the BEOG—Basic Equal Opportunity Grant—application). Don't sound like an eager beaver Joe High School or Pete Preppie and write a collection of clichés about high ambitions or goal-oriented achievements or team-spirited efforts. At the other extreme, don't try coming on like some punk-rock-and-dope freak who's been around and is street-wise but print-illiterate.

It's difficult, of course, to recommend specific information that you should include in your essay that will assure your admission. Even the best and most carefully crafted essay can still turn off a reader who happens not to like the style or substance of what you say. Still, however, the most successful essays in general are those that display some individuality: they may relate an incident or tell an anecdote that reveals your nature, your character, your aspirations, or the particular flavor of your life to this point. Perhaps you have a strong interest in a certain field or have zeroed in on a certain career goal. If so, use these as starting points for your essay. But in general, you should try to let the essay speak for itself—short stories or other "creative" pieces, photos, films, poems, unless specifically called for, sometimes can give the impression of overloading the admissions committee with more data than it can handle. A general rule of thumb: save the "creative" expressions for schools which have the reputation for liking—and requiring—this sort of activity.

In general, the more you can avoid the current clichés of your peer group—both the self-expressive yawping of "Me! Me! Me!" on the one hand and the hard-sell "getting mine at any cost" success rap on the other—the better for you. The best voice or "stance" to adopt is that of a mature, straightforward person who is eager to start college and wants to learn, but has little of the starry-eyed idealism of the Joe Colleges of the fifties, the flower children of the sixties, or the eco-freaks of the seventies. These are the eighties, you're about to enter the adult world, and you're offering the college a set of unique talents and experiences.

Now read over the rough draft one last time. Could any one of your 968 other classmates have written it? If so, tear it up and start over. You want your essay to be one that makes the admissions officers sit up and take notice, not one that causes them to sigh, "Oh, another of *those!*" as they pitch it in the Out box.

• Once you've got all the materials together, the essay written, application blank filled out, and other credentials on the way, take a last look to check over all the forms. Make sure you haven't omitted anything. Make sure there isn't a line somewhere saying, "On a separate sheet of paper list . . ." or "Write a short essay of not over 500 words on. . . ." Also make sure you've enclosed a check for the application fee, if there is one. Most schools do require a small fee for processing the paperwork of all those hundreds of candidates who apply each term. Again, pay it now and make sure the check is good. A rubber check leaves a bad taste with Admissions and assures you'll be relegated to the "On Hold" file.

• What about "early admissions"? It isn't always necessary to wait for your senior year to start the application process. Some topflight schools do have an early-admissions plan to enroll particularly motivated or talented students who have finished the eleventh, even the tenth, grade and are seen as "admissible" without the formality of a high school diploma. If you're one of these exceptional ones, check it out—you may be able to start college a full year early. And in our youth-oriented, early-success culture, that's an important year saved.

There's another plan, called the Early Decision Plan, in which good students who make outstanding scores on the eleventh-grade CEEB SATs (or PSATs) and also have high rank and academic marks are assured of college admission as early as December of their senior year—but only if they apply by October 1 and only to the one institution. There's no risk involved for you—in fact, it's often a way to assure yourself a place in that tough first-choice school, since few other admissions will have been received by that time. Clearly you must be qualified to participate in the program at all. But if you're a strong student, check it out. If nothing works out, you still have the rest of your senior year to apply to other schools.

You may hear the term "open admissions" and wonder what it means. Some colleges may literally admit all who apply, but a more common practice is for several schools in the same system to allow for open admission to the *system*. You don't always get your first choice of individual schools under this plan, but you will usually get entrance to at least one college within a state or city system. For example, you would apply to the City University of New York system, listing six possible choices, and in turn receive an answer from the admissions committee which in effect decides for you which school(s) on your list you're qualified to enter.

Another admissions plan you may want to consider is "deferred admissions"—a plan by which you are admitted to the college of your choice but delay your actual matriculation for a year in order to work, travel, or take special training in a field such as theater, dance, music, or art. The college and student must plan this deferment jointly and the college must approve of the activities you will engage in during the year (you can't attend another college or just "hang out" with friends on another campus, for example; you must have a real *plan* for additional work, experience, study, or training).

There are pros and cons to this system, as with anything else. The advantages are the increased depth and breadth of experience that an extra year of travel, work, or specialized study might give, plus the added maturity that an extra year brings. The disadvantages: you lose your good high school study habits, find it harder to get back into a school routine, are separated from your peer group for an important year, and may find it harder to get recommendations from high school teachers and principals, whose memories of your work may have dimmed during the year. You can solve this last problem by getting the recommendation letters on record before you take off for your free year. Also, make sure to pay a deposit to reserve your place in next year's freshman class—if the school's admissions policies toughen up during the year, you may find it harder to get into the freshman class unless your fee is already paid.

As far as lateness and promptness go, it's always better to be among the early applicants than among the latecomers. All things considered, an earlier application is nearly always more favorably received than a late one. Particularly if the school is highly competitive, the earlier the better. But if for some reason you're delayed in starting the application process or find that early choices don't pan out, don't feel that you're excluded from starting to college because it's later in the year than is normal for beginning the admissions process. Unless you're applying to a highly competitive, prestigious school, take the trouble to inquire about late admissions. Remember that even very good schools will often have unfilled slots up to several months before the fall term begins. You'll probably have to pay some late fees—often considerable ones—but it's money well spent.

SCHOLARSHIPS AND FINANCIAL AID

Grades and other credentials aside, let's talk about another aspect of college education: money. Let's not delude ourselves—college is expensive. And it's getting more expensive every day; inflation, stagflation, and the recession haven't spared higher education. Students often deplore the high cost of college, forgetting that universities are like any other business. They have to pay staff salaries, keep the lights and heat on, repair the physical plant, and do the million and one other things that businesses must do to stay afloat. It would be nice if all institutions of higher learning could give away their services for free and so opt out of the inflationary spiral, but that's just not the way it is.

Let's face up to another hard fact. More and more, it's the case that the very rich and the very poor are the groups that find it easiest to go to school: the rich, because they have the backing of family wealth, "strings" to pull, and business or ancestral ties; the poor, because they can demonstrate family incomes far below the minimums required for eligibility for some of the most attractive grants-in-aid.

Unfortunately, most of us are neither super-affluent nor at the poverty level. We're simply the children of middle-income families who'd like to afford some higher education. We lack the connections and "clout" necessary to win a prestigious Ivy League scholarship, yet our family income is far above the poverty level required by many state and federal grants.

What are the options? Let's first discuss how to decide on the right approach. Then we'll show you some of the options available to you.

First of all, sit down with your checkbook, savings passbook, and calculator and do a little simple arithmetic. It's unlikely that you'll receive an all-expenses-paid, full-tuition scholarship for your four years. So your first task is to determine how much the total costs are, then how much you and your parents can contribute to those costs, and finally, how much supplemental aid you will require.

So start by figuring out the total cost of your first year at the colleges of your first, second, and third choice. A few rules of thumb: large urban private universities cost more than junior colleges, particularly those that are part of a state or city system. Exclusive eastern schools tend to cost more than comparable schools in other sections of the country. State-supported colleges and universities are generally less expensive to state residents (although out-of-staters and residents of less than three years often have to pay hefty sums). Junior colleges are usually—but not always—cheaper than four-year colleges or universities.

Start with the college catalog or bulletin. Get the exact cost of tuition and fees for your first year. Often the costs are given per semester hour, so you'll need to multiply by 12, 15, or whatever comprises a full academic load to get the total figure. Be sure to include both semesters, plus special short terms or summer school if you plan to go year-round. Also note special fees such as testing, laboratory, matriculation, or registration costs. And do be aware that many colleges explicitly reserve the right to raise or change fees without prior notice. Don't figure your budget so close that a $100 miscalculation can blow the whole thing.

Tuition and fees are "fixed costs"—that is, there's no way

of changing them short of dropping out. They will come in at about 10 to 20 percent of the total cost at a public institution and about 35 to 50 percent at a private institution. Your next item, room and board, can run from 35 to 50 percent of the total package. Remember, however, that if it's a dormitory situation, or any other on-campus living arrangement, meals are usually included (hence the "room and board"), so you need budget only for off-campus meals and extras.

Now fill in some other categories. Your situation may be unique, but here are some categories to get you started:

Books, supplies (paper, pens, typewriter, calculator, drafting materials, art materials), other required materials such as workbooks or cassettes for the language lab.
Club or professional association dues.
Fraternity dues (if applicable).
Medical care (doctor's and dentist's bills, medicines, over-the-counter drugs, infirmary fees and insurance if these are not provided as part of your student health care package).
"Activity fees" (usually paid to the Student Union to cover admission to on-campus activities of all sorts).
Laundry and dry cleaning.
Clothing and accessories (including briefcases, luggage, umbrellas, athletic gear, and casual wear).
Haircuts, shaving supplies, or grooming sundries.
Transportation, on- and off-campus (include a minimum of two visits home per year—Christmas and summer vacation—if you are going away from home; be sure to budget more if you intend to go more often). On-campus travel should include car expenses, repairs,

gasoline, and all the standard things if you plan to keep a car on campus. Otherwise, figure whatever mode of transportation you plan to take: subway, trains, bicycle, buses, taxis, car-pooling with friends. Any one of these will involve costs—be sure they get figured in.

Recreational expenses (dating, social occasions, sporting events tickets, films, concerts, nights out on the town, restaurant meals, and so on).

Incidentals (budget $20 to $50 a week for these, depending on how well you're covered in the other categories. This includes magazines and newspapers, snacks, sodas and gum from the vending machines, cigarettes if you smoke, and all the little extras that you tend to forget in making a budget).

Equipment and furniture for your apartment or dorm room (more on this in the next chapter, but you need to plan for the throw rugs, coffeepots, clock radios, popcorn poppers, and yogurt makers that you'll use to stock your new lair).

Postage, stationery, and telephone (yes, it *costs* to communicate with the folks back home. And while you're at it, add some change too—you'll need dimes and quarters for the pay phone, and it's nice not *always* to call the folks collect).

Hobby and craft expenses (include your camera, film, musical instruments and sheet music, theatrical makeup, art supplies, jogging gear, tennis racquets, backpack and hiking boots, and whatever else you'll use to keep you sane in your spare time).

Well! Quite a list, isn't it? Now make a rough estimate of each category and decide on what you *think* each of the items will cost. Be honest! If you're a camera freak, include plenty of money for film or you'll find your budget shot. If big evenings on the town, or trendy clothes, or art books, or new jogging shoes are your secret pitfalls, include them too. You'll have to make some cuts, but right now you're arriving at an idealized bottom line that includes both necessities and frills.

Next give a ballpark figure of what you yourself or your parents can provide—through savings, a part-time or summer job for you, and/or an outright gift or loan from parents or other relatives. Whatever the source, be sure it's realistic and doesn't involve your working to the detriment of your studies. If you're smart, you'll already have planned for this and will have squirreled away some money for two or three summers prior to senior year.

Do this exercise for at least your three top-choice colleges so you can get an idea of what the relative costs are. Maybe Crawling Ivy is out of the question, but you may be pleasantly surprised that Sprawling Juniper U. is so inexpensive. And by looking at the categories carefully, you'll see how you can plan to cut some corners and still swing one of your first choices.

Then get together what the financial aid offices now call a "student resources package." Sit down and list all your sources of cash in the following categories: parents or other relatives, Social Security benefits, veteran's benefits, summer earnings, part-time work, student savings, interest on savings accounts, insurance (probably your parents' rather than your own), and other sources. Total up this list, subtract it from the total costs of a year at Crawling Ivy, and you'll see what you need to get in the way of financial aid.

Why do it all in such a complicated way? Very simple:

you may not need to apply for financial aid. Or you may not need to apply for as much aid as you thought at first. We tend to panic and overestimate how expensive college is going to be. And most colleges today talk of financial aid "packages"—that is, monies from several sources to supplement sources the student already has. So hang onto the worksheets. Your financial aid officer will be impressed and glad you've done some of the preliminary paperwork. He's tired of people coming into his office and saying "I need lots of money for college." The question is: How much?

The next step is to write to or call the financial aid officer of the school(s) you're applying to. Here again, multiple admissions may be a solution: the school that comes up with the best financial aid package may be—may have to be —your first choice. So talk to them all, keeping these hints in mind:

· Start early. In fact, when you write for the admissions materials, dash off another letter to the financial aid office for information on scholarships available to you and the necessary forms. Sometimes, in addition to the national and state programs, there will be local opportunities available through the school or certain programs or departments. Again, start early; here the early bird often does get the worm.

· Remember that if cash is still tight when the entire package is assembled, you can cut costs in some categories. Living at home is no long-term solution, but it can get you through a semester or two while you build up your cash reserves. A local or junior college may also offer more flexible time for part-time employment—a real boon to those on tight budgets.

· Don't despair of getting aid just because your family

has a decent income. Scholarship and grant committees understand this: they understand that just because your father is a decently paid executive doesn't necessarily mean that *you* have access to any of the cash. You may have a bad relationship with Dad and not find a single sou forthcoming toward your education. Or the cash may be tied up in investments, or earmarked to pay for Mom's recent surgery, sister's private-school tuition, a nursing home for Great-grandpa. Often the space marked "approximate family income" is misleading, so be honest about it. If your father is a recently fired executive from a prestigious firm, you may have no more available cash than the lower-income kid.

· Be reasonable. Remember that there really *is* less money available today than in the easier, more affluent sixties and early seventies. Congress in the fall of 1980 passed a $140 million cut in the federally funded BEOG program (Basic Educational Opportunity Grant, in case you haven't learned your alphabet soup). Eduardo Wolle, legislative director of the U.S. Student Association in Washington, an organization which has been fighting the cuts, estimated in an October 1980 *Oui* interview that this reduction alone would cut each student's grant by about $50.

· Learn to talk the language of financial aid "packages" —by which most financial aid officers mean a collection of several funding sources that can be balanced, juggled, and tapped at various stages in your career as a student. Since this takes time, effort, planning ahead, and expert counseling, make friends with the financial aid people from day one. "Grantsmanship" is a complex game, and you'll need some pros to help you play it right.

· First, in order to decide what type of financial aid to apply for, you need to understand the difference between the various types of aid programs. *Scholarships* may be either direct gifts of money or, more typically, remission or waiver of fees and tuition for a student. Scholarships don't require a return of services or repayment either during your college career or after you graduate. However, *scholarship loans* (grants to students advanced as loans) are canceled either totally or partially only if you provide services to the grant agency—as for example, with state government assistance to prospective teachers or medical students, who agree to teach or perform medical services in a specified area for a certain length of time.

A *grant* generally refers to a stipend given a student for services. The funds are not tax-exempt and should be declared as income on IRS returns. Often grants are awarded in combination with campus employment or student loans.

Finally, *loans* are really advances of credit or funds to an undergraduate student. Repayment is usually required in the form of either services or cash payments (usually in installments, and typically with a reasonable interest rate) after the student graduates or leaves the college.

· Typically, an aid package to a bright student might include a university scholarship, a job (perhaps a part-time job on campus), and a loan in varying amounts each term. Public colleges typically provide about $400 per student in various kinds of aid; private universities can go as high as $900 or more. And don't forget that private institutions also have access to certain forms of public aid as well.

The package approach, by the way, is the current one. A survey sponsored by the College Scholarship Service and the U.S. Office of Education, conducted by ETS and reported in *Barron's Handbook of American College Financial Aid*, shows that the more aid you need, the more likely it is that the aid will come in the form of a package or combination of sources. And remember, family income and scholastic record are only two component parts of the criteria used to determine who gets aid and how much. (Other criteria include availability of funds, the complexities of packaging the total aid plan, and of course, the qualifications of other candidates.)

• When you present your list of incidentals, be modest and realistic. Don't include first-class airline tickets and a week at Club Med under "travel," or dinner for two at Le Frogpond or upkeep for your Excalibur as miscellaneous "necessities" that you expect the financial aid office to help bankroll. When you appear for interviews, look neat and clean, but not too affluent. We've seen students swathed in full-length fox coats and dripping Vuitton and Gucci accessories who wonder why Financial Aid was so short with them. You don't have to look poverty-stricken, but you shouldn't exude wealth either.

• Worried about the portion of the package that you and your parents have to contribute? Send for the *free* pamphlet *Meeting College Costs*, which is published by the College Scholarship Service and is available in most college financial aid offices. It should give you an idea of what your share will be and how best to handle it. (Some seasoned players in the game of grantsmanship claim that the best way is to be declared "independent" by your parents—meaning you're totally self-supporting and on your own. But there are legal niceties [chiefly tax considerations] in acquiring this status, so proceed with caution.)

• A good source to check: large data banks with funding information such as The Scholarship Search Company (1775 Broadway, New York, N.Y. 10019), which has listings of over 250,000 sources of funding for students. You have to pay for the info, of course, but in return you'll get a printout of many relevant sources. Some will apply to your situation; others won't. Best finds are the odd once-in-a-million chances, like the $1,000 stipends to all Yalies whose names are Leavenworth or DeForest. These *do* exist. If you fit the category, you're in luck.

The advantage of the computerized search is that it uncovers many sources of funding you might not normally know about: the Gannett Newspaper Carrier Awards (for former employees of newspapers, or their families), E. C. Halbeck Scholarships for sons and daughters of postal workers, Methodist National Scholarships for good (or bad) Methodists, Sons of Poland awards for Jersey City residents, and so on. Often these obscure sources go begging because no one takes the trouble to research them and apply.

· A few scholarships and grants require essays or documentation: for example, the National American Legion Auxiliary Presidents' Scholarships, for which any student whose parents were in any war and who is willing to write a short essay can qualify—for $1,000 to $1,500 in funds. Often local businesses and chambers of commerce have scholarship funds that literally go begging because no one bothers to write the essay. So it takes two hours of your time. What better investment can you make in your future?

· Considering a loan? Naturally, you'd rather have an outright grant or another source of funds you don't need to repay. But usually a typical package is going to include some money for day-to-day expenses, and unless you want to work full-time or hold down two or three part-time jobs, a loan is often the only alternative. Consider, then, sources like the Guaranteed Student Loan program (funds guaranteed either by the state or federal government, with payments beginning nine months after you graduate, and the balance not having to be paid off for ten years). Payment schedules are arranged with the college from which you borrowed the money. Some pluses here: the modest payments (a minimum of $30 a month), the lenient criteria (family income doesn't matter), and relative indifference to the economy. The criteria that *do* apply are simple: you have to be accepted as a student at an accredited institution; have to allow six weeks for loan approval; and must have credit insurance. Interest rates on student loans tend to be lower than conventional bank loan rates.

· If you're interested in the whole field of loans, consider these other sources: National Direct (formerly Defense) Student Loans (which allow for borrowings up to $2,500 each academic year depending on need, with repayment postponed until nine months after graduation); United Student Aid Funds (state plans for residents backed by state or Federal Reserve funds). Write United Student Aid Funds in care of 6610 North Shadeland Ave., Box 50827, Indianapolis, Ind. 46250. The National Direct Student Loans *do* require you to demonstrate financial need, but if you teach for five years or go into the service, or become a full-time staff member in an Operation Head Start preschool program, the debt is erased entirely.

More sources: the Law Enforcement Education Program (LEEP), which has money available to people who study police science, criminal justice, and other related fields. This program makes available ten-year low-interest loans up to $2,200 per academic year to students in programs related directly to law enforcement. Try also college or university loans (usually emergency short-term loans available in real crisis situations such as illness or a death in the family), loans for community and junior college graduates, nursing student loan programs and other sources. Finally, if nothing else is available, consider the deferred tuition payment plan. Some colleges use quarterly payments, others monthly payments, sometimes financed through a local bank. Check out three such sources: Tuition Plan, Inc., 1 Park Ave., New York, N.Y. 10016, or 400 North Michigan Ave., Chicago, Ill. 60611; Tuition Plan of New Hampshire, Inc., 18 School St., Concord, N.H. 03301; and Funds for Education, Inc., 319 Lincoln St., Manchester, N.H. 03102. Also check out Parents Loan Plans for the pricier colleges—some will have their own financing plan—and ROTC scholarships (worth $10,000 to $33,000 over a four-year period, *if* you put in six years of service, with at least four on active duty after you graduate. Here, SAT scores matter greatly: testing abilities are among the top-rated criteria for these lucrative awards.)

 · On to the grants and scholarships! The most popular ones are the Basic Educational Opportunity Grant (BEOG), the Educational Opportunity Grant (EOG or SEOG), LEEP grants, and state and institutional grants and scholarships.

Forget the myth that your family has to earn under $12,000 a year for you to qualify for BEOG. In November 1978 the rules were changed so that your family can now earn as much as $25,000 yearly. (For this grant you have to be a U.S. citizen or permanent resident, be enrolled at least half-time in college, and be judged worthy of a grant by the U.S. Office of Education.) You can get from $200 to $1,800 per year for BEOG, so it's well worth pursuing. Get the info through the special forms available from the College Scholarship Service (Box 176, Princeton, N.J. 08540) or pick up the BEOG forms in the financial aid office and mail them to: Basic Grant Program, Box A, Iowa City,

Iowa 52240. And if BEOG can't cover the expenses and you and/or your parents can't make up the difference, the federally funded SEOG (Supplemental Educational Opportunity Grant) can cough up $200 to $1,500 a year, depending on need, academic promise, and seriousness of purpose. You can pick up SEOG applications from the financial aid office or write the BEOG address above. Or write directly to the U.S. Office of Education, Washington, D.C. 20202. Students don't need to repay the SEOG grants, but colleges must match them with other aid for the student, such as a National Direct Loan, a work-study program, or a local scholarship.

Bright, academically inclined, and a good tester? Consider *winning* your scholarship on the basis of your test scores. The most publicized competitive scholarships are the National Merit Scholarships.

The National Merits are based on both academic excellence and financial need. Three types of scholarships are awarded: (1) those based solely on merit (not financial need), which are worth approximately $1,000 for a total of about 1,000 stipends per year; (2) National Merit awards sponsored by some colleges and based on financial need, ranging from $100 to $1,500 for four years (you should contact the college of your choice to see if it sponsors these scholarships); and (3) corporation-sponsored National Merit awards in a range of $250 to $1,500 a year, based on financial need (parents should contact their employers to see if the company sponsors such awards).

Again, eligibility for the awards depends on your taking the PSAT/NMSQT in October of your junior year. If you qualify as a semifinalist, you will take the SAT in November of your senior year and will be notified four to six weeks later if you are the recipient of an award.

There are also scores of other scholarships based on academic prowess—like the journalism and literature full-tuition scholarship, funded by a newspaper magnate, that sent Valerie through four years of undergraduate school. Most don't give additional stipends for books or room and board, but if you're resourceful, part-time jobs and additional grants or loans can fill the bill here.

Finally, one of the best and most widely accessible funding sources is your state office that is responsible for financial aid for education. For example, New York State has a Tuition Assistance Program that offers from $200 to $1,800 a year to over 350,000 resident students. Illinois is similarly blessed with about $78.1 million in Illinois State Grants. California comes up with $78.9 to $79 million annually. On the other hand, smaller and less well supported states offer far smaller sums for education. Check out your state office, which is usually listed under a title something like "Council of Higher Education Assistance." Ask for an application and a list of regulations. Some states are surprisingly lenient; several years ago, for example, Illinois began to award the grants to part-time as well as full-time students, thus making it possible for many working adults to return to college. (Right on, Illinois!) Check it out—you can only lose by not applying.

· Finally, there's the old standby, the campus work-study program that helps students find work to pay for their tuition. This is a federally funded program which provides part-time employment for lower-income full-time students. Students work an average of twenty hours a week during the regular term, forty hours in summer and vacations. Standard minimum wages are usually paid. Sometimes colleges will have agreements with affiliated nonprofit organizations, such as museums, foundations, historical societies, and social service institutions, that take the overflow from this popular program. There are fairly stringent restrictions as to income, but if you qualify the program is a real lifesaver for many.

Even if your family's income is too high to qualify for work-study, consider enrolling in a co-op program or another off-campus, part-time work program sanctioned by your school. Such a program enables you to alternate periods of study with full-time employment in off-campus jobs. The range is enormous: journalism, publishing, public and private schools, city, state, and federal offices, labs, hospitals, museums, banks, public relations firms, and ad agencies. It's a terrific way to gain actual work experiences and also make money for college expenses at the same time. No wonder the "Learn while you earn" motto has become so popular. It's an ideal program for highly motivated, career-minded students who are eager to experience the world of work as well as the one inside the walls of old Crawling Ivy.

SCHOLARSHIPS FOR WOMEN

Although many scholarship and loan sources—the majority, in fact—are for both men and women, there are an increasing number that are earmarked "For Women Only." Not all will fit your needs or qualifications, but out of the growing number of such grants, there might just be one that seems tailor-made for you. Here are some sources of information on available funds and also the names of some scholarships and loans earmarked for women.

· The American Association of University Women (AAUW) annually publishes a booklet entitled "Educational Financial Aids." Order from: AAUW Sales Office,

2401 Virginia Ave. N.W., Washington, D.C. 20037. The cost is $1.00. Clairol (which itself sponsors a scholarship program) also publishes a (free) booklet, called "Educational Financial Aid Sources for Women." Write: Clairol Loving Care Scholarship Program, 345 Park Ave., 5th Floor, New York, N.Y. 10022. Together, these two booklets should give you most of the information you need to determine which scholarships, if any, you're qualified for. Also check out the following scholarships and loans:

· Florence Eagleton Grants Program (to help conduct research on the roles of women in public life). For information, write: Center for the American Woman and Politics, Eagleton Institute of Politics, Rutgers University, New Brunswick, N.J. 08901.

· Diuguid Fellowships (intended to provide women whose career and professional goals have been deferred with an opportunity for study; applicants must live in the southern U.S.A., be twenty-one years of age or over, and have had their careers or education interrupted because of family or work duties). For information, write: Council of Southern Universities, Inc., 795 Peachtree St. N.E., Suite 484, Atlanta, Ga. 30308.

· Helen Malloch Scholarships (for upperclass undergraduate women—juniors or seniors—or graduate women majoring in journalism). For information, write: National Federation of Press Women, 7005 Park Ave., Richmond, Va. 23226.

· The Fred A. Hooper Memorial Scholarship (intended to encourage advanced study in transportation and traffic management for women). For information, write: Traffic Clubs International, 1040 Woodcock Rd., Orlando, Fla. 32803.

· Internship programs for women interested in politics.

For information, write: Washington Institute for Women in Politics, Mount Vernon College, 2100 Foxhall Rd. N.W., Washington, D.C. 20007.

· Soroptimist International Awards (offered by Soroptimist International of the Americas, Inc., as regional or local awards for women returning to school to train for a higher-level job). For information contact your local chapter of Soroptimist International, or write: The Soroptimist Foundation, 1616 Walnut St., Philadelphia, Pa. 19103.

Note: The following four grants and one loan are administered by the Business and Professional Women's Foundation. For information, write: Scholarship Department (or "Loan Fund for Women" for the last item), BPW Foundation, 2012 Massachusetts Ave N.W., Washington, D.C. 20036. The awards are:

· The Kelly Services Second Career Scholarships (for women twenty-five and over who have spent five or more years in full-time homemaking and are either widowed or divorced).

· Florence Morse Scholarships (for women twenty-five and older who are in their junior or senior year of a business school accredited by the AACSB (American Assembly of Collegiate Schools of Business).

· Clairol Loving Care Scholarships (for women of thirty and over).

· BPW Career Advancement Scholarships (awarded to women twenty-five and over).

· BPW Loan Program Loan Fund for Women in Engineering Studies ($80,000 a year in loans given to women for study in engineering programs accredited by the Engineers Council for Profesional Development; the study can be full- or part-time but must account for at least six hours per semester).

- More engineering scholarships are available from two sources: Women in Engineering Program, University of Missouri, Rolla, Mo. 64501; and Society of Women Engineers, United Engineering Center, 345 East 47th St., New York, N.Y. 10017.
- Interested in athletic scholarships? Check the January issue each year of *Women's Sports Magazine*. Reprints are $1.00 if you miss the yearly issue. For information, write: Women's Sports Foundation, 195 Moulton St., San Francisco, Calif. 94123.
- Loans in varying amounts with about 4 percent annual interest are available to women. Write PEO Educational Fund, 3700 Grand Ave., Des Moines, Iowa 50312.
- It's not a scholarship, but it does bring money, perks, and recognition. Enter *Glamour's* Top Ten College Women Contest (deadline is usually around mid-December each year). Watch the November issue of the magazine for details or write to *Glamour* Top Ten College Women Contest, 350 Madison Ave., New York, N.Y. 10017.
- Some final notes on guides and publications to send away for: *Association for Intercollegiate Athletics for Women* (AIAW) *Directory* (write for information and current price to AAHPER Publication Sales, 1201 16th St., Washington, D.C. 20036). Also write for *Selected List of Postsecondary Opportunities for Minorities and Women*, published as a free booklet by the U.S. Office of Education, Bureau of Postsecondary Education, Washington, D.C. 20202.
- Finally, while you're in your local bookstore browsing, pick up the following two guides: *A Woman's Guide to Career Preparation: Scholarships, Grants and Loans*, by Ann J. Lawlin (New York: Anchor Press, Doubleday,

1979), and *Directory of Financial Aids for Women*, by Gail Ann Schlacter (Los Angeles: Reference Service Press, 1979).

THE INTERVIEW

Once the financial problems are settled—or are in the process of being settled—you can relax a bit. The long admissions process is nearly over. You've only one more hurdle to jump: the admissions interview.

This process is often optional—in fact, with rising transportation costs and scheduling difficulties, more and more schools are dropping this portion of the admissions procedure, or at least making it strictly voluntary. This is especially true for students coming from great distances; the school just can't afford to require that Joe or Jane pack up for a leisurely weekend at Crawling Ivy.

Even if an admissions interview is not mandatory, we strongly recommend making one on your own initiative. If you can swing the travel money and the time away from your studies, plan to spend at least a day or two on the campus(es) of your choice. Often the difference between two prospective students is very slight, and the fact that you called and made an appointment to come in person to the campus will weigh strongly in your favor. Consider the interview as a positive opportunity to learn more about the school of your choice and to allow the school to do the same with you. It's a positive opportunity, not a chore or an ordeal to be faced!

Things may be different if you're a local student. You may well be asked to come in for a personal chat for any of a variety of reasons: as a final screening for a scholarship or other award; to discuss financial aid packages or other options; to confirm or verify materials on your application; or in some cases, to discuss low test scores, especially if they're at variance with your overall record.

If you are asked to go for an admissions interview, look back over the advice we gave for College Day participants. The same rules apply. Look neat, clean, and well groomed. Remember the obligatory hair trim, manicure, and shower, plus a beard trim for men and light, natural-looking makeup for women. Good casual but tailored clothes are appropriate: the jeans can be saved for postadmission days.

If you're asked to see the financial aid office about qualifications for a scholarship or grant, then be as punctual, businesslike, and pleasant as you can be. Don't rant on about your superior academic accomplishments or gripe about your great financial "need." Be sure to have supporting documents. And if it's a merit or academic scholarship you're competing for, have some facts at hand and in your head in case you're asked to talk about why you want to attend Crawling Ivy.

If the admissions office calls on you to confirm, deny, or add to material on your application, don't panic. Very often your information is simply inadequate and some additional data is desired. Or if the discrepancy between high school grades and test scores is too great, the school is looking for an explanation. Here's where it helps to mention that you were ill or injured, that there was a crisis at home, or that you are simply a bad tester. Honesty and straightforwardness pay off in this situation. If necessary, offering to do some remedial work or get tutoring in an area of weakness can help—particularly if you're a marginal case. But bluster, bluff, and belligerence will get you nowhere. If you go in and berate your high school, criticize the tests, curse the ETS, and verbally abuse the admissions counselor who interviews you, forget it. "Winning through intimidation" is not a game your friendly admissions office loves to play.

If it's a simple interview to help Admissions decide between two or more likely candidates, you can't know the competition and so can't plan your strategy accordingly. But our usual sage advice still applies: be calm and collected, present a "mature" appearance, be articulate. Stress your strengths but also mention your weaknesses so as to present a balanced view of your record. Be honest in mentioning anything—low test scores, a couple of lower grades, a possible weak recommendation—that might offset the record. But don't be afraid to "blow your own horn"; in a casual way, be sure to mention all your special extracurricular accomplishments or areas where you shine academically. Best of all, if there's a steady record of improvement, point this out to the admissions counselor. That's precisely the kind of growth that universities look for.

And once you've survived the interview, go relax. Walk around the campus. Get a cup of coffee in the Student Union. Talk to some people. Get to know the place. You'll be spending a lot of your time there for the next four years.

Then go home and wait for the mail. And don't forget to celebrate when the letter of acceptance arrives!

PART TWO

GETTING READY TO GO

5

What to Do When You're Accepted

ALL RIGHT, the hardest part is done. There are a couple of possible scenarios here. The best possible one is the happiest: you got into the college of your first choice. Terrific! You're happy, your parents are happy, the admissions office is happy. All systems are GO.

But suppose things didn't work out quite so well. You bombed out on Number One and possibly on Number Two as well. You *did* manage to get into a couple of other just-average places, but neither of them particularly turns you on.

There are several different moves left at this point. One is, obviously, to wait for a year, reapply to Choices Number One and Two, and sit it out. Another is to investigate how close you came to admission to the place of your dreams, put yourself on a waiting list (if one exists), and wait for the mail each day. A third alternative, and probably the one that most students pick, is to settle for third or fourth best and get on with it.

It's not an easy decision to make. A great deal depends on you and your temperament. Could you sustain your interest in Crawling Ivy for a full year if it were necessary to wait that long? What would be your alternatives if you were rejected for a second time? Can you really afford that critical lost year?

A better alternative—unless you have a sensational job, a year of travel, or some other activity that can fully engage you for a year—is to take a long hard look at those third and fourth choices. Ask yourself at least the following questions and try to decide if you can live with the place for at least a year:

Is the college academically adequate for my purposes: that is, does it have the courses, programs, majors, minors I am most interested in at this point?
What is its general academic reputation? How does it stack up against other colleges in the area? nationally?
What is the faculty like? What percentage of them have Ph.D.'s or other professional degrees? Are they distinguished scholars and writers, or merely teachers?
What is the school's record for publishing and research? What significant books, articles, or research projects and grants have originated there in the past five years?
Would a program from this college transfer to the schools of my first and second choice, should I choose to transfer there a year or so later?
Is it geographically suited to my needs? Close to family, if necessary? Convenient for travel? Does it offer good housing, cultural activity, an interesting environment?
Is the library adequate for research at the undergraduate

level? Are other facilities, such as gyms, athletic programs, and extracurricular activities I'm interested in, also present?

If you can answer yes to a fair percentage of these questions, then you probably can live with your third or fourth choice. If not, start making inquiries about late admissions *at once*. You may find that you're in luck and several good schools have unexpected late openings (due to cancellations and other accidents) that now put you into the running for some good schools you hadn't considered when your sights were set so firmly on Crawling Ivy U.

One possible strategy: if possible, place yourself on a waiting list for your first and second choices. You might write a carefully phrased letter to the admissions office saying that you regret that you were rejected, understand that they had many well-qualified applicants, but are still interested in the place and would like to be put on a waiting list, if such exists. Often such lists are made up of, say, the top twenty or thirty or fifty applicants who had to be rejected at the last minute but who had very strong records. Most admissions officers won't tell you what position you occupy on such a list, but most will be helpful in telling you exactly what getting on such a list "means" and when you can expect to hear the outcome of this final list.

Meanwhile, as you wait to hear from Number One, keep busy getting yourself admitted to one or two other good, acceptable second-string schools. The state university, if it's a good one, is usually a safe bet, as are large urban "commuter" colleges. In general, stick with four-year institutions if you're thinking of transferring; there will be more transferable programs than at the local junior college.

If your waiting-list strategy pays off, then be sure to write promptly to the schools you decide not to enter; they may have waiting lists too, and that place you vacate may just go to some student whose heart's desire is to go to the place you're just lukewarm over. Write a courteous letter and ask if it's possible to get any part of your fees back. If it's very late, the answer is probably no; earlier in the year, refunds are often possible. And be sure you complete the paperwork and send in fees and deposits to the school you finally choose, regardless of how late in the year it is. Promptness is always impressive to the university officials.

If the waiting-list maneuver doesn't pan out and you have to attend your second or third choice for a year, don't let a "second-best" attitude creep into your work. Study and play as hard as you would at your first-choice school. Give the place a chance. A year later, you may not even want to think of transferring. And even if you do give the first-string place(s) a whirl again, you'll be one up on the GPA game with your good record from Sprawling Juniper State U. under your belt. Ironically, it's often easier to get into the Crawling Ivies of the academic world as a transfer student than as a green freshman!

We hope, however, that you've been accepted at the college you really wanted to attend. You've got that all-important letter of admission in your hand—the document that certifies that you're good enough to get inside the halls of old Crawling Ivy, if not out of them. You've got your admissions materials in hand, an admissions officer's or counselor's card (or at least a name of a human being that you can call), and a catalog. But that's all, except for possibly a campus map. The rest is up to you. *You*, all by yourself, now have to create the rest of your college career out of nothing.

So it's now up to you. The days of being treated like a

kid are over. High schools may pamper their students and take *in loco parentis* seriously, but colleges and universities nowadays seldom do. They just can't afford the time, personnel, or effort it takes to coddle their students. Besides, what with increasing numbers of students over twenty-one and even over thirty-five enrolling in the classroom, it seems a little artificial to send out detailed lists of instructions on choosing a roommate or being on time for meals. Most campuses, therefore, leave it strictly up to you to take care of the thousand and one details that need to be attended to before you finally settle into your new dorm room or apartment.

At times, these details will seem overpowering. After all, you're leaving a safe and secure nest where Mom and Dad took care of most of the details of nitty-gritty daily life. Now it's all your own show: laundry and dry cleaning, shoe repairs and shines, breakfast coffee, snacks, transportation, cash for books and other supplies, tuition, housing regulations, insurance, forms for financial aid, and in most cases, a part-time job to bring in some bread while you are in school. So let's try to sort out some things you can do before even the first day of registration. You can use this chapter as a sort of checklist for organizing your own activities in the month or so before school starts.

ON- AND OFF-CAMPUS LIVING

First, you've got to find a place to live. Time was when life was simple and the dorm was the major—sometimes the only—scene for college living. Along with your registration or admission forms you got dorm applications, which you dutifully filled out and returned. You were accepted, of course, since there was plenty of room for everyone, and that was that.

Not so anymore. Times have changed, and campus housing has changed quite as radically as the rest of higher education. Now the options are endless—in addition to the dorm, you could opt for an apartment, either shared or alone; a rented room in a nearby house; a communal living arrangement; a frat house or house for students of a certain ethnic or religious persuasion; a nearby loft or studio; or a move-in arrangement with friends or family.

Basically, however, all these options can be sorted out into two broad groups: on-campus and off-campus housing. The on-campus alternatives are more complex than they were in the old days. The simple sex-segregated dorm has given way to a variety of coed and "semi-coed" arrangements. Typically, there is a floor for women and one for men, with separate shower and bathroom facilities but common study and recreation areas. Or sometimes men and women are mixed on a floor, with roommates of the same sex specified. Some dorms do allow mixed-sex roommate pairs, but they are far rarer than the movies would have us believe! If your school is one of these, consult with the housing office to discover whether or not roommates are assigned or are a matter of personal choice, and what options you have if you prefer *not* to live as half of a male-female pairing. And relax: you're not likely to draw Bo Derek or Robert Redford on your first venture into coed living. Just investigate your options, stay cool, and enjoy.

In addition to the old-style dorm room with a shared bath or shower there are usually other options, including studios and efficiency apartments. Now many newer dorms have private or semiprivate baths or showers and small kitchens (or at least a fridge for light snacks and soft drinks). Some of the more elaborate arrangements are really small studio or efficiency apartments with Murphy or studio beds or sleep sofas that double as couches. Some will have tiny dining L's and partitioned-off eating and shower facilities. Some are barely big enough for one small person; some are roomy enough to accommodate two or three comfortably.

If you crave dorm living, there's no substitute for the preregistration visit to find out the facts before you move in. When you visit the campus, drop by all the living quarters available to freshmen. Sometimes there are several dorms, some student apartments, fraternity houses, an "international" or religious house, and a variety of off-campus boardinghouses. Go visit all of them. One dorm doesn't necessarily give a true picture. You may detest one and be turned on by all the rest. Or vice-versa. But go visit everything available. While you're there, talk to some residents. Hang out in the lounges or coffee shop. Check out the TV and visitors' rooms (could you *really* study with that orgy of disco beat around you?). Check out the practical things, too. See if the place has a laundry room (a real drag it is to schlep your dirty clothes three blocks away in foul weather). Vending machines, a snack bar, a coffee shop, or a nearby cafeteria are also a plus if there are no kitchen facilities in your room. Check the visitors' regulations if you intend to have out-of-town guests (either sex); many schools have visitors' dorms or rooms especially for that purpose.

Also ask how roommates are assigned—do you pick your own or are you at the mercy of the housing office's files? (Many housing offices provide roommate-preference forms and questionnaires that are useful in matching persons of similar tastes and interests.) Are food and drink permitted in the dorm, and if so, under what conditions? Is there a lights-out policy or curfew? Any quiet hours? (Surprisingly, this isn't a bad policy: dorm parties and beer blasts can continue into the wee small hours, and fun though it is, do you *really* want to prepare for your economics final with the sound of Coors cans hitting the pavement outside, cries of "Toga! Toga! Toga!" and some turkey playing his new CW albums full-volume on a commercial stereo outfit he undoubtedly retrieved from Studio 54?).

Then think about all these points and weigh them. The freedom from regulations may not be an unmixed blessing. Sure, you want to have some fun, but you also want to study. Finding a place that allows freedom and flexibility during off-hours but also imposes restrictions on the perpetual party-givers is what you're aiming for.

While you're at it, check out regulations on supposedly "innocent" things such as pets in the room; hanging pictures and otherwise "defacing" the walls; putting "coloration" on the old tatty furniture, as one university of our acquaintance put it; keeping food in the room, and so on. Most dorms officially ban dope and booze from the room, although actual practice may conflict with the published regulations; campus officials in one place will close their eyes, while in another they'll hire bloodhounds to track down your beer or stash. Dorms often have weird rules that are leftovers from some archaic era, so that a place that winks at your sleep-over friend and smuggled six-packs may end up fining you for putting holes in the wall. Be warned!

Why go off-campus to live? By the time you've toured all the available dorms, you may be thinking that all the action is there and little or none in the bleak little student apartments down the road. Well, take another look. Dorms are convenient, sure, but they can also be costly, restrictive, noisy, overcrowded, and just plain dull. So check out the off-campus listings before you sign anything. There are often some real bargains to be found in off-campus arrangements—but only for those who are willing to look, compare, shop, call, search out the want ads, and otherwise do their homework.

As with any kind of house hunting, the off-campus housing game is largely a matter of luck in locating good leads. It takes time to find exactly what you want, so start early in order to cover all the sources. Check out the college newspaper, the local papers (including suburban and neighborhood tabloids). Then get listings from the campus housing office and the student activities office, from bulletin boards scattered around the campus, and from the "roommate wanted" ads of the local frat house or student newspaper. By the end of a day of searching, you should have quite a hefty list of numbers and addresses.

Next, arm yourself with a campus map that includes the surrounding area (a three-to-five-mile radius should be sufficient). You'll need to locate all those "charming 1 bdrm/r.grdn/wdbrn frpl/b w. shower" lodgings before you go calling. Perhaps the fact that something is a good hour from campus explains why it's so cheap and still available! Here, a friend or acquaintance who knows the area can be invaluable help. Check out what's walking distance or easy commuting/driving distance before you make that first call. Also, find out what the desirable locations are. You may have been a champion athlete in your old high school and think you're well able to take care of yourself, but you can still be robbed or mugged if you live in the local skid row and wino area. Try to pick a good section that's inhabited by other students and has easy access to some campus watering-holes, restaurants, coffeehouses, museums, theaters, and bookstores.

Then start making some calls. Access to a free phone helps; otherwise, you're going to need a pile of dimes. Ask about space (how much?) and facilities for showering or bathing, cooking, refrigerating or freezing food, doing laundry. Also ask about pets, visitors, "decorating" and planting restrictions, what's supplied, and what you need to furnish. It does no good to save $75 a month on rent over the dorm prices if you've got to invest a bundle in furniture (the charming 1 bedrm w. wdbrn frpl has no bed, desk, chair, stove, or refrig).

Once you've made inquiries and narrowed down your list, put on your walking shoes (your well-worn Adidas or Nikes are ideal for this) and go house hunting. Travel the way you plan to get around once you're settled: take the bus, commuter train, bike, or shank's mare just as you'd do if you were leaving campus and going home for the day. Time the trips you make. That's the only way you'll know exactly how to interpret "convenient to Crawling Ivy campus life."

While you're checking out the environs, also notice the availability of other facilities. Are there groceries, delicatessens, drugstores, coffee shops, a laundry and dry cleaners, and a bank within easy distance? Or do you have to take yet another bus, train, or bike ride to get to a place to do your wash, buy a paper, get a check cashed, pick up some yogurt for tomorrow's lunch, or buy a cup of coffee to see you through a late night of study? If there's nothing nearby, don't rent, charming and inexpensive though the lodgings may be.

As for the advantages of off-campus living: the chief

ones are that it's likely to be less expensive, less noisy and "social," and hence more conducive to study than the dorm. If you pick the right place, it's also less restrictive (yes, dorms may still try to pull the *in loco parentis* bit) and generally allows you a more self-reliant, adult style of living. Remember, however, that dorms do provide a good way to meet people and become involved in college life. Off-campus living may tend to isolate you, especially if you're a freshman or transfer and don't know many people.

There are also disadvantages to living off-campus. Especially if you rent furnished rooms or an apartment in someone else's house, that "someone else" may place restrictions that cramp your life-style even more than the dorm: no loud music, lights out at a certain hour, no noisy guests, no food or drink in the room. In general, you're better off with a large multi-unit apartment building (a medium-priced high rise is ideal) rather than just one unit in a private home. The anonymity of the larger building gives you a welcome alternative to the little old ladies trying to mother their renter.

Then, too, there's the comfort and convenience factor. Make sure that the heating or air-conditioning is adequate, the hot water works, the shower has sufficient water pressure, and the place won't blow a fuse if you switch on both TV and typewriter simultaneously. Often "student" apartments are cozy and charming all right—but they're also relics of the nineteenth century in terms of heat, plumbing, and electricity. Make sure that yours has all the necessaries *before* you sign that lease.

Also, think out the furnished/unfurnished argument carefully in advance. Much depends on what "furnished" means. Apartments in old houses tend to be furnished in Early Victorian Attic and lean toward lavender sofas with faded cabbage roses, dusty rose and institutional green walls. Can you really survive this tacky decor for a full year? You're better off with a sparsely equipped pseudo-Danish-modern high rise; at least these places tend toward rusts, browns, golds and avocado tones—a lot less offensive than Old Lady Edwardian. Best compromise: find a simply furnished modern efficiency or studio with a Murphy bed, studio couch, or convertible sofa, a couple of chairs, decent tile floors or carpeting, a snack bar with chairs or stools or a kitchen nook with a table, and a fully equipped bathroom. Then you can supply nothing more than kitchen utensils, linens, stereo, and TV, plus knicknacks and pictures, and you're set (more about equipping your digs in style in the next section: keep reading!)

Once you've located a satisfactory place to live, get a lease if it's off-campus, a letter of agreement or contract if it's a dorm. Make sure everything is spelled out in both arrangements. Don't depend on goodwill in either case. Your landlord may take a dislike to you and try to impose restrictions that weren't in the original agreement in order to get you out of your quarters. Or the dorm may raise the room-and-board fee to a point where it's impossible to pay. Having everything in writing will keep things a lot cleaner on both sides. For your part, you know what agreements you must live up to and what are the consequences of not doing so. Our advice: don't assume anything; set clear limits, particularly about raises in rent or room and board during the academic year.

ROOMMATES

The question then arises: what about sharing with a roommate, or several roommates? Much here depends on your personal temperament, your study habits, and your social life. But here are the pros and cons that will help you make the right decision.

On the plus side, a roommate (if he or she is the right person) can be a study companion, a tennis/racquetball/poker/running/badminton/chess partner, a handy double-dating extra, a sounding board, an extra pair of wheels, and a source of record albums, stereo gear, cameras, and swim fins, not to mention a joy forever. If he or she is the wrong person . . . well, more of that later. Roommates can share in the cooking, housecleaning, laundry, and carrying-out of garbage. They can lend small sums of money, cash checks (sometimes), lend you a sweater in an emergency, arrange (and break) blind dates, argue about Proust or Nietzsche or Hesse, get freebie tickets to obscure foreign films, and find the best buys in used televisions on campus.

But wait: all is not sweetness and light. Roommates can also borrow your favorite Harris tweed blazer and return it, sans buttons and elbow patches, six months later; burn holes in your favorite pullover; steal your latest (and best) girlfriend or boyfriend; drink up all your liquid refreshment and never offer to replenish it; scoff at your vegetarian diet; throw noisy parties when you have a final coming up; keep obnoxious pets; smoke foul-smelling cigarettes; laugh at your accent; and pull your cat's tail. They may also cop out of KP duty; let the garbage accumulate in overflowing sacks in the kitchen; heap up wet towels on the bathroom floor; bathe rarely, use deodorant never, and generally behave like pigs. These relationships have a way of ending badly—for example, you may throw the offender from a twentieth-story window the night before your big economics final when he invites half the We Tappa Keg fraternity in for brew and assorted smokes, not to mention a sampling of your very own *Best of Disco* double album. In return for the attempted murder, he may retaliate and steal away in the night with your Justin boots, two Donna Summer albums, assorted edibles and drinkables, and your little black book full of phone numbers.

Picking a roommate is a little like getting married: it's wonderful when it works out, sheer undiluted hell when it doesn't. Unless your dorm is in the habit of assigning roomies at random, our advice is to live alone for the first term, case the place until you find a *simpatico* soul (or souls), and then set up housekeeping together. Often a group will naturally emerge from a term's living in the dorm—a sort of battle camaraderie grows from enduring the cafeteria food and the clowns down the hall—and sooner or later someone will say, "Hey, what if we got our own place? . . ."

But let's say you're not so lucky. You get to campus and find a pink slip in your mailbox: "Your dorm room is 811 Creeping Vineweed and your roommate is Morton Groinstern [or Marian Geek]." So off you go, only to discover that you, the perpetual party person, have been assigned to Mort (or Marian) the Grind. Or vice-versa. How to survive? True, you may never really relate to old Mortie or Marian, but here are a few ideas to help you last out the year:

· Remember that your roommate is, after all, human (though some cases are clearly marginal). Even if you don't *like* the person, you can respect his or her wishes and privacy. Who knows? You might even learn something from each other.

- Do you have a roommate of a different race/culture/socioeconomic background? Colleges today are more of a melting-pot than ever, so the chances are good that you'll end up sharing a room with a foreign or minority student. The same rules apply as with someone from your own background: respect the person's privacy and customs, learn to give and take, and try to learn something about this other culture while you're living together. It's an invaluable chance to broaden your own horizons and shake yourself out of that high school provincialism.
- How about borrowing and lending things? Polonius' advice to Laertes in *Hamlet* was well taken: "Neither a borrower nor a lender be." But don't be inflexible. There are times when your roommate's stickpin or blouse or record album is the very thing you need for the evening ahead. If he or she is willing to lend and you're a conscientious borrower, go ahead. But expect to reciprocate sometime. And don't let the borrowing on either side become burdensome or embarrassing for either one of you. Whatever you do, don't borrow without asking—especially cars, bikes, or other wheels. If you should have an accident, the liability laws can get sticky.
- Ideological conflicts over drinking/dope/dating/religion/politics? Remember, again, the rule of thumb is tolerance. Hold your ground if you feel strongly about your position, but show sympathy and tolerance for the other point of view. Remember that part of the package deal on a "liberal" education is learning to live with people of different persuasions. Show respect for your roommate's point of view and insist on the same for yourself. And remember

that while arguments about politics and religion can be stimulating and entertaining, they're not definitive. Two freshmen arguing in a dorm are not going to settle such profound questions as predestination vs. free will, capitalism vs. Marxism. Keep your cool and your perspective and enjoy the discussions for what they are: the immortal tradition of the dormitory bull session.

• While questions of religion and politics are abstract, issues involving noise and privacy are concrete and very real. If your roommate dotes on loud music played full volume, watches TV incessantly, types until the small hours, sings or whistles while reading tomorrow's chapter of Aristotle, talks nonstop on the phone, or invites guests without asking first, you're in for trouble—especially if you need total quiet for concentration. Or perhaps the roles are reversed: the roommate insists on ear-splitting silence when *you* need the local rock station or your favorite record as background for study or conversation.

If you're too incompatible, you may simply have to part company over this all-important noise vs. quiet issue. But it's also possible that you could work out a compromise. For example, the quiet-lover can designate certain "quiet hours" for study when TV, radio, stereo, and phones are shut off (might just help raise the party-lover's GPA too!). If the silence is too oppressive, you (or your roommate) can retreat to the dorm lounge, student commons, or Student Union, or a local hangout that's equipped with Muzak, a jukebox, or a band. Also, consider investing in a pair or two of headphones. A great solution to the noise issue, and you can also use them when you walk, run, jog, or bike back and forth to class. If you're the quiet-lover, it's also important to give your roommate some time for the noisy parties he or she digs. Take some long weekends or get off on your own for a while and turn the place over to old Born-to-Boogie. If worse comes to worst, you can always part at the end of the term.

- But let's say that tolerance and understanding aren't met in return; let's say your roomie ignores your pleas and attempts at compromise. Your sleep is punctuated by shouts, pounding heels, knocks on the walls or ceilings, whoops, yells, and the ongoing beat of the Top Ten. It's time, then, to complain. If the dorm counselor, dean of students, or dean of men (or women) hasn't already come down on your companion, make sure their offices have full noise or nuisance reports—from you or (preferably) someone else. If you can make your complaint in confidence, so much the better; you're less likely to find your favorite posters shredded or cherished souvenirs ripped off. But stick to your guns. If the noise approaches critical level in your room, it's also disturbing the entire dorm. It's a public service to come down on this kind of sound freak.

- Sharing the household tasks? It's up to you to work out an equitable arrangement. In a dorm where "room and board" are provided, meals are no problem—you eat in the cafeteria, snack in the room (see our guide to stocking your kitchen in the next section), or eat out with friends or a date. Cleaning is usually taken care of by the university's janitorial or cleaning service, so household chores are confined to doing the laundry and dry cleaning (each of you does your own, or you alternate weeks), picking up the room a bit between cleanings, emptying the wastepaper baskets, and making sure the wet towels get thrown into the hamper. The simplest way is the best: if each one of you straightens up your own desk, makes the bed, hangs up clothes, and picks up your own towels, the place won't become too much of a wreck.

Dorm rooms are traditionally a little cluttered and, shall we say, lived-in. Not to worry: that's a necessary part of going to college. The problem, again, is with the extremes. If you're compulsively neat and your roommate's a hopeless slob, or vice-versa, you're in for a long and bitter feud. If you're the neat one, try to relax a bit and accept a little clutter. The only time to rebel is when El Slob poses a threat to your health. Piles of garbage, unwashed clothes, ripening towels, and rotting leftover pizza and apple cores—not to mention the half-smoked cigarettes smouldering in the ashtray on top of a pile of papers—are health and safety hazards you should not tolerate. Better you should live alone. Pick up once, twice, and then complain. A slightly scruffy dorm is one thing; a pigsty is another.

• Finally, while we're on the subject of delicate subjects, what about money? If you're both average working stiffs, both cobbling together a living out of a scholarship or loan, a part-time job here and there, a monthly handout from Dad, checks from your great-aunt's birthday cards, and the money you won playing penny-ante last night, no problem. You'll borrow five, lend ten, get back $11.50, and blow the next windfall from home on a big Italian meal. Problems are much more likely to arise if you were born with the proverbial silver spoon in mouth and your roommate's trying to figure out where the next month's dorm rent will come from. Or vice-versa. The struggling one is bound to resent the affluent one and envy his or her possessions/freedom/clout/connections. (Interestingly enough, the moneyed one of the pair often comes away envying the other's freedom from possessions and snobbery: after all, genteel poverty and asceticism *are* old campus traditions.)

A few general rules, whatever your circumstances. Don't brag about your money (or whine about the lack of it). Keep your finances to yourself. Don't borrow sums over $10, and always repay what you owe. Don't enter into long-term loan arrangements. If you buy, sell, or trade possessions, get fair value for fair value—don't cheat the other person or yourself. Don't show off your expensive stereo/camera/clothes/luggage/jewelry if your roommate isn't similarly blessed. And don't rip off your roommate's things, or tolerate being ripped off yourself.

- Now, with all these caveats: relax and enjoy! At worst, you've added another story to your repertoire for future bull sessions. ("Let me tell you about this turkey I roomed with freshman year. . . .") At best, you've made a new friend, possibly a lasting one. It can go either way. It's up to you both to make it work out.

AND DON'T FORGET . . .

Once the living arrangements are complete and the roommate question is settled, you're practically home free. There's time to relax and savor the last few weeks of your vacation. But while you go to those farewell parties and exchange addresses with friends, look over this checklist to see if there's anything left to do:

- Taking a car to campus? Make sure you've checked out all the car regulations. Most campuses require that student vehicles be registered (usually for a fee), have a sticker, and confine parking to designated areas. You'll need a map that tells you where you can and can't park. Same applies to a motorcycle or Moped. While you're at it, check out driver's tests and licensing in the state where you plan to go to school. If you plan to be there four years, invest the time in getting the proper state license. It's instant ID for check cashing and a tremendous help in case of accident or injury.

· Check out your car insurance (or your parents') to make sure you're covered while in the state or on campus. If you need to get insurance for yourself, consider the school's policy if one is available—you might save money if the college has such a plan.

· Speaking of insurance, also check on student health plans, which can save you a bundle in doctor's, dentist's, and lab fees, plus hospital costs if you're ill or injured. Get a student health card so that you can get into the infirmary your first week on campus if necessary. We hope you don't use it, but be prepared just in case. Valerie once celebrated her arrival back on the Emory campus by driving a metal bookcase wedge into her thumb; a student health card saved her the hassle of finding a doctor on a weekend in a strange town.

· Make sure you have a campus schedule for the year so you can plan vacations and trips home. Know what academic schedule your school is on—semester, quarter, trimester, 4-1-4, or whatever. The 4-1-4 plan, which is so popular now, allows for two major terms plus an "off-season" for short courses and workshops. During "mini-terms" ambitious students can take three-week concentrated courses and earn up to six hours credit. Or you can use these special terms to travel, vacation, visit the folks, or work. And don't forget to check on summer programs. Many schools have excellent co-op, workshop, and travel programs during the summer. It's a fine time to make your first jaunt to Europe, learn a new language, study poetry writing, co-op with an ad agency, brush up on your tennis, or earn a semester's credit in two months.

· Do you have to make a decision as to whether or not to sign on for the campus meal plan? The obvious alternative is cooking for yourself, but consider also that you might find it cheaper and more interesting to buy meals on demand from the student snack bar or cafeteria. The reason? Most meal plans include three squares a day, and if you eat according to a different pattern, don't like or need the amount or kind of food the cafeteria offers, or are away at mealtime, then the food ticket is a waste of time and money. Much depends on your own habits. If you want a quick guide to help you make a decision, take a day or two to study the meal-plan choices in the cafeteria. How much of the food would (could) you eat? Are any of the items counter to your dietary or religious habits or preferences? Will you be away at mealtimes a good deal? Do you habitually eat on schedule or at irregular hours? If you like the regularity and convenience of structured mealtimes that you can count on, by all means sign on for the plan—it's cheap, balanced, and usually fairly nutritious. But it's also high-calorie and high-carbohydrate; if you're on a diet for reasons of health or weight reduction, or as part of a training program, a good portion of the chow may go to waste. Our advice: check the meal plan out carefully before you sign on.

· Use some of your last vacation days to read over your catalog. Carry it around with you. Read it at bus stops, in the dentist's office, waiting in line. Remember that this is the place where you're probably going to spend the rest of your college career. Get to know the place in print. Study the regulations. Know the requirements for your major. These are all things that will help you in the long run.

- Get a campus map and study it. You'll be considerably less lost than the run-of-the-mill freshman. Amaze your friends! Know your way around!
- If you have scholarship or grant (or loan) money forthcoming, check out when and where you'll get the cash in hand. Often you'll need to process this paperwork before you can register. If so, plan on arriving a day early to complete the financial details; otherwise you can be stuck in registration line with a whopping tuition bill and no money in sight.
- Is there a registration fee or matriculation fee? Sometimes entering freshmen are unfamiliar with the university's fee structure and do not include these in their budgets. Make sure you allow for such special fees when you get your finances in order.
- If you'll be writing checks on a hometown bank, make sure you have a supply with you plus identification. Many campuses won't accept or cash checks from out of town unless you have a student ID card (a campus Catch-22). Better yet, get some traveler's checks, a cashier's check, or a certified check to tide you over. Or open an account at a local bank. Also investigate the "student bank" on campus—it's a big time-saver if one is available.
- See about getting a student activities ID card early (your first day on campus, for example). There are usually some good (free) films, lectures, concerts, and exhibitions in the pre-registration week—they're a good way to get you out of your dorm room and into circulation. And remember: with the student ID card come discounts in local museums, bookstores, and theaters, even shops and restaurants. A real recession-proof way to travel in style for rock-bottom prices!

What to Do When You're Accepted

- Scout your hometown friends, acquaintances, and relatives for the names, addresses, and phone numbers of other students from your area who have also gone to Crawling Ivy. Look them up. Give them a call if they're home for the holidays. Sure, they may turn out to be losers but they may also become your best friends. At the worst, they're good for more introductions and an occasional night out of the dorm. And don't forget that local alumni, especially the ones only a year or two out of school, will also have contacts, phone numbers of people to meet, lists of places to go, off-the-cuff evaluations of the faculty and classes, and lots of helpful hints on surviving the rigors of Crawling Ivy. Look them up before you go, too. As the Ann Beattie character who could tie one hundred different knots once said, "It pays to know everything."
- Invest a little time in getting your act together. We know: it's the In thing to leave it all to the last night, which you'll spend hyped up on coffee and No-Doz or worse, throwing your gear into any available carryall. Resist this temptation. A little organization never hurt anyone. The more planning you can do now, the easier your unpacking job becomes. Take time to clean your closets, sort through notes and books, get repairs and alterations made. If you're buying new luggage, opt for the soft, stuffable kind; nylon duffels and carryalls are ideal. Or check out the canvas luggage in sporting goods departments—often cheaper and sturdier than the pricier specialty shop versions.

Also investigate alternate ways of schlepping your things. If you're traveling by plane or train, you'll need to stay within a certain luggage allowance. You may need to ship some books or out-of-season clothing by UPS or mail. If you're doing the car routine, invest in a sturdy footlocker for the bulky items like sporting equipment, boots, and winter coats. It can always double as a coffee table or extra seating once you're settled.

Even if you're traveling to college by plane, consider checking some of the extra gear. Many airlines will ship even large items such as bicycles for as little as $12, provided the carrying cartons or suitcases conform to their size requirements. American Airlines even provides "Flying Footlockers" which will hold up to 500 pounds. And in case you favor trains over planes, Amtrak will charge approximately $10 per 100 pounds.

If you elect to ship things by mail, compare UPS and mail rates. Fourth-class book rate, for example, is around $6 or $7 for a 40-pound package—if you can stand the slow delivery time (one to three weeks). It may be smarter to use UPS: $9 to $11 by ground transportation and $27-plus by air for 40 pounds, as of this writing. One obvious solution: carry or ship at priority or first-class rates the things you'll need immediately; send the other things a slower but less expensive way and wait for their arrival.

· Need extra money for that expensive first semester, but don't want to take on an extra job? Consider free-lancing by turning a hobby or special interest into fast money (and advertise your service in the school newspaper). A few ideas: a "fast food" or catering service (assemble and sell deli packages or snacks on dinnerless nights in the dorms; put together "exam week" survival kits of healthful munchies to keep late-night study sessions going; bake specialties such as carrot cakes or other goodies). Other hobbies-into-money ideas: play your instrument or lend out your stereo outfit for hire at parties (at so much per hour); teach music or dance to other students or faculty members' families; tutor in foreign languages, math, or English; work in the

What to Do When You're Accepted

school's language or writing lab; set up a campus moving service (your clients rent the van or truck, and you and your friends pack, load, and unload for an hourly fee); set up an apartment-cleaning service for harried movers in and out; set up a photography service (bread-and-butter passport and ID photos and an occasional model's composite; arty shots for sale at local fairs and exhibitions); sell craft items such as leatherwork, jewelry, or ceramics.

· Keep health-care costs and drugstore bills down by going to the student health center or infirmary for common, nonprescription drugs: cold pills, aspirin, antihistamines, antacids, salves, ointments, cough medicines, eye drops. Check out these services before you load up on half the medicine cabinet from home or buy out the hometown drugstore. It may be that you can get all your health supplies and medicines at a fraction of their usual cost. Free Ace bandages, Band-Aids, knee wraps or pads, and even crutches are sometimes available through the campus athletic center.

· Finally, before you leave for campus, check out the local exercise facilities situation. Don't join a health club until you have looked over your gym, since many gyms now have a vast array of exercise equipment and machines, including free weights—sometimes even a complete Olympic free-weight room. The gym may be free to all full-time students or available for a small extra fee. Chances are it's far better than your local health club—and much less expensive. And most schools today have at least a fair-sized pool and running or jogging track, which may be yours free of charge. If the school's facilities aren't up to snuff, call up the local Y. Often its free-weight facilities are superb, and there's almost always a pool. Plan to stay in shape—you're much less likely to pick up the proverbial twenty pounds of freshman flab; and you'll keep your energy level high as an added benefit.

And in case you're still in doubt about what to take and what to leave behind, read on. We've made all those hard decisions easier by weeding through your closets for you, sorting out the must-haves from the leave-behinds, and reminding you of all the things you'll need to survive your year at old Crawling Ivy.

6

Putting Your Pad Together

WE'VE ALL been through it: the last frantic back-to-campus rush. You've just filled three large footlockers with every scrap of clothing you've ever owned (plus a few goodies ripped off from Mother or Sis—along with an old high school football jersey and ID bracelet). Now you're loading the family car, minus back seat, with all the books in your shelves, your dad's old portable typewriter, two dozen sheets and pillowcases, a Salvation Army coffeepot, assorted golf clubs, tennis racquets, softballs, and running shoes, and the entire family's record collection.

OK, you're going off for a year. The dorm room or apartment looked pretty bare. But do you really *need* all this stuff? This isn't an arctic expedition, you know—just a trek to Crawling Ivy, two hundred and fifty miles from home.

It's always hard to part with treasured junk, especially

high school mementoes. You need some links with your immediate past and with your family to ease the transition from Living at Home to Being on Your Own. But you don't need to take the contents of the family attic or basement with you to make your new digs liveable. Here's a quick checklist of some essentials and a few optional items that will get you through in fine style:

· Clothes, casual and dress (heavy on the casual, lighter on the dress-up wear). Complete details of putting together your campus wardrobe are covered in our next section, but in general, your best guide is what the other students wear (you *did* notice on your last trip to campus, didn't you?). What to take: jeans, jeans, jeans; chinos, cords, good flannel dress pants; skirts, and knit or jersey dresses for women; sweaters of every type; shirts, casual and dress; polo shirts and knit turtlenecks; boots; loafers and other casual shoes; jackets, coats, and raincoat; a good dress outfit or two. What to leave behind: out-of-season stuff (you can retrieve it on your next expedition home); your high school prom outfit; high school letter sweaters and jerseys (unless your school is particularly famous or notable); worn-out things; scruffy jeans; anything too high-school-looking.

· Your trusty warmup suit or sweatsuit, running shoes, athletic bag or carryall, and sporting equipment (but only for the sports you actually will play).

· Towels, washcloths, and bed linens (unless these are furnished by the dorm—check this out in advance). A minimum of two pairs of sheets and pillowcases, six large towels and washcloths. A large bath mat and bath blanket are nice but not strictly necessary.

· Bedspread, blankets, curtains, rugs. These are optional. Some schools do provide them, so check first to make sure what you need. Even if the blankets and spread are provided, some inexpensive curtains and a throw rug or two will make the place look cozier. Pick washable stuff that you can throw in the machine. A big down comforter is warm and can double as a bedspread—and needs no tucking in. Instant bed-making!

· Medicine and prescription drugs (take along refills for the hard-to-get items, or have a prescription from your doctor with you—but only if the local drugstore fills out-of-state prescriptions. Check this one out also).

· Shaving supplies, razor, after-shave lotion, cologne, and other toiletries for men; cosmetics, a stand-up mirror, curling iron or hot rollers, and blow dryer for women.

· Small electronics gear: bedside clock or clock-radio, tape recorder, stereo, portable TV (if permitted), stereo headphones, CB set. Take whatever will fit into your quarters that you need to feel comfortable and "at home."

Don't try to save space here. Why buy what you already have? Besides, the more of these items you have with you, the less you'll tend to rush out after classes and spend your cash on movies, discos, country-western bars, or whatever the latest campus fad is.

· Kitchen utensils, if you're living off-campus: a coffeepot, a few pots and pans, a skillet, cooking and measuring spoons, some simple dishes (paper or plastic will do just fine for starters). If you can also swing an electric skillet, popcorn popper, toaster, hot plate, crock pot and/or can opener, you can cut your food bills in half and still eat well. Even if you don't have a full kitchen, a small ice chest, some good thermos jars, and an electric skillet or hot plate —plus the inevitable coffeepot—can keep you going on snacks and light meals when you miss the last call for dinner.

If you're planning to live in the dorm, the kitchen list

will be much simpler. But try to swing a coffeepot, either a hot plate or electric skillet, perhaps a popcorn popper, and a small ice chest anyway. You'll need a couple of glasses, a coffee mug, a plate, a bowl, and a few utensils. Add a corkscrew and bottle opener, and you're equipped to survive even the institutional food.

· Plenty of clothes hangers: the ordinary wire kind from the cleaners, but also some heavy padded hangers for coats and knitwear, and some pants hangers. A shoe bag is also a good closet-stretcher (remember that closets, especially in older dorms, are often miniatures). Any kind of space-saving hanger is welcome.

· Cleaning supplies. Believe it or not, you may find your dorm room dusty from a summer of sitting unused. Some sponges, a mop and broom, and scouring pads or disinfectant may help get rid of dust and musty odors.

· A calendar (desk or pocket type). You might want to keep two calendars—one on the desk (perhaps a desk-pad variety) or wall to record assignments or due dates for papers; another, pocket-sized one for social events and out-of-town trips.

· Books. Proceed with caution here. There's no use in taking all your old high school texts unless you plan to use them for review. OK, you might take your trig or French texts for reference, but the civics and health ed. texts stay home. Take a few paperback novels you're particularly fond of, art or photography books, and any recent acquisitions you're still reading. But be warned: you'll shortly be inundated by books of every description, so keep the traveling library to a minimum.

· A dictionary. A must regardless of what field you're in. Pick a good hardcover and supplement it with a small paperback version that you can carry in your briefcase or knapsack. It's the wisest investment you can make.

• A good research guide. Kate Turabian's guide to term and research papers is a classic of the genre; another good one is James Lester's *Writing Research Papers*.

• A calculator (small briefcase or pocket-sized ones are ideal) if you'll be taking accounting or math courses.

• An umbrella. One of the folding collapsible styles is ideal; you can stick it in your briefcase or backpack without stabbing your fellow classmates on the way across the commons.

• A typewriter (portable). If you can't type, learn. Take a crash course or teach yourself. This small miracle will help you win good grades, speed up your paper writing, and tremendously simplify your whole college career.

• A steam iron or steamer. Remember, Mom is no longer there. You're on your own, and that means keeping the crease in your pants and making sure your shirts or blouses are pressed. Another essential investment, it will save you a bundle in dry-cleaning bills.

• Sewing gear. No, you don't need to get a needlepoint-emblazoned wicker sewing basket like Grandma's, but you do need one of those little plastic gizmos that are fitted out with needles, thread, some straight pins, spare buttons, a thimble, and all that good stuff. It's up to you to put on those shirt buttons!

• A collapsible clothes rack or a clothesline with pins. Again let us remind you: laundry facilities can seem miles away on a snowy night when you've a term paper due. Some packets of Woolite and a clothes rack or line can assure a clean shirt and socks the next day without the polar trek. You'll also need a laundry bag. If you get a brightly colored

one, it can double as a sort of mammoth pillow between washings; use it to hold clean pajamas or bed linens.
- Stationery and stamps. Of course you can buy these at the campus bookstore, but often the choices are limited and prices are surprisingly high. If you have an unused supply left over from graduation, take it along. Throw in some inexpensive felt-tipped pens, a roll of stamps, some postcards or self-sealing notes—it's a nice gesture to write the folks back home and tell them you arrived in one piece.
- Change for pay phones. It may surprise you, but you may have trouble finding change on campus. The bookstore may require a purchase and the cafeteria, like as not, uses a meal ticket or card instead of cash. Just to be safe, get your local bank to make up a roll of dimes, quarters, and nickels for vending machines and phones.
- An extension cord. You can't have too many of these —the outlet is always a mile away in old dorm rooms.
- A small tool kit. You'll be amazed at how often you need to use a small screwdriver, hammer, or wrench while you're setting up your new quarters. This is a must if you're moving to an off-campus apartment.
- A bathroom scale. Essential if you intend to fight off the freshman flabs. Everyone—but everyone—seems to gain weight the first semester away from home: too much junk food, too much high-carbohydrate cafeteria fare, too much brew, and not enough exercise. Take the little monster from home to keep yourself honest, or buy an inexpensive one for yourself.
- An electric fan or heater. Depending on whether you're heading to a warm or cold climate, consider the possibility that the heat or air-conditioning may go off or may function at less than peak efficiency. Your small fan or

Putting Your Pad Together 123

heater may get you through a heat wave or cold snap in more comfort than your less-prepared classmates.

· A desk lamp. Check to see if one is provided. If not, take along a small one for late-night study sessions.

· Personal knicknacks: trophies, framed photos, souvenirs, mugs, assorted junque. Here's where you need to be selective. A little of this goes a long way, but a picture or two, your favorite mug, your track trophies and plaques, and a few other odds and ends will help personalize your sterile little cell. You don't have to emulate Ye Olde Curiosity Shoppe, however. Easy does it with the memorabilia—you'll be collecting more in very short order.

So much for the essentials. Now for some of the optional things—the frills and extras that make the anonymous dorm room or apartment into something special. Some of these you can bring from home; others are fairly large and bulky and can better be purchased closer to campus. (Thrifty consumers, note: if you live in a small town or rural area and plan to go to college in the big city, expect a steep hike in prices. It might just pay to buy some of the extras in your hometown and rent a small U-Haul or trailer for the goodies.)

Wherever you get them, here are some instant decorating items that will make your place look not only presentable but downright homey.

· Posters and photos for the wall. These can be pricey, if you insist on art posters and signed lithographs; but they can be as inexpensive as the local record store's freebies (used as advertising; you pick them up when the display comes down). In between, there are all sorts of handsome, inexpensive posters and signs that can be bought for very little money. And check out other freebies: movie posters, advertising posters, travel posters, giveaways, and throwaways. If friends want to give you a going-away party, a clever trick is to ask everyone to forego expensive gifts and chip in on a poster. Instant camouflage for dirty or paint-flaked walls!

• An "occasional" chair (preferably something portable and foldable). A collapsible beanbag is fine: so are the big overstuffed canvas pillow chairs. For rooms that are short on space, try some folding high-tech metal chairs, a big canvas butterfly chair, or a collapsible woven chair that can hide in the closet when you aren't using it. Lightweight directors' chairs or even beach and outdoor furniture are also good choices.

• Some big throw pillows, in enormous floor-size, and also some small scatter pillows for bed or sofa. A quick decorating touch that's practical as well—guests can use the floor pillows for sitting and you can prop yourself up with them when you want to study in bed. Pick bright colors like red, aquamarine, and emerald or go with the dark jewel tones—burgundy, rust, brown, navy blue. Stay away from anything that will soil or stain.

• Throw rugs. Again, stay with darker tones and sturdy, wear-resistant textures; the multicolor shags are practically impervious to wear and dirt. Get something washable, if possible. If you're in the mood to splurge, a *kilim* (a small Eastern rug), woven rug, Greek *flokati*, or perhaps a South American copy of a Navajo design are all colorful, chic, and durable.

• Baskets, lots of them, in every size. Big oversized hampers can stash old newspapers and magazines and even hold the wash—they're wonderful ways to keep the overflow out of sight. A medium-sized one can be lined with plastic and used for a trash can. Small ones can hold mail, notes, bills, pencils, stamps, jewelry, and odds and ends.

· Some In-Out boxes or bookends for your desk. A nice high-tech extra, and they will keep your desk from becoming a disaster area quite so rapidly.

· OK, you shouldn't overdo it, but if your walls and ceilings look grungy, go out to the dime store and invest in some huge paper kites, paper lanterns, soft sculptures, mobiles, fans, models of the *Enterprise* or any of the *Star Wars* ships—something to hang that's inexpensive, splashy, and covers the peeling paint. (We used to have a huge map of the moon hanging above our bed; try it if you're a space buff.)

· A big plant or two. Again, don't overdo it. One or two large ones will go a long way toward brightening the place. Pick something that doesn't require a lot of care: a cactus or a sturdy plant like the *dracena marginata*, which, some plant buffs say, "can live under the bed." Philodendron and rubber plants are also good choices—easy care, little watering, and they grow to alarming sizes.

· A shelf or case for your stereo records. Take along just a small assortment of your favorites, then get a good shelf or case or rack to avoid ruining them.

· Attractive glasses, an ice bucket, a serving tray. You don't want to become a dish collector, but these items are nice to have when you've invited special guests.

· Some good-looking coffee mugs and a rack. It's ecology-conscious to drink from china mugs and saves not only waste but the cost of paper cups. Get giant china or ceramic mugs and use them as kitchen decoration in between coffee breaks.

· Some colorful bedspreads, throws, shawls, or blankets to drape on beds, overstuffed chairs, or that monstrosity of a sofa. Colorful, inexpensive Indian-print spreads are wonderful ways to disguise the Goodwill rejects and other tacky furnishings that you inherit or buy because it's the only thing you can afford.

That should just about complete your average furnished dorm room or apartment. Remember, how much of this gear you buy or bring from home depends strictly on how much space you have. Don't take so much that the place is cluttered; you'll find it hard to concentrate with so much distraction. But if you have plenty of space and nothing to fill it, some giant pillows, rugs, and a plant can do a lot toward filling up that yawning empty room.

But suppose you're furnishing from scratch yourself? Sometimes it's the only reasonable alternative. Or you may prefer taking your chances with your own finds to living with the lavender damask sofa of 1930s vintage. Funky may be in, but pure schmaltz is hard to take. So you decide to go out on your own.

Wait! Before you pitch the Early Landlady cabbage roses, take another look. What would the overstuffed pieces look like slipcovered in a rugged stretch terry or velour? Or draped with one of the Indian-print bedspreads you so cleverly brought from home? Think about the alternatives before you pitch anything out. Could the hideous coffee table or lamp stands be painted a deep lacquer-red, burgundy, or hunter's green? Try to see all the uglies through fresh eyes as they might look with some paint or upholstery.

If you must pitch out the existing stuff—or if you're moving into four bare walls—start your scavenger hunt at the local Goodwill, Salvation Army, or thrift shop (use the Yellow Pages to locate them). Check out campus bulletin boards, want ads in the local papers, moving and rummage

Putting Your Pad Together

and garage sales in nearby blocks. Campuses being what they are, there's a lot of moving in and out, and consequently a good many sales. People often would rather sell it cheap than take it along. If you're patient and resourceful, you can get most of the items you need secondhand. Look for convertible sofas or daybeds, an easychair or two, small tables, bookshelves, a desk or a big dining table that can double as work space. Your whole place can be furnished, very attractively, too, from rummage sales, friends' and relatives' castaways, throwaways in the street or local garbage dump (yes, you read it right—people do throw furniture away), and other scavengers' havens. But you have to be willing to search, sift, scrounge, paint, sand, clean, strip, and varnish if you take the low road—and all that takes time from your studies. Best solution: if you're really into redoing your new digs and transforming Tacky into Funky, start early. Come to campus at least a week or so before registration, make a maximum effort to get all the basics together, and have it functional by day one. Don't get so involved in the intricacies, pains, and pleasures of your decor that you forget why you're there.

But assuming worse comes to worst: you arrive on campus the day before registration and confront institutional green walls, grungy floors, and hopeless furniture in your new abode. Let's make it a typical place: tiny galley-type kitchen with ancient stove and fridge, antique bathroom with pedestal sink and antique tub. What to do? Not to worry: here's a two-hour instant makeover that will make the place presentable until the next check comes and you can get something to replace the overstuffed horrors.

· Clean up! Mop the floors, disinfect kitchen and bathroom, wash the kitchen shelves and lay fresh shelving paper. While you're at it, put some cedar-scented paper in the drawers and spray on a little insect and roach repellent to keep down the big crawlies. (Remember, Muhammad Ali doesn't want you livin' with roaches.) Dust the furniture with lemon-scented polish. The place will look better instantly.

· If the bed is rickety or ugly, discard the headboard and frame. Put the mattress and box springs on a throw rug or square of carpeting (a remnant is fine) and spread your down comforter, or *duvet*, over it. Now arrange some throw pillows. Instant Turkish-harem daybed, and a place for guests to lounge as well.

· If you keep any of the overstuffed pieces of furniture, wrap them in spreads or even attractive printed sheets. Use pins or Velcro strips to hold the fabric in place.

· If the lampshades are unbearably tacky, throw them out and substitute inexpensive paper or plastic shades.

· Desperate for a coffee table? Try your footlocker, spray-painted a bright red; an unpainted wooden cube (you supply the paint); a big piece of glass or mirror on top of (yes!) a new shiny aluminum garbage can or a big wicker wastebasket. Or consider a huge tree stump, a railroad crosstie cut to a height of fourteen inches (Ralph's invention for our home in North Dakota), a nest of high-tech stacking baskets, or some wire shelving turned sideways. A big wooden movers' pallet or packing crate will also do handsomely. Look around. Be inventive.

· Go for a walk in the woods or a nearby park and bring back sprays of fresh leaves in brilliant fall colors, a basket of pine cones, or some interesting rocks and pebbles. You've got an instant table arrangement.

· Consider improvising. Bricks and long boards are the staple of student apartment bookcases—but how about

Putting Your Pad Together

painting the shelves lacquer-red, black, or chocolate brown? Make an interesting display of posters or plants on top.

- Use interesting clothing and accessories as wall hangings. Your Mexican sweater, cowboy hat, serape, and bright football jerseys can make a super-looking wall display. Use pushpins or thumbtacks to drape them across the wall like a window display in a store.

- Colored lightbulbs and lots of outsize candles provide interesting, inexpensive lighting for parties and special evenings. Take some of the big fat Christmas candles back from your holiday visit home. You can set them in a nonworking fireplace, group them on a table, or use them for a centerpiece.

- Need a desk and dining table all in one? An unpainted standard-size door on two sawhorses fills both bills. Paint the door red and the sawhorses black or battleship gray. A smaller version could be a bedside or lamp table. And a movers' pallet, stripped and bleached or sanded, can hold plants and big art books.

One final thing: the kitchen. It used to be Mom's domain; now it's yours. You have to find your own way through the maze of mysteries that surrounds food and cooking. We won't tell you how and what to cook, but we will suggest a quick list of staples that you should have on hand.

1. Measuring spoons.
2. Cooking spoons in two or three sizes.
3. Paring knife.
4. Eggbeater or whisk.
5. Salt and pepper shakers.

6. Paper napkins, plates, etc. (for emergency use until you collect enough dishes to use).
7. Paper towels.
8. Dishpan (large plastic variety).
9. Dish rack or drainer.
10. Sponges or dishmop.
11. Small saucepan and skillet (we assume you have the coffeepot already).
12. Mixing bowl.
13. Two or three plastic refrigerator containers.
14. Dishwashing detergent.
15. Plastic (or inexpensive stainless steel) knives, forks, spoons.
16. Can opener and bottle opener.
17. Tea and coffee.
18. Sugar, salt, spices, catsup, mustard, mayonnaise, powdered milk, cereal, rice or pastas, etc.
19. Sodas and fruit juice or milk.
20. A few canned or frozen quick meals (canned chili and tuna, frozen pizza or fried chicken) for emergencies.
21. Snacks: dried fruits, sunflower seeds, other nuts, raisins, fresh fruit, yogurt, raw vegetables, granola bars, cheese, hardboiled eggs.

Once you're home with your load, get the utensils organized on the shelves and put the groceries in the refrigerator immediately. Keep the kitchen operation as simple as you can; that way it will be less of a chore.

Probably you will not do much in the way of fancy cooking. Unless you or your roommate(s) are interested in *nouvelle cuisine*, your staple diet will probably be chicken, turkey, hamburgers, tuna fish (salad or casserole), and more hamburgers. Not an exciting diet, but a pretty healthy one. Just be sure to supplement it with fresh salads, fruits, and juices, plus bran and unsweetened granola for roughage and fiber. Anyone can learn to broil chicken, mix up a quick tuna casserole or meatloaf, and fry a good hamburger. Ask your mother for how-to-do-it instructions and write them down on an index card to post on the refrigerator door.

One last topic to cover before we leave the subject of your new surroundings, and that's the problem of rip-offs. For the first time in your life, you're in complete charge of your life and all your possessions: camera, stereo, TV, calculator, tape deck. It may not be much, but it's valuable to you. Unfortunately, it may also be potentially valuable to someone else. There are thieves who prey almost entirely on dorms and student apartments. Not everyone who enrolls in college these days is there for the intellectual or social action; some are just plain rip-off artists. So take some simple precautions. Install your own burglar alarm or burglar bars if permissible. If you're in the dorm, ask about the downstairs security system. The tighter it is, the less you have to worry about—but don't be thrown too much off your guard.

If you have a small lock box, file cabinet, or safe, consider locking up small valuables such as jewelry, rare coins, cameras, or calculators. It's true that a pro will know how to get through such defenses—but an amateur might be deterred by all the locks and steel.

Remember, also, that the less you talk about or display your possessions, the less likely you are to be ripped off. Keep curtains and blinds closed at night. Don't hang your beloved Gibson classic in the window or you'll come home some night to find it gone. Keep a low profile with regard to your things, especially with new acquaintances and people you don't know well. Don't invite strangers to your place unless they're friends of reputable friends, and even then, don't show off your new stereo or CB the first night you meet.

The usual targets for robbery are items that can be resold easily—small appliances, cameras, stereos, musical instruments, typewriters, watches and other jewelry, radios—in other words, all the items a college student is likely to keep in a dorm room or apartment.

Consider taking out a household furnishings insurance policy on your valuables. For a few dollars each month you can insure everything in the place and be assured that if you are ripped off, you can at least be repaid a fraction of the items' current value.

Finally, if you are the victim of robbery, be sure to notify school officials or your landlord or building owner. They probably won't assume responsibility for your bad luck, but at least they stand warned that their property is not secure. Maybe at the very least they'll beef up their safety precautions and prevent a recurrence of the theft.

Now that you've got your security in line and your kitchen stocked, your living room redecorated and the whole place cleaned and dusted, let's turn our attention to you. And that's what the next chapter is about: your wardrobe and grooming needs and how you can get your best campus look together with a minimum of time and money.

7

Putting Your Wardrobe Together

YOU CAN SORT through books and mementoes, neatly stow your gear in footlockers, suitcases, and packing crates, and otherwise be a model of organization when it comes to getting your campus packing done. But even the best of students seem to fall apart at the thought of organizing the all-important campus wardrobe.

Fashions come and fashions go, but the back-to-school wardrobe still looms as the biggest item on most students' autumn agenda. Just watch the department store ads, show windows, and special promotions if you don't believe it. From the week after July 4 until mid-September, we're inundated by fall clothes, back-to-school wear, campus fashions, endless lists of Ins and Outs, Do's and Don'ts—all bearing the not-so-subliminal message that clothes are a vital part of going back to college.

You may take the position that you're above all the fashion hype. *You're* going to college for the intellectual stimulation, not to turn into a clotheshorse. For you, clothes not only don't make the man or the woman, they have absolutely nothing to do with his or her future and success or failure in college. (You're not alone: it's a kind of academic orthodoxy on many campuses, among both students and faculty, to affect a studied indifference to clothes.)

So you put down the campus "peacocks" and "fashion plates" for their bizarre, colorful plumage and sneer at their Shetlands, kilts, designer shirts, and crazy accessories. *Until,* that is, one fine day when you notice that it's often the fashion-conscious people who get the dates, the campus offices, even the good grades and good jobs. And as for women: the local clotheshorses, with their artful makeup and clever tricks with scarves and belts and jewelry—they can somehow make the same old jeans and shirts look new and different day after day.

That's when you go home, look through your closet, and decide you'd better rethink some of that fine contempt for clothes.

It helps in putting all of this in proper perspective to remember that a campus wardrobe is not a Platonic ideal of "wardobe-ness," nor is it any other system of "perfect" clothes for a "typical" or "average" college student. (We know: there's no such thing!) It's simply a well-thought-out collection of the things that you yourself can wear, day in and day out, for classes, social occasions, work, vacations, and general tooling around and hanging out. It includes active sportswear and special uniforms that you may wear in the lab or studio, or on the job. It's first of all functional and *then* funky/individualistic/expressive/fun/fashionable—or all of the above. In most cases, that adds up to a wardrobe built on some simple classics and staples to

Putting Your Wardrobe Together 135

which you can add some "frills" and special items for dress-up occasions.

If we start with "the basics," we have to begin with jeans. For both men and women, the wardrobe staple for the eighties is jeans, in literally dozens of fabrics, colors, styles, and brands. But the jeans that you'll find walking the campus today are not the faded, rumpled, pre-worn, and much-patched Righteous Funk jeans of the sixties and early seventies. Today's jeans are neat, pressed, narrow or straight-legged, more often new than secondhand. You'll need a minimum of three pairs; there's no top limit until your small closet begins to scream for mercy. You can't have too many jeans! One pair should be denim, of course—at least one pair with narrow legs for pairing with boots. One pair might be western-style, and one pair for dress-up might be velvet, leather, suede, polished cotton, or raw silk for a casual, uncontrived look that's very handsome.

Supplement the jeans with a pair or two of good chinos or cords if you plan to affect the preppie look (it's coming back on many campuses now). Add a pair of good lightweight wool or gabardine dress pants in a basic color like charcoal gray, navy blue, camel, black, or loden green. Also consider army fatigues and painter's pants—they're popular jeans-alternatives on many campuses, and they're inexpensive and fun to wear for class or as casual garb.

Women take note: skirts are now running a close second to pants on many campuses. Styles like the A-line, wrap, soft dirndl, kilt, straight skirt, and pleated skirt are real basics that crop up year after year. If you pick lightweight wool flannel, gabardine, jersey or wool challis, or even a synthetic like Quiana, you'll be way ahead of the game. Your skirts will go from winter to spring and still look good when you unpack them next fall. If you want to start a basic skirt collection, begin with a soft black gathered or pleated skirt in lightweight wool jersey or a silk blend (dressy enough for evening, basic enough for day). Add a plaid kilt, a muted tweed, and a charcoal gray or navy wrap or A-line and you've got a whole skirt "wardrobe" that can take you everywhere in style.

As for tops: for everyday wear, casual shirts or blouses in plaids, stripes, small prints, or solids can be paired with sweaters for a cold climate. T-shirts and knit tops or polo shirts work well for summer or for Sun Belt campuses. Crewneck and turtleneck sweaters are campus classics whatever the climate. Choose big, thick, rugged wool versions for cold midwestern and eastern colleges, lightweight knits and cotton blends for more moderate climates. Cardigans are good coverups for cold weather and make attractive toppings for the popular "layered look" that's so chill-dispelling. (Remember, the extra layers trap warmth; often three lighter sweaters spell more protection than one super-heavy coat.) Some of the blazer-type cardigans are good investments that offer an inexpensive alternative to a real jacket when you want to "dress up" a casual look. Women can pick one that harmonizes with both skirts and pants for an instant "suit" look. Try the cardigan both belted and unbelted for a change of looks.

You'll certainly want to add a coat or heavy jacket if you're heading for a cold climate. Down-filled parkas, quilted jackets and vests, ski wear, and the ever-popular shearlings and suedes are widely seen on most campuses. In a rainy climate like that of the Gulf Coast, a raincoat or rain slicker (preferably with a zip-in lining for cooler days) may be preferable to a "real" coat. And almost everywhere, for one reason or another, boots are a must for rain, snow, sleet, or slush. Invest in a well-made pair of waterproof vinyl, rubber, or treated-leather boots. Later, save your pennies for a dress pair in fine leather, suede, or reptile skin. Western boots are always popular, and they are super-stylish now. Justins, Dan Posts, Fryes, and Tony Lamas are the *crème de la crème* of the western boots, but there are many other brands that also show a lot of style for considerably less money.

Women will sometimes find that fashion boots have higher heels, classier designs, and prettier colors than "utilitarian" boots, but they also have little weather resistance, are seldom lined, and often don't have skid-resistant treads on soles and heels. You may want to buy two pairs of boots: one no-nonsense pair in rubber for sloshing through knee-high drifts, another "dress" pair in a more fashionable style and material.

What about dress-up occasions? Here, it helps to know your campus. For many schools, a pair of dress slacks and a navy blue blazer is the most formal outfit a male will ever need. A woman might well get by with a wool skirt or tailored pants worn with a sweater or silk blouse and topped with a jacket or short vest.

But if you're heading for a super-dressy campus, plan to work in town, or expect to spend a good many nights dancing or eating out, you'll want to invest in some party clothes. Believe it or not, dress-up evenings are back in full force on many campuses, so you may be surprised at how often you'll get to wear your spiffiest gear.

Males who go for dress-up will probably need at least one good suit, preferably a three-piecer in a basic fabric and cut. A charcoal gray or navy blue pinstripe is one choice that's safe for almost everyone. If you're feeling affluent, add a good-looking velvet or suede blazer to team with everything from jeans to silk shirts and dress slacks.

Women have many more options for dress-up occasions, depending on the campus, the surrounding town, and the nature of the occasion. A simple silk or jersey dress, a long skirt and dressy blouse or silk shirt, or silk pants with a dressy sweater and/or silk shirt are always safe bets. But there are literally dozens of other options: jumpsuits, halters, tube tops, scarves wrapped sarong-style over leotards, bodysuits worn with silk skirts or pants, long dresses, short dresses, tunics, and ethnic looks such as Chinese kimonos, Mexican wedding dresses, kurtas, and caftans. It's up to you to choose the look that's best for you and your campus. But in general, opt for less expensive evening wear (take advantage of those options!) and save the biggest slice of your clothing budget for day-in, day-out wear, since that's what you'll need 90 percent of the time.

As for shoes—well, your knockabout and dress boots will both become wardrobe staples for fall and winter weather. We predict that you'll even wear the rubber boots quite a lot for sloshing around a newly thawed campus in the spring. So be sure to treat the leather *before* you're rained on the first time; also protect leather against salt, slush, and snow if you're headed for the Snow Belt. For non-boot weather, fill in with hiking shoes, moccasins, slip-ons, loafers, ghillies, "earth shoes," sandals, running or tennis shoes, jazz oxfords—whatever the latest campus footwear fad is. If you're in doubt about the current In footwear on your campus, save a few sous so that you can invest in the latest rage in shoes and other accessories to update your look when you arrive.

For women, again, the options are almost overwhelming. If you're in doubt about some "safe" shoes to take along, try moccasin or loafer styles with small stacked heels, plain pumps or T-straps for dress-up, and city sandals in dark or luggage-toned leather. These styles are basic and vary very little from year to year except in heel height and trim.

Speaking of accessories: here as with other things, casual and understated is the rule of the day. A briefcase is really necessary only if that's the current status symbol on your campus (usually a professional or business-oriented campus rather than a liberal arts one). Most undergraduates carry backpacks, knapsacks, the popular rubberized canvas or parachute cloth totes, or book bags. "Male handbags"? Forget it unless you're on a very sophisticated urban campus (for example, we *do* see quite a lot of these in downtown Chicago among Roosevelt, Northwestern, DePaul, and Loyola students). But they should be real leather or an excellent imitation, masculine-looking, rugged, and fairly large, preferably in a shoulder-strap style. The best ones are really large shoulder-slung duffels or carry-on bags in leather or canvas that hold books, notebooks, pens, pencils, snacks, and gym clothes. A safe bet is always a big sports carryall such as Addidas or Nike makes. Ditto for the oversized leather knapsacks that are almost big pieces of luggage: they're very handsome and wear well year after year. Women may find that they can double as handbags—or supplement smaller purse-size bags that hold the usual money, credit cards, keys, and makeup.

The choices in women's bags are so varied that it's almost impossible to recommend a single style. But in general, we've found shoulderbags work better than clutch or handle styles for campus wear; you'll often need both hands free for books, totes, and all the things you seem to amass during the course of the day. Pick a medium- to large-size bag so that it can accommodate extra pens, pencils, notebooks, snacks, makeup, even a book or two.

If you're on a status-conscious big-city campus with a bit

of snob sense, signature bags can make a big impression—but check it out first. You don't want to invest a fortune in a Gucci briefcase or tote, or a Vuitton duffel, only to learn that just this month they're passé, gauche, and Out with the In crowd, who now favor Wilderness gear and L. L. Bean. Before you go designer-mad, watch what the campus trendsetters are carrying; you may save yourself some big bucks.

Once you've got your basic clothes, a coat, footwear, and a handbag or book bag, you're almost home free. But wait: let's not forget the accessories. They're the small touches that liven up a basic outfit and often make a basic shirt-and-slacks or sweater-and-jeans look into something special. Men first. Let's start with some canvas, webbing, and leather belts; ties for dress-up wear; casual and dress socks; a functional watch and a good pen; ascots, scarves, and pocket squares, plus a muffler for winter; a short vest in knit fabric, suede, or leather; winter gloves; and a few pieces of jewelry. Again, nothing fancy: at the most, a gold neck chain or link bracelet, a tie tack or clip, cuff links, and a simple ring. (Be careful here: your prized high school class ring is considered crassly adolescent on some campuses, while it's acceptable on others.)

With the "male jewelry" question, there's really no substitute for knowing your campus. You may be able to get away with tons of gold chains dropping inside your open-to-the-navel shirt. Or you may find that anything more than watch and cuff links brands you as an effete snob, a discomaniac, a latter-day hippie, or worse. Psych out the campus mood before you put down the big bucks for gold chains. Less often *is* more. And the general mood of the eighties is toward understatement and quiet conservatism rather than the flamboyance of the sixties and early seventies.

In accessories, women have an infinitely greater range of

choices, styles, and items than men. But many of the basics remain the same: belts, ties, scarves, pocket squares, socks, watches, jewelry, vests and other "third layers" *ad infinitum*, gloves, and totes or bookbags. But to this you can add wraps, shawls, leotards, bodysuits and tights, pantyhose, hair accessories, ribbons, headbands, detachable collars and dickeys, small hats, caps, and assorted other headgear. To simplify it all, start with an accessory "wardrobe" made up of these items: one good dress leather belt and one casual belt (perhaps in canvas or webbing) or a "fun" belt in an Indian-beaded or western style; two or three scarves in oblong, square, and shawl styles; a silk handkerchief square; a wool muffler or long scarf; four to six pairs of stockings, tights, or pantyhose (some plain, some colored or patterned to coordinate with the basic colors in your skirts and pants); hair accessories (combs, picks, headbands, or ribbons); a handbag or tote/book bag; a cap and gloves for cold weather; a short knit sweater-vest to layer over pants and skirts; a watch and two pairs of earrings (one dress, one sporty); a gold or silver link bracelet and one or two thin gold or silver chains. You can add to this list as more items (and cash) come your way.

Although we love to talk about a certain campus "style" or "look," it's often very hard to define or describe a single outfit that sums up an entire campus or region. More commonly, various clubs, cliques, majors, schools, sororities, or fraternities will have their own distinctive looks. For example, business types may affect three-piece suits (skirted for women, please), while liberal-arts majors may sport long hair, jeans, turtlenecks, and ethnic jewelry. Performers in dance and theater may go in for leotards and tights with leg warmers; campus jocks may live in warmup suits and jogging shoes; and various ethnic groups may cling to their native dress. There are really only two universal American college looks, and these are jeans-dressing and a sort of bastardized Ivy League/preppie look: cotton polo shirts in pale colors, Brooks Brothers Oxford-cloth shirts, beige chinos or cords, webbing and leather belts, loafers or tennis shoes, Shetland or Irish fishermen's sweaters and well-worn tweed jackets for winter, a navy blue blazer and charcoal gray slacks for casual dress, and the inevitable beige gabardine raincoat with houndstooth-check lining. You almost can't go wrong with this look, particularly if you mix in some good-looking jeans for a denim-oriented campus.

But we can't emphasize strongly enough that you should plan to take only the basics with you and save a part of your clothing budget to fill in with the really "hot" campus items for fall. If everyone who is anyone has: a Lacoste shirt/designer jeans/an Eddie Bauer backpack/Nike running shoes/a monogrammed Shetland sweater/a western belt and Indian headband, then you too can travel in style for a minimum investment. Fad items tend to be inexpensive, one-season sorts of things. But take time to look. Don't rush out your first week and put a whole new wardrobe together based on your impressions of registration week. You may just have been watching the wrong people!

If you're still worried about your budget, there are plenty of ways to get good looks at low prices. Don't go on a credit-card binge at your local department store. Instead, try the following ideas and sources for inexpensive but good-quality functional clothes and accessories:

· Try your luck with wholesale or discount outlets for reasonably priced merchandise—most of it surprisingly good. Many cities now have shopping complexes that specialize in seconds and sale merchandise from pricier shops.

Putting Your Wardrobe Together

With luck you can find handsome items for a fraction of their original price.

· For staples like jeans and cords, try army-navy and surplus stores. The color and styling of these items are basic anyway, so you can find duplicates of department and specialty store merchandise at much lower cost. While you're at it, pick up some army fatigues, a battle jacket or two, some duffel bags in canvas, a rain slicker or poncho, and a couple of belts. And don't forget to check out boots, sweatsuits, and T-shirts. With a little luck, you could find literally half your wardrobe here.

· Check out secondhand stores, thrift shops, neighborhood rummage sales, Salvation Army and Goodwill stores, and other sources of secondhand goods. Often you'll find little-worn, nicely broken-in jeans for $2 to $5. (Remember that jeans have now become such classics that there's a brisk underground market in buying, selling, and trading styles and shades ranging from faded to indigo blue.) Also consider swapping or trading with a friend if your supply needs replenishing. Barter is the wave of the future!

· Consider jeans alternatives, such as fatigues, painter's pants, overalls, or cotton drawstring pants for summer. Check out sales and discount outlets for these as well as for your regular supply of jeans.

· Learn to think of "active sportswear" as good day-in, day-out garb. Your warmup suit, jogging pants, and running shoes can go to class as well as the track or gym—and they're also perfect lounging and study gear. Even if your school has dress codes about what you can and can't wear to classes, you can still spend the better part of your weekends around the coffee shop, cafeteria, library, and dorm wearing your warmup suit and tennis shoes.

Women especially can experiment with this form of dress. The exercise leotard and tights can be the basis for a whole day's worth of looks. Add jeans, boots, a plaid shirt, and a scarf, and you're ready for both your exercise group and a day of classes. Peel off the jeans, replace them with a wrap skirt or colorful shawl knotted sarong-style. Add jewelry, belt, and dressy sandals and you're ready for a night on the town. Back in the dorm later, shed the evening accessories, strip down to the basic leotard and tights, layer on sweatpants and a T-shirt, and you're ready to relax.

· Watch department-store sales for several months in advance of your departure for college. The January before you leave isn't too early, especially if it's winter stuff you're after. Back-to-school sales can produce good bargains—and so can late-summer sales on summer overstocks just before the fall merchandise arrives. Since jeans aren't really "seasonal" items, they don't go on sale as often as seasonal things do, but keep a sharp eye out for two-for-one jeans sales. Also look for fast sellouts on styles that bombed, were overproduced, or were overpriced. Stay away from extremes and go for the classics, though: otherwise, you'll look as if you're stuck in a freshman-year time-machine.

· Want to put a little fun and pizzazz into your wardrobe? Check out the secondhand stores, vintage clothing shops, ethnic stores, and import emporia for unusual items: a novelty belt, a lapel pin, a pair of *real* jazz oxfords, a Hawaiian shirt, an authentic English hacking jacket or World War II bomber's jacket, an army officer's trenchcoat. Who knows what you might unearth in all those bins of secondhand junk? Women take note: these shops are also great sources for antique lingerie, lace handkerchiefs, Victorian slips that can double as dresses. Deco-style beaded tops and dresses, and other finery. If nothing else, you may spot unusual laces and trims that can be cut off and used to trim your own shirts and sweaters.

· If you're yearning for really classy boots, duffels, briefcases, watches, or luggage, watch the want ads in your local newspapers. Keep an eye on weekly trading papers too. You can find prices up to 75 percent less than brand-new. If you're patient and careful to shop around, you might just put together a real class act for pennies.

· Want to keep the total wardrobe small? Here's an entire twelve-piece wardrobe for men and women that you can pack in a large suitcase: three pairs of jeans, three T-shirts (or polo shirts or pullover sweaters), two shirts (one wool or cotton, the other silk), a pair of dress pants, a cardigan sweater or jacket, a lined all-weather coat, and a warmup or jogging suit. (Women can add one leotard with matching tights and a skirt to extend the possibilities of mixing and matching.) All you'll need besides are socks or stockings, underwear, shoes, boots, and a book bag or carryall.

· If you're a small woman, do try an unorthodox solution for finding quality clothes on the cheap: the boys' section of large department stores or men's specialty shops such as Brooks Brothers. An Oxford-cloth shirt with button-down collar or a Lacoste pullover that fits a twelve-year-old boy may also fit you. What's more, it will be half the price of its equivalent in the women's section. While you're at it, take a swing through the junior and teenage girls' department; even if the clothes are too small (try the big sweaters and down coats anyway), you can find good low-cost jewelry, bags, belts, and hair ornaments. It's an especially fine source for fad items when you're looking for the newest look at the lowest cost.

· Don't neglect your friendly dime store as a source of thrifty chic either. If you're short on cash but long on imagination, take a $10 bill, go to the local Woolworth's, and see how far you can stretch it. You'll find such collectibles as plastic bangles and hoop earrings, scarves, cotton and straw hats, straw and wicker bags, baskets and carryalls, colorful espadrilles, ballet-style flats and Chinese-style Mary Janes, totes, book bags, inexpensive cosmetics, and a profusion of belts, combs, headbands, and hair-ribbons or clips. Men can find T-shirts, cotton bandannas, shower thongs, even shorts and bathing trunks.

· Do get to know the shops in your college town or village. Even if home is the big city, don't turn up your nose at local merchants. Often they'll have those big-city looks at lower prices to fit student pocketbooks. Don't overlook local crafts and ethnic shops—they may be full of wonderfull belts, jewelry, bags, and other accessories that can help you start a collection for the future.

· Also find out the names of sample shops and designer outlets near your school. Especially for smaller-sized women, they're a real boon, often allowing you to get super-looking clothes at a fraction of their original prices.

· Don't let your campus activities turn you into a "fashion dropout." It's easy to get so engrossed in your studies and campus life that each morning you reach for the same comfortable old jeans and T-shirt or sweater. Keeping your looks current requires only a little time and money—and it's amazing how quickly you can change those campus basics and turn them into fresh looks. If you need inspiration, check out the "College Clothes on $150 a Year" section of *Cheap Chic*. Women should watch especially the August issues of *Glamour*, *Mademoiselle*, *Seventeen*, and *Self*. These are usually special college issues packed with good ideas on updating your old clothes, picking new ones, and generally putting together a versatile, fashionable college wardrobe.

· Do learn to use accessories imaginatively to change the looks of your outfits. Scarves can be bandeau bras, turbans, hobo-style handbags, headwraps, ties, belts, sashes, even necklaces and bracelets. Big shawls can double as classy midcalf skirts over a leotard or body suit. Belts can become necklaces and vice-versa. Big canvas duffels can do double duty as handbags or backpacks and also as weekend luggage, totes, portfolios, and exercise-gear carryalls. The more versatile your accessories, the more mileage you'll get from them. Learn to think "multiple purpose" about every single item you buy.

And men: don't think the accessory advice is for women only—you can use many of the same tricks. You can even raid a sister's or girlfriend's closet for scarves, mufflers, pocket squares, and other "unisex" accessories.

· Do use friends and roommates (with their permission, of course) as a source of clothes or accessories for special occasions. Always—but always—ask when you borrow. Return the items in good condition and be prepared to reciprocate. Often your roommate's closet will supply the missing shoes or belt you need to perk up an outfit but haven't time or cash to shop for. Another idea: organize a Saturday clothes swap. Have each person in your dorm bring a certain number of items, group them by categories, and then let people swap one-for-one. A good, inexpensive way to recycle your wardrobe and get some fresh looks without a cash outlay.

· Do use your talents to personalize inexpensive staples like T-shirts, denim jackets, jeans, and plain pants. Dye the T-shirts offbeat pastels and "hot" shades. Add transfers or sew on appliqués for more personalizing. Tie-dye or fringe vests, skirts, and shawls. Embroider or appliqué a denim shirt. Use a wood-burning kit to personalize a plain belt. Try handcrafting some jewelry from papier-mâché or tin. Try macramé, weaving, knitting, crocheting. Hand-paint or embroider a top for evening or a Chinese silk kimono to wear around the dorm.

· Don't overlook the catalogs. Sears Roebuck, J. C. Penney, and Montgomery Ward all make good, inexpensive shirts, jackets, and jeans. All your "staples" can be found in the big wish books—including western-look clothes and footwear. Check out their prices and styling before you pay specialty-store prices for essentially the same items. And if you want the best in outdoorsy gear that's also classy campus wear, check out the L. L. Bean and Eddie Bauer catalogs: lots of good down jackets and vests, sweaters, and other rugged stuff, reasonably priced. Aspiring preppies take note: the Talbots and Carroll Reed offer down-to-earth prices on rich-looking Ivy League and prep-style clothes.

· Do use college as a time to experiment with fashion. It may be the only chance you'll have to experiment freely before you enter the "adult" world. Besides, it's a perfect period for discovering your own fashion identity: you're young and have free time to try different looks. Also you aren't yet hemmed in by the conservatism of the business world and the dress-for-success ethic. Unlike the working person, you can pair wildly printed T-shirts with fringed jeans, a beaded bag, desert boots, and ethnic jewelry and no one will be upset. Instead, people will marvel at your "creativity" and "originality."

· Another word for women: learn to use makeup and hair styles imaginatively to help create the look or mood of an outfit. Makeup, remember, is just as much an "accessory" as a scarf, belt, or hat—and often it offers better returns for a smaller investment. Sometimes a new hair style or a new color of eye shadow or lip gloss can transform the look of an outfit as nothing else will. And often the key to transforming day into evening looks turns on the way you decide to twist or braid your hair, and the deeper, murkier makeup tones you choose for evening.

· Looking for a basic four-minute makeup for day? Start with a tinted moisturizer as a base to even out your natural color. You probably won't even need makeup base over the moisturizer. A touch of blush across the cheekbones and temples will give the color that you need. Apply a neutral-colored eye shadow in earth tones (brown, gray, khaki, pale mauve, or olive) and blend up to the crease. Line the eyes close to both upper and lower lashes about halfway around the eye—any further and you "close" the eye instead of opening it up. Smudge the liner so that it's just a suggestion of color, not a definite line. Add mascara on upper and lower lashes, a touch of lip gloss, and you're off and running for the day.

One word of general advice: dress for the campus you're actually on, not some fantasy place or "ideal" college. Don't affect the Ivy League look if you're in the middle of a blue-grass-and-country-western-look campus, or dress Sun Belt or West Coast style if you're actually in northern Minnesota or North Dakota. Dress according to the climate, the activities your school is into (forget the tennis whites or rowing or polo gear unless your school excels in that sport), the kinds of things your fellow students wear, and the location. College towns look different from big-city streetcar colleges, which in turn differ from suburban junior colleges and big state universities. Tailor your look to your locale if you want to fit in.

Finally, remember that nothing, not even the most expensive clothes, looks good if you're carelessly groomed and out of shape. Start off your college life with a good haircut and shaping. Follow a regular program of hair and skin care. Take along a blow dryer, a styling comb, and manicure kit—along with a shoeshine box, sewing kit, clothes brush, and spot remover. Spend a few minutes each week checking for loose buttons and making minor repairs, shining shoes, getting dry cleaning done, and getting rundown heels fixed. Keep your nails clean and shaped.

And keep your *body* in shape too. Substitute healthy snacks for high-cal munchies. Pass up the mystery meat, mashed potatoes, and high-calorie desserts in favor of grilled fish or chicken, salads, yogurt or fruit. Run, bicycle, jog, walk, play racquetball or tennis, take up aerobic dance. Take advantage of the local Y, the school gym or weight room. If you have access to a pool, use it. Stay well, stay fit, and stay in style. You'll feel and work better if you do.

8

What to Do if You're a Special Case

THE FIRST THING to realize if you're a special case is that it's probably up to you to solve whatever problems you have. We don't mean that there aren't dozens of offices, bureaus, counselors, faculty members, deans, and other people who stand waiting to help you. But your problem, whatever it is, is basically your responsibility, and it's going to be up to you either to solve it or to find somebody who can help you solve it.

Let's go over a few categories, so you'll know what we're talking about.

PHYSICAL DISABILITIES

Depending on the nature of the disability, you may have an easier time of it than you might think. For instance, almost any university will make provisions for blind students. There are cassette tapes of various subjects, and there are people who will read to you. If you are having this book read to you, you already know the score.

The important thing here is not to become discouraged. It's going to be rough, and you may as well make up your mind to the fact that you're going to be competing with other students under a definite handicap. On the other hand, the yearbooks are full of people who've not only gotten through college while blind but have gone on to graduate school, earned an advanced degree, and made a success of their chosen field.

Ralph lost one eye in a hunting accident years ago. There was nothing wrong with the remaining eye, but long hours of study took their toll. When he graduated from high school, he applied for a job as a state counselor for the blind. He thought that he might understand some of the problems that vision-impaired people would have. The head of the state office for the blind told him that few blind people ever succeeded, and that he should simply try to get them into some kind of work at which they could make a living. When Ralph suggested that a higher education would outfit blind people to better cope with their problems, the administrator scoffed. Ralph told him where to put the job, and left.

Years later, when he started college himself, Ralph met two blind students, both of whom were in their freshman year. One had lost an eye in a rodeo accident. The other had glaucoma. The rodeo rider became a successful businessman, and the glaucoma victim became a very successful lawyer. They didn't believe the bureaucrat at the state office building, either.

Think of it this way: modern communications media

have provided you with dozens of substitutes for learning through sight. Take advantage of them. Get a tape recorder that's small and easily used. More than likely, the state vocational rehabilitation office will buy it for you. Use it, and use the wealth of information available to you in the form of counseling and rehabilitation. The aim here is to get through college with more than merely a diploma. You can do it, but you're going to have to work harder than most people. Our friend Leon Lucabanne did it, finished an advanced degree, and along the way earned a black belt in karate in the All-America Karate Federation. Leon has only peripheral vision, as a result of retinal breakage caused by diabetes.

What about other disabilities? Ralph had a friend in college whose father carried him to class every day in his arms. He had literally been wrecked physically by paralytic polio. But he persevered, finished college, went to law school, and wrote a definitive book on minorities and the law. Another polio victim, Jack Emmott, is a successful lawyer in Houston.

And then there's Lisa Boynton, whose IQ is high enough to get her into Mensa but whose dyslexia makes it difficult for her to read rapidly. Through sheer determination and raw intelligence, she made it not only through an undergraduate program but through graduate school in accounting, and then through law school. She's now a successful businesswoman in Chicago.

What about all the guys who were disabled in World War II, Korea, and Vietnam? Ralph's cousin, Sonny Buttram, overcame paraplegia (he was shot in the back by Korean machine-gun fire) to become a successful businessman and dental lab owner. The world is full of stories about people who overcame handicaps and went on to succeed.

If you have no handicap, you may want to skip over the next few paragraphs. On the other hand, you might want to read them. You'll learn something about yourself and about the people who have the handicaps.

OK, guys and girls. Some straight talk. All the inspirational jive in the world isn't going to get you over that curb and onto the sidewalk when there's nobody to help and there's ice on the street. Neither are success stories going to get the day's reading done when you have no eyes to read with. Maybe you're hearing this right now, instead of seeing it.

At various times in his life, Ralph has spent a long time in a wheelchair. He has one eye, and a heart murmur that has restricted his activities all his life. So, let's talk about practical things.

If you're in a wheelchair for good or for an extended time, you know that it's possible to get state aid to help you go to school. You should ask your vocational rehab counselor which schools make provisions for people in your position. They'll know, because they'll have gotten some feedback from others in the same predicament. Furthermore, they'll know which colleges have inclined curbing, ramps, and all the other things that are important to you. The law requires these things. If the school of your choice doesn't have them yet, tell the state vocational rehab counselor. They'll do something about it, and you won't get any flak.

You might also check out the possibility that the school of your choice gives "working scholarships" to people who help people in wheelchairs. Many schools do it.

Don't forget that many campuses are spread out over a large area. Plan your classes so that you don't get stuck on one side of the campus with a class five minutes away in time and six blocks away in space. No matter how understanding your prof is, he or she will eventually get tired of your coming in late.

If you have a powered chair, you already know what to watch out for, especially in the winter when there's ice and there's the possibility of your battery freezing up: another plus for the urban school that is all in one building, such as DePaul, Spertus, or Roosevelt.

If you're blind, you can benefit from a tremendous number of advances that have been made in the last few decades. Miniature tape recorders have replaced Braille styluses for taking notes, and most schools now have Braille or other numbering systems for elevators, classrooms, offices, and equally important, rest rooms.

Also, there are tapes in the library, with trained personnel to help you find them and use them. Many libraries have tapes of book or text readings that you can check out the same way that a sighted person would check out a book. These tapes are made by thousands of volunteers all across the country, who are picked for the clarity of their voices and their enunciation.

Moreover, many campus counseling offices have ongoing programs to help you prepare for the world outside the university. They have the techniques and the personnel to teach you how to get through school and become self-supporting after you graduate.

When you choose your school, make sure that it is large enough and has enough money to support the kinds of programs that you are going to need. You've got enough problems, whatever your disability, without putting yourself into a situation in which you can't take advantage of the advances of modern technology. Take any help that's available, and don't be bashful about asking for it.

If you have neuromotor problems, if you have trouble

either walking or writing, getting up stairs, or using the library facilities, look before you make your choice. If you have trouble with your vision, with your heart, with your reading ability, with any of the myriad illnesses or conditions that make you a special case, make sure that the college you've chosen knows how to help you to help yourself. If no provisions are made for special cases like yours, chances are that the faculty and the administration are still living in the Dark Ages as far as handicapped people are concerned.

That you don't need.

Remember, no matter how racked up you are, it's your mind that counts in college. Use it. Learn with it. Take advantage of any help that's available, but realize that you've got to make your own way. You've got to use college as a stepping-stone to a career, to gainful employment, to self-sufficiency.

Don't expect a hell of a lot of sympathy. You undoubtedly already know that it's up to you to do what has to be done. But there are many people who are genuinely interested in your success, and who will help you rationally and objectively to reach your goals.

You won't have to seek these people out. They'll find you, not because they're "do-gooders," but because they're the kind of people who like to help other people, no strings attached.

So, hang in there. You may be in for some pleasant surprises. And you *will* make it. We're pulling for you.

LIVING AT HOME

Some people might ask, "This is a problem?" Well, for most people it is, especially if you're the first person in your family to get a college degree.

Don't expect your parents, brothers, or sisters to understand that whatever the world/state/local/home situation is at the moment, there will be times when there is nothing, repeat, *nothing* that is more important than that exam you have to take in the morning.

Also, don't expect them to understand why you're staying up late at night, eating poorly, wearing yourself out, and "straining your eyes" studying something like the contributions of the pre-Socratic philosophers to the concept of a substratum for existence. They won't understand, and you may not either.

The fact remains, it's a r-e-q-u-i-r-e-m-e-n-t, and you have to learn the stuff to get through the course. And you have to have the course to graduate. So you have to stay up all night studying (because you spent the time you should have been studying watching the Bears lose to Pittsburgh).

Parents and siblings also have a tough time leaving you alone when you're trying to study. Don't forget, solitary behavior is suspect in middle-class America, and nobody will really believe that you're locked in your room *studying*. You're actually looking at *Playboy* magazine and smoking funny cigarettes, not learning how Milton justifies God's ways to man.

Your mother will want you to come downstairs and join the family. She'll also bring you food. And your father will be proud, but puzzled. Your sisters and brothers will not be concerned. They will simply drive you crazy.

What to do? If you can't live away from home, then sit down with the family and lay out for them the requirements for graduation. Tell them how much you have to do if you're going to succeed in college. Have a rational discussion with them at the outset, and explain to them how much you have to study, how much you have to read each night, and how much you want to do well. They're usually on your side, and a solid understanding from the beginning will save you a lot of grief later on.

Your changing life-style may also cause some problems with your parents. One of the best ways for some people to study is to get together with other people in a class and go over the material. These rap sessions can really be beneficial, but they sometimes sound like nothing more than bull sessions to people who don't know what taking college courses is like. Again, explain the situation to your parents, so that they'll understand that some education comes through osmosis as well as through listening to lectures and looking at lab slides.

If you're working on a part-time or a full-time job, you will be getting in at all hours. This is another source of friction between you and your family, so spell out your schedule for them before you get caught in a crossfire.

Also remember that if your mother is like most, she'll worry about your health, what with your increasingly long hours of work and study. Don't hold it against her. She may get on your nerves, but she has your best interests at heart.

Your dad will worry more about your changing personality than about your eating and sleeping habits. Learn to handle the changes. That's what they're trying to do, too.

If you absolutely can't stand it at home, then get out before it gets any worse. Share a room with another student, or get a room in the dormitory. If you can't swing the cost, get a part-time job so you can be on your own.

You should be out on your own, anyway. Our advice is never to live at home while you're going to college if you can possibly avoid it. This is true even if the college is in the same town you've been living in all the time. No matter how much you may love your parents, and no matter how much they may love you, you're better off away from home. Simply, the demands of college and the demands of fully integrating into the life of the home don't often mix. College is often the transition between dependence on the family and real independence. It should be a rite of passage between adolescence and adulthood. It'll be the place where you learn about the rest of the world, the world that lies outside both the home and the historical present in which you live. It's the greatest time you'll ever have in your burgeoning adult life, and you should jump right into it without a lifeline back into the living room or the family den.

Besides, you'll be growing farther and farther away from your parents as you go through college. Better to make a clean break at the beginning, and get used to visiting them on holidays. Ask anybody who's tried it both ways. They'll tell you to get out of the house.

But what if you're married, and have no choice but to live at home? What if you're married, have children, are a little older than most of the other students, have a part-time job, and can attend school only at night or only during the day? Don't feel left out or alone. Times have changed. There are a lot of you these days.

Once upon a time in the fifties, at Crawling Ivy University in the nation's heartland, you would have been dismissed by the campus cognoscenti as merely a "day student." That meant that you weren't a bona fide member of the student body, since you had responsibilities that encroached on your party time. You also probably had a part-time or a full-time job, were going night and day to survive, lying to the dean about how much you were working so you could carry a full load of courses, and keeping up with your wife or husband and family, too. If you were smart, it compounded the trouble: even with all the responsibilities, you were doing better in class than the full-time, live-in students. They were fraternity or sorority denizens, for whom college was either a social occasion or an opportunity to make contacts that would open doors for them after graduation. You, on the other hand, obviously didn't have the money to participate in campus life. Which meant that you weren't socially acceptable.

This kind of narrow view of what college is all about unfortunately still prevails on some campuses. Either develop a thick hide or go somewhere else. You won't educate these people, so there's no use wasting your time with them. But remember: they're still holding to a college world view that dates back to the twenties. If you run into these types on today's campus, you should feel sorry for them, but not much.

By the time you graduate, you will already have learned how to cope with hardship, money problems, frustrations, conflicting schedules, conflicting priorities, deadlines, and budgeting your time, energies, cash, and attention. In short, you will have learned how to survive in the modern business or professional world, which is definitely *not* a continuous round of cocktail parties as some people would have you think.

But how do you do all this budgeting? It ain't easy, but

the methods are easier to learn than you think. You've just got to face the facts.

Let's go back to our hypothetical character, the one who's a little older, is married, has children, has money problems, and can go to school only during the day or at night (depending on which shift he's on at work). Let's call him "Joe Garble" (that's the way his name always comes out of the little paging loudspeaker at the hospital when the nurse calls him to tell him that he has yet another mouth to feed). There are a lot of Joes around these days. People have learned that though it's difficult, it is possible to go ahead and get married and start a family while attending college. As a result, Joe is becoming the rule rather than the exception, especially at urban universities.

Here's Joe's schedule. This is not made up, but is an absolutely accurate account of a typical day.

7:00 A.M.   Joe gets up, wakes Beverly, and starts getting the baby ready to take to the sitter (or the day-care center). Beverly starts breakfast, and gets ready to go to work.

7:45 A.M.   Joe and Beverly leave their apartment. Joe drops Bev off at the hospital (where she's a nurse) and heads for the sitter's. Upon arriving, he carries in the baby, the bottles with formula, extra diapers, whatever medicine the baby may be taking for whatever may be ailing it, and extra dry clothes.

8:30 A.M.   Joe arrives on campus and spends twenty minutes looking for a parking place. He finds one, and rushes to the cafeteria for a quick cup of coffee before Francis Benjamin's History of Greece class.

9:00 A.M.   An hour of the history of Greece. Benjamin (now deceased) is so good, he makes Joe forget how much he has to do when he gets home. Beautiful class. High point of the day!

10:00 A.M. On to the Human Values Seminar, with assorted profs from the theology school. Dull and dry, a mixture of God's Grace and Existentialism, threaded through the Methodist Church. Escape at 11:00.

11:00 A.M. Another brilliant seminar with John Doby, who can't understand why Joe is wasting his time in the Graduate Liberal Arts Institute but admires his logical analyses. Joe feels refreshed, having washed God's Grace and Existentialism down with a good swig of small-group social dynamics.

12:00   Lunch at the Chow Palace. Argument between one classmate, who believes death to be an aesthetic necessity for the introduction of variety into the universe, and another, who thinks that Wittgenstein really solved all the problems with the *Tractatus*. This argument is replaced by another, between a born-again Japanese and a Chicago-born Irish kid who has become a devout Buddhist, Each accuses the other of being a traitor to his heritage. Joe leaves as the Chicago Buddhist cites "Buddha is and is not" as being a genuine instance of X and non-X existing in the same universe.

1:00 P.M.   Joe spends an hour looking over the re-

	search paper he has to present to his humanities class.
2:00 P.M.	Joe leads a discussion of Rabelais' small piece on the walls of Paris, from *Gargantua and Pantagruel*. Several women take exception to the piece, and a nun leaves in disgust, on her way to the dean.
4:00 P.M.	Joe picks the baby up and heads for home. He has an hour before he has to report for duty at the ambulance company where he works every other night.
5:00 P.M.	Joe arrives at the ambulance company, having picked up Beverly at the hospital, gulped down a Big Mac, changed clothes, and fought the rush-hour traffic, all in an hour.
6:00 P.M.	The first wreck call of nine that night.
8:00 A.M.	Joe leaves the ambulance company for home, not having slept a wink all night. Nine calls: four deaths, five survivors, two of whom will be permanently maimed.
9:00 A.M.	Another episode in the continuing saga of the Diadochi and the Epigoni: Alexander is dead, and the generals are taking their places in history.

Joe will get to sleep at midnight. Another day, and he will begin the cycle again.

Farfetched? Not on your life. We know the guy, and he made it all the way through a Ph.D. program, and has enjoyed a long, successful career as a professor and an administrator. How did he do it? Here are a few general tips.

- First and foremost, nobody's going to help you but yourself. Even if this is not strictly true, you'll be better off if you operate on this assumption.
- You're going to have to budget your time correctly, both in terms of what you want to get out of school and what you want to get out of your home life. The child needs attention, and it really isn't his or her fault. Don't take it out on the kid.
- Don't take it out on your wife, either. It takes two, you know, and now that you have the child you've got to do what you've got to do.
- Which means, learn to run your life like a good railroad. There are a lot of hours in any day. Most people waste an incredible amount of time. Don't do it. Learn to use your time to your advantage.
- Look back at Joe Garble's day. It's a tight schedule, but he kept it up for seven or eight years without going off the deep end. Look at it closely, and you'll see how he did it:

7:00 A.M.	He and Bev share the morning tasks.
7:45 to 9:00 A.M.	Joe allows himself an hour and fifteen minutes to get from home to class. This gives him enough time to get a cup of coffee before class, and enough time to make the passage from family man to student.
9:00 to 12:00 NOON	Solid three hours of class. Rough? Joe planned it that way. This schedule gets all the classes over by the middle of the day, and leaves him time for lunch and a look at the material he has to teach. He has two

	hours' leeway before he has to "make his next appearance."
2:00 to 4:00 P.M.	He's a teaching assistant in humanities class, which pays his tuition.
4:00 to 5:00 P.M.	A little tight here, but only every third night.
5:00 P.M.	And on through the night. Why work as an ambulance driver? Because Joe can study between ambulance calls. If there aren't many calls, he gets a lot done. If there are a lot of calls, he doesn't get much done.

But how about staying up all night? This phase of Joe's college career lasted only three years, but he adjusted to it. And he always planned his schedule well in advance.

It was a tradition at Crawling Ivy that professors gave out syllabi on the first day of class. Joe took these sheets eagerly, because they enabled him to plan the entire semester. Certain exams came on certain days, as did deadlines for papers, research work, and other assignments.

Joe worked out a large chart, representing the entire semester. He plotted his work days (or nights) on the chart, and then drew in the class times, the papers, the exams, and the teaching responsibilities. By the morning of the second day of class, Joe knew what he had to do, how much time he had to do it in, and where the fudge factors were. Nobody could figure out how he did it. He was simply realistic about budgeting time, that's all.

Which is why years later, when he became a university administrator, he was able to publish five times as much as anybody on his faculty while at the same time holding down a forty-hour-a-week administrator's job.

"Waste not, want not" applies to the use of time as well as food and money.

TRANSFER STUDENT

We'll cover the details of transferring in from another school in another section of the book, with some tips on credits and working with your adviser. There are a few general considerations as well, so let's cover them here.

First, a lot depends on where you're coming from. If you've just graduated from a junior college, have an associate degree, and are beginning your junior year, you're already savvy about school and what it takes to get through.

But if your junior college had lower standards than the school you're now entering, you may expect some trouble. The most frequent kind of trouble is the qualifying exams that are a must for graduation.

The English qualifying exam or its equivalent is common to almost all universities. It tests (more or less accurately) your ability to write and to express yourself simply, effectively, and correctly. Unfortunately, many junior colleges give easy grades in English, and leave it to the senior institutions to do the work. The result? Large numbers of people who thought they could write, but who now have to go back and take freshman comp again.

Not only is it embarrassing, it's costly as well. If you're on a state grant or a scholarship, you may not be able to get the extra courses paid for. That means that your tight budget is going to become even tighter, which in turn probably means that you'll have to borrow more money or work longer hours on your part-time job.

So if you're still in junior college, plan your schedule well and make sure that you get what you need to compete in the senior institutions. And if you're planning to enter a junior college remember that there are good ones and there are bad ones. A beautiful campus and sparkling clean halls and classrooms are no guarantee of a good education. Many junior or community colleges have low standards because they are populated with people who do not plan to go to senior institutions. Others have low standards because they have fallen victim to state departments of education, and are testing grounds for every half-baked educational theory that the Board of Education pushes through the legislature.

Several years ago, for example, many community colleges instituted curricula made up completely of "modular" courses. These courses were our old familiar ones, broken down into component parts. The trick was that you took, studied, and passed one part at a time. It was like taking fifteen tiny courses, all of which made up one regular course. Consequently, instead of a solid program in, say, English that taught effective writing, there were modular courses on "The Sentence" and "The Paragraph," or on "Vocabulary" and "Common Usage." As a result, many people now attending senior institutions have a disjointed, fractured conception of language and how to write. They've also been following a method of learning material that gives them little preparation for the syntheses of diverse fields that makes higher education so valuable.

This is not to say that all junior or community colleges are bad. Far from it. However, the standards in these colleges are usually below the standards of senior institutions.

The gulf between bad junior colleges and good senior colleges is sometimes simply too wide to cross. Remember that many students in community colleges do not intend to go on to senior institutions. They'll stop with the associate of arts degree. They're in for a rude shock, because they'll find out pretty quickly that such a degree is practically worthless in terms of developing a career plan that will put them on a sound financial basis for life.

So if you're transferring from a junior or community college, your greatest hurdle will be standards. The senior institution will probably be harder, with more material to study for each course and more depth in the courses. Further, many senior colleges are oriented toward graduate studies, and the curriculum tends toward tough courses that will prepare students for graduate school.

The greatest contribution that community colleges can make is to enable people with the necessary native intelligence to get started in college despite poor preparation. Many colleges have programs especially designed to find these "diamonds in the rough." And many a top-notch grad student started out several years behind in a little country college. In fact, Ralph spent his first two quarters in a little college in the north Georgia mountains. It was a way to get started after a five-year hiatus since graduating from high school.

By the time he got to Emory in Atlanta, Ralph had gotten up a head of steam. Then, it was a long roll to the Ph.D. nine years later. As grateful as Ralph is to the little college, it was a shock when he arrived on the Emory campus. Nothing in the community college had prepared him for the realities of a genuinely high-quality, pressured program like the one at Emory. More time spent at the small college would have hampered his progress severely.

It is an old complaint at senior institutions that the junior colleges don't do their jobs. This is not entirely a prejudice; the senior institutions more often than not have the thankless task of filling in the gaps left by amateurish curricula and second-rate faculty. It's no joke to get all A's at Chicken Lick and not be able to pass the English qualifying exam at the state university. We would be dishonest if we told you that you'll have smooth sailing when you make the transition to the bigger institution.

On the other hand, thousands of community colleges across the country are doing a superb job of preparing people for just such transitions. How can you tell the sheep from the goats? Here are a few tips:

· Again, read the catalog! Find out the faculty's credentials.

· Does the school have a reputation in the community for doing its job? Or is it the place to go for easy grades?

· What do the senior institutions in the area think of it? Here's the important one: do the senior institutions accept credits from the junior college in question? If they don't, forget it.

· What is the success ratio of people who've gone on from Chicken Lick community college to State? Look up the graduates and ask them.

· Compare Chicken Lick's catalog with the catalog of a reputable senior institution. If Chicken Lick is loaded up with courses such as "The Human Condition" or "The Understanding of Man," approach it carefully. It's probably not running on a track parallel to the one the senior institution is running on.

One last piece of advice. Make the transfer as soon as you can. Don't wait for the Associate of Arts degree if you plan to get a bachelor's degree anyway. It won't do you a bit of good. It'll have little to do with job opportunities if you go on and finish college. If you plan to go all the way, get into the senior institution as soon as possible, and start working on your four-year plan that will take you through to the degree you need. The atmosphere in senior institutions is markedly different from that of junior colleges. The sooner you learn to survive in it, the better off you'll be.

SHORT OF CASH

If you're short of cash, you have a variety of choices besides dropping out of school. You can borrow money through student loan funds at your school or at a local bank; you can apply for financial aid through the financial aid office at your school; you can check with the various state agencies to see if you qualify for grants; or you can get a job on or off campus, part-time or full-time. (See Chapter 4 for complete details about available sources of money and how to apply.)

Our friend Joe Garble got a state grant. He also got a government loan and a loan from a bank where he used to work. These loans, plus his tuition scholarship and his job, made it possible for him to complete his education. As Joe would be happy to tell you, he lied to the dean's office about how much he was working so that he could continue to take a full load in graduate school. This is not wise unless you're pretty bright. However, if you've got enough nerve you may be able to work full-time and go to school full-time. For many people, especially in the middle of a recession, there's no other way. So take heart. Others have gone before you, and you are definitely not alone.

If you're already in school and running short of change, go directly to the financial aid office. There may be funds available now that weren't available when you applied earlier. Our friend and former colleague Bob Franklin, the financial aid officer at Roosevelt University, tells us that many people who qualify for aid don't know it. They drop out of school instead of dropping by his office, where they could get some help and advice. Take advantage of every funding source you can. If you're afraid you don't qualify, either because of grades or other circumstances, you might be surprised.

Joe Garble's "part-time" job was full-time, of course. He was on ambulance call from 5:00 P.M. until 8:00 the next morning, a period of fifteen hours. Within any seven-day period he worked an average of forty-five hours, since he reported for duty every third night.

It sounds like a lot, but there were always quiet nights when he didn't have to go out at all. Those nights, he was able to study and prepare for the class he taught himself. The nights that he was busy, he did no studying. Careful planning was necessary in order not to be taken by surprise if he couldn't put in a full night of poring over the books. Again, you can make it if you approach all of this in a serious, businesslike manner. If you are planning to glide through, forget it.

We had many students at Roosevelt who worked full-time and took a partial load of course work. Sometimes this is the better idea, since you can devote more time to the few subjects you are taking. Far better to take fewer courses and do really well in them than to take a full load and flunk out or make a poor showing that would mar your record later on.

If you can, try to land a job that has something to do

with your educational goal. Joe had no intention of driving an ambulance for the rest of his life, but he took advantage of the possibility of being able to study between trips. Better that he could have found a part-time teaching position in another university in the same city, but his field demanded at least a master's degree before he could do that.

Many schools now have cooperative education programs which enable you to work at the career of your choice at a low level, receive credit for the work that you do, and tie it into your university education. Consequently, many English or journalism majors also work at newspapers or magazines, and many budding architectural students are already working as draftsmen for architectural firms.

We had a friend, Dwayne Clark, who worked on a degree at Georgia Tech during the winter, and worked during the summer at Huntsville, Alabama, with Wernher von Braun on solutions to the problem of precessing liquids in the rocket fuel tanks. His answer to the problem was a mathematical model of the surface of the fuel, based on the concept of a ballbearing moving inside of a parabola, with a little spring on it. It worked, and ole Charlie (as his Georgia Tech buddies called him) made his contribution to the space program. Ralph once used this story in defense of the proposition that cooperative education programs were more than worth their while. Thanks in part to Dwayne, not only did the rockets get off the ground, so did the coop program at Roosevelt.

When you get a part-time job, try to land one with somebody who knows what you're up against as a student. Also, try to get a job with somebody who has a college education. If you don't, you'll probably be resented by the boss or the rest of the employees. This is no joke, as Joe Garble found out to his dismay at the ambulance company. Everybody there knew that Joe would someday leave them to go on to greater things. None of them had the initiative to go to college. Consequently, they took out their frustrations on Joe. Not a good situation.

Some part-time jobs, although they are mostly menial, seem to be tailor-made for students. They don't take much intelligence, and they don't entail much responsibility. If the boss knows what you are trying to do with your life and he's not jealous of your future, you may have an easy time of it, just putting in your hours and drawing your money. On the other hand, you're spending a lot of hours doing something that has absolutely nothing to do with your ultimate goals. Again, try to get your short-term goals and your long-term goals together. Cooperative education may be just the ticket for you.

When you find a job, make it clear to the people you work for that you are serious about doing a good job for them, even though you'll be temporary help. Many employers have been badly burned by college students who slough off on the job. Let them know that you're honorable from the beginning. It'll save problems later.

On the other hand, don't let some jerk exploit you just because you're a student. College towns are full of employers who look upon the student body as a ready source of slave labor. They know you need the money, and they'll work you right into the ground for peanuts if you let them. Don't fall for it. Check with the campus placement office before you look for a job. Ask them who's who and what's what. They'll have a file on the good employers and the hustlers. Take their advice. Their data comes right from the students.

The campus itself may be a source of employment. Many students never have to leave the campus: they work there, take courses there, and live there. If you're attending a northern school where the climate is beastly and transportation is at a premium, there are some real arguments for accepting less money on a campus job rather than making more money at a job across town.

Unfortunately, many campuses are as bad as other employers about exploiting the student labor force. They feel that they've got a captive audience, and they'll use you in any way they can. Don't let them get away with it. If the campus employment service has a bad reputation, don't mess with it. Remember: although there are many people who are willing to help you, you should go on the assumption that nobody is going to help you but yourself. That way, real help will be a pleasant surprise. And you'll be able to maintain control over your life, besides.

TO RECAP

If you're a special case—if you have a physical handicap or a learning disability, or if you're loaded down with family responsibilities and are short of cash, or if you have a job and can't take part fully in campus activities—remember the following:

· You're not alone, and you're not the first person who's been in this position.

· There are dozens of offices, both on campus and off, where you can go to get advice, help, tests, and a host of other services just for the asking.

· Keep looking for a job, and when you find it make sure that it doesn't take over your life to the detriment of your studies.

· Don't get bogged down in your problems. Turn the

problems into projects. Projects can be worked on and brought to constructive results. Problems can only drag you down. Map out your strategy for success, and get on with it.

· Your greatest source of strength is yourself. Learn to rely on yourself. Be a self-starter. Don't let other people drag you down. Operate on the assumption that nobody is going to help you but yourself. Make your own way, the only way you know how, but *make it*.

· And when you get discouraged, think about ole Joe Garble and his schedule. Then get to work.

9

For Women Only

WE ALL KNOW that in the 1980s college populations are at least 50 percent female—in fact, some campuses are as much as 60 to 70 percent women. This represents a real reversal of the days when men practically owned the universities and writers were safe in referring to the typical college student as "he." It's not just in the student body that the change has taken place; women are now more prominent than ever in every phase of academic life. They're faculty members, administrators, counselors, deans, even college presidents. There's now a healthy percentage of women serving on college and university boards of trustees, as well as holding office in the national educational associations and professional organizations. You're now much more likely than a decade ago to find that your history professor/department chairperson/counselor/college dean is a woman. No longer is it true that the only visible females on campus are the dean of women and sorority housemothers.

Given this increased visibility of women on campus, and the rising enrollment of women in all areas of the university—undergraduate, graduate, business, and professional schools—there are, naturally, resources and services available to you that just weren't there a decade or so ago. There are special women's studies programs, counseling services, health-care clinics, women's organizations, even day-care facilities that are yours for the asking. All you have to do is to identify them and know when and where they can be of help to you. What follows is a quick re-cap of some of the special problems and areas of concern confronting women students in the eighties. (Some, not all, will be of equal interest to men, especially men looking for a good campus for a wife, a girlfriend, or sister—so you men shouldn't skip over this.)

Still pondering campus choices? The old coed vs. girls' school question is still very much with us. In fact, the all-girls' schools have been regaining their popularity recently. And for good reason: less complicated social atmosphere, less pressure to "dress up" for every day (it *is* a relief to be able to go to class in sweatshirt and jeans and no makeup, then go all out for glamour on weekend dates). Then, too, there's a different competitive atmosphere in class when it's all women. Some students say they feel freer to express ideas, and enjoy the all-female intellectual interchange. But there are drawbacks: a more artificial classroom environment (after all, you'll work with men on the job in the "real" nine-to-five world, so why not learn the rules of that interchange in school?). Also there are fewer chances for meeting men in casual campus-type environments when you're on an all-girl campus. Introductions have to be arranged by friends or engineered through contacts on coed or all-male campuses. We can't make this important decision for you. Much depends on your personal tastes and inclinations: do you find men a disruption and distraction, or a source of challenge and fresh ideas? Our advice: if you're considering an all-female campus, go visit several; then look over some similar coed places before you make your final applications.

Whatever your campus choice, try to locate at least one interested, sympathetic, reasonably liberated female in a position of authority who can be an informal mentor to you. She might be a favorite faculty member, a department head, a counselor or adviser, the dean of students, or even a bright grad student or teaching assistant. She may just prove more sympathetic to, and knowledgeable about, your special problems and projects than a male adviser—and she can also serve as a role model as you start to firm up career plans.

If you're interested in women's studies, check out your school's offerings. There may be a formal women's studies program that offers a major and/or minor. Or there may be simply a selection of courses offered each term on topics such as "The Woman as Artist," "Women in the Novel," or "Women's Politics." Often they're fascinating, creative courses, but occasionally they're ill-conceived and too trendy to be really useful. Ninety percent depends on the instructor and on the coordinator who oversees the offerings. Listen to the student grapevine carefully and pick the really good ones: they can prove immensely rewarding and enlightening, regardless of your major area. But think twice before getting typecast as a women's studies major unless the program is really distinguished. The area is so new that often prospective employers dismiss it as less serious than it in fact is. Often your best bet is to use the women's courses as a strong minor area to supplement a major in journalism, politics, history, or business. That way, you'll have the strong background in a career-oriented field with a specialty in women's roles within that area. And do consider going on for a master's or Ph.D. in women's studies; many fine schools now offer these programs, which provide specific preparation for you to oversee or coordinate—even create—such a program when you graduate.

On the subject of majors: don't allow yourself to be sex-stereotyped into "traditional female" majors such as crafts, elementary or secondary education, home economics, nutrition, art or music history, or nursing. Sure, these are all interesting areas—and incidentally, not confined to women, as witness the number of male majors. But don't exclude business administration, accounting, pre-law, pre-med, math, economics, and political science. Pick the area *you* are most interested and talented in, not a field that has a reputation for being "feminine." And while you're at it, notice the number of men who are opting for the arts, elementary ed., kindergarten teaching, and nursing. The old sex stereotypes, thank goodness, just don't apply anymore. In today's liberated working world, *she's* just as likely to be a construction worker or a CPA, while *he* runs a day-care center or studies *nouvelle cuisine*.

Like sex-stereotyped majors, the old female "play dumb" attitude that ruled coed campuses in past decades is passé. You're still living in the past if you believe that women must play dumb in order to attract dates. Today's college men, for the most part, enjoy and expect intellectual excellence in the women around them. They *like* bright, witty, articulate females and consider Betty Boop types as bits of fluff. Don't let yourself get hemmed in by catering to a man's *macho* need to dominate a brainless lady. In the end, it will all fall apart when he discovers your hidden stash of A-plus term papers and your library of writings on logical positivism, contemporary ethics, and cultural anthropology. You can't go through life as a closet intellectual, so pick a male who respects your academic prowess and ready wit.

Don't fall prey to another feminine stereotype: the athletics-is-for-men-only trap. Remember Yvonne Goolagong, Chris Evert, Peggy Fleming, Cathy Rigby, and the host of women athletes who are making waves these days—not to mention bodybuilders like Rachel MacLeish, Patsy Chapman, Stacey Bentley, and Rosina Ravalli. Or powerlifters like pretty Pam Meister and seventeen-year-old beauty contest winner Melissa Orth, who regularly sets world records with her bench press. There's something in athletics these days for every woman. Try marathon running, racewalking, ice skating, bodybuilding, powerlifting, Olympic lifting, swimming, tennis, gymnastics, aerobic dance, racquetball—even baseball or football if you wish. There's a lot more to women's college athletics these days than trying out for the cheerleading team or keeping score at the sorority volleyball game.

Athlete or not, you'll feel better and like yourself a lot more if you stay in decent shape during your college days. We all know about the "freshman flab" syndrome, usually experienced by reasonably shapely women who leave Mom's nutritionally balanced, low-cal meals for high-cal, high-carbohydrate cafeteria fare and forsake the active life they led in high school for days of sitting over their studies and evenings of sitting in the movies or the local watering-hole. Result: you're fifteen pounds heavier at Christmas than in September, and by spring none of last year's jeans and tops will fit. The solution: take off the first five pounds when they first appear on the scales rather than letting them turn into twenty or thirty. And keep moving. Break up long periods of sitting with short walks or jogs. Bicycle or walk wherever you can instead of taking your car or the bus. Opt for shopping, browsing museums or antique stores, dancing, or recreational sports instead of eating and drinking for relaxation.

If you find you're having problems, either personal or academic, seek out the school counselor or find a sympathetic ear in a faculty adviser or administrator. Look up the dean of women or get to know your dorm counselor. And don't forget the local YWCA, which in large cities will have a variety of counseling services available for members. Or perhaps all you need is a support system—a group of other women to brainstorm and talk with, bounce ideas off of, get contacts from. The current buzz-word for these support systems is a *network*. Networks come in all sizes and shapes from high-powered, high-prestige exclusive clubs for top women executives all the way to small, loosely knit informal campus groups of teachers, students, and office workers who meet monthly in Student Unions to share grievances and triumphs. Check it out—perhaps your campus has a network of its own, or can put you in touch with a local one. For locating a network near you, look at Carol Kleiman's *Women's Networks* (Lippincott and Crowell, 1980), which has complete, up-to-date listings for most major cities.

Having career-choice problems? Again, your women's studies division can be a real source of help, as can the college placement office. Chances are there will be someone on the staff who specializes in women's career counseling. If your campus offers you no special aids, turn to the local YWCA, a junior college in the area, or a division of adult or continuing education (which is usually happy to help both younger students and older ones). Or look to a nonprofit organization such as Flexible Careers or Women Employed in Chicago, both of which sponsor annual women's career conferences. So do groups like Women Owners of Small Businesses. And the Chicago-based Leigh Associates now plans to make its annual women's career conferences regular happenings in many major cities outside the Midwest. The earlier you locate and affiliate with these resources (many of which are free to students or charge only nominal student fees), the more direction your academic career will have.

Personal safety problems on campus are still very much with us even in the enlightened eighties. It's a matter of fact that women still are the primary victims of campus crimes. If you live alone or with roommates in an off-campus apartment, observe normal safety precautions. But also get to know campus police and security officers in case problems do arise. If you live on campus, come and go in well-traveled and well-lighted areas. Travel in groups if you go off-campus at night or must cross deserted paths on the way back to the dorm. And no matter how fitness-minded you are, do your running or jogging during daylight hours—preferably with a group of friends. Have a few friends who know your habits and schedule and will miss you if you fail to show for breakfast or class. And don't assume that everyone who is a student is "safe"—some, unfortunately, are potential thieves or rapists. Make sure you know the people you let in the front door.

We hope it never happens, but if you should be assaulted on campus, please don't keep it quiet, either through shame or fear of the consequences. Rape or attempted rape is a serious offense, whether you know the male or not (yes, authorities do now recognize that "date-rape" occurs more often than we once imagined). Run, do not walk, to your campus infirmary or security officer. Take a witness, if possible—at least a supportive friend who can testify as to your physical and mental distress. Make sure you get medical attention at once. And do report the incident to the campus police or security office as soon as possible. You may well furnish the lead they need to arrest the offender.

Harassment on campus? Yes, unfortunately it sometimes happens: the persistent acquaintance who calls, visits, trails you to the library, hangs around your dorm; the young professor or teaching assistant who seems to have more on his mind than the assignment. You've given clear "Get lost" signals and *still* he hangs around. If the attentions of this Harry Hands-on become more than annoying, report him to your dorm counselor, dean of students, or, in desperate cases, the campus cops. Just don't write off Harry as a harmless nut, particularly if his brand of action involves physical violence, obscene phone calls, or threatening notes. Harry may just be a socially inept nerd who can't take no for an answer—but he might also turn out to be your friendly campus version of Jack the Ripper.

But suppose you'd *like* to date your prof and find your eyes meeting his more and more frequently during the lecture? If he's single or legitimately divorced, and so are you, there's no problem on most campuses. There may be a little coffee-shop gossip, but most campuses these days accept student-teacher romances pretty matter-of-factly. You may want to cool it until you've finished his course to avoid shrieks of "Favoritism!" from less fortunate students. But if he's married, think twice. Questions of morality aside, you don't need the hassle and negative publicity of being named in a divorce or custody case. And don't bank on his leaving a comfortable marriage for a semester's fling. Unfortunately, Part I of *Looking for Mr. Goodbar* is more typical than the story of Abélard and Héloïse. And if the man in question is a pedophile Humbert Humbert working out his Lolita complex, beware: he may abandon you when you reach voting age. In any case, do you *really* want to marry a father-substitute?

Returning to school after a few years off? Don't fall into the timid, self-deprecating "I'm too old to go back" trap. (For some reason women seem more self-conscious about this than men—perhaps because they see themselves surrounded by bevies of long-haired, lissome, brainy coeds, who usually don't exist in real life.) Valerie heard the "I'm too old" story from literally hundreds of women, ages twenty-five through eighty-nine, in her three years of counseling adult students. Invariably they came back six months later, bursting with energy, optimism, and new ideas.

So if you're returning to school after a break, start getting yourself together a few months in advance. Buy some current-looking casual outfits (see our chapter on wardrobe for advice). Update your hair and makeup. Take a few days away from the toddler, soaps, or job and brush up on current films, news, records, magazines. Get to know your classmates and profs, regardless of their age. One of the most delightful things about large campuses nowadays is their totally eclectic mix of students. One classroom may house a retired army officer, three returning housewives, office workers on lunch hour, a few odd freshmen, a senior citizen or two. These people are not threats but potential friends and colleagues, regardless of their age. Enjoy them and the varied flavor they bring to your classrooms.

If you need inexpensive child care while you go to class, check out campus child-care facilities. Often they're free or minimum-cost to faculty and students. If there are none, don't panic yet. Look around your classes and spot women with similar problems. You might form an informal babysitting pool as a series of trade-offs. A group of six women we knew brought their toddlers to the university each Tuesday and Thursday, then arranged class schedules so that one of the mothers was always "on duty." The women sat with the kids in the school's student lounge near the TV; helped them draw, color, and work puzzles; and bought them light snacks. Warm days were occasions for walks and strolls through a nearby gallery. And remember: if you're desperate, you can always take a school-age child to class with you for one session. Most instructors won't mind if the child is well-behaved and not disruptive. It's not a permanent solution, but it will save you on days when the babysitter doesn't show.

You don't have to be married, working, mothering—any or all of the above—to fall prey to the Superwoman myth. You know Superwoman: she's the lady in designer clothes who's always photographed cooking gourmet meals with one hand and changing the baby with the other, all the while cradling to her left ear a phone which she uses to close her million-dollar business deals. She's the lady who manages with perfect ease a city condo, a country estate, two large offices, a family of five, and a social life that would rival any jet-setter's.

Her unmarried version is the girl with the perfect ash-blonde mane, perfect teeth, and perfect size-6 figure who maintains a straight-A average in an Ivy League school, dates an equally handsome male Ivy Leaguer—and also wins marathon runs, goes to aerobics class three times a week, lives on a strict 500-calorie-a-day vegetarian diet, dances with the local ballet troupe, plays third violin for the symphony back home, works for every women's cause imaginable, handcrafts exquisite silver jewelry, and knits her own sweaters in her spare time. And she just happens to hold down a full-time job in a prestigious law firm as a legal assistant, in preparation for her own legal career. And—oh, yes, she's also a dorm counselor, edits the school newspaper, is active in five or six clubs, acts in two theater productions a year, and does a little free-lance modeling on the side.

You read this in your glossy magazine and go slump into the Slough of Despond for a good evening of junk-food munching and watching the soaps. Superwoman has scored again.

Yes, Superwomen like these do exist—but chiefly, we suspect, in print and photos. Don't let their stories lay a guilt trip on you. It's a fact of life that getting through college in itself is a full-time job—and coupled with full-time or part-time work, housekeeping, raising a family, extracurricular activities, or any combination of these, it's a *full* full-time job. Some things just have to be allowed to slide. You can't maintain a high average, work at your job, devote time to family, keep a spotless dorm room or apartment, and keep yourself in top condition all the time. Learn to make some trade-offs. Devote exam week to term papers and final cram sessions and let the laundry go. When finals are over, there's ample time to wash your hair, towels, dog, and bathtub before the new term starts. Even Wonder Woman needs a day off now and then.

And finally, don't let yourself become a casualty of the new success ethic for women. The pages of newspapers and magazines and the racks in bookstores are full of articles and books telling women how to become corporate VPs, knowledgeable money managers, real estate investors, savvy world travelers, expert gamespersons and politicians. The covert message, however, is that in order to do this you have to be good—twice as good as any man—and that being this good requires a full-time, twenty-four-hour-a-day commitment.

We know: it takes hard work to succeed as a woman, even with the increased opportunities that the 1980s afford. But whereas books like this once had to warn women not to party their college years away, now we have to warn against incipient "workaholism." If you find yourself overscheduled with classes, work, family commitments, and extracurricular commitments, now's the time also to schedule in some unstructured time for yourself. If you have to do it on paper, then block out some chunks of time each week for a long walk, a shopping trip, a stroll through the museum or bookstore, a long dinner with friends, or just an evening off to go to bed early with a good novel. Don't subject yourself to so much pressure and desire to succeed that you lose sight of the very real pleasures of college as a time to explore, grow, change, and learn. Your future schooling and career plans will go better as a result. Don't be pressured or burdened by your status as a woman of the eighties: career success, grades, jobs, earning power all have to be measured against the real pleasure you receive in acquiring them all. It's an ideal time to be a college woman—make sure you enjoy every minute of it!

PART THREE

DIGGING IN FOR THE DURATION

10

Sources of Information

UNIVERSITIES ARE CENTERS for information. That was the original purpose of universities, all the way back to Plato's Academy. Universities are traditionally repositories of every conceivable kind of information about everything anybody could possibly want to know. The libraries teem with books, reference texts, video and audio cassettes, films, journals, magazines, and pamphlets. Professors are walking encyclopedias, at least in their own field of study. People come from all over the globe to study and learn at places like Crawling Ivy University.

Why the hell, then, can't you find:

A good mechanic
A little information on off-campus housing
A good doctor/dentist/lawyer
A hi-fi place that won't cheat you

Somebody who sells La Bella Flamenco strings for your guitar
A baby-sitter or a day-care center
Some money
A good psychiatrist who doesn't charge an arm and a leg
A church, synogogue, or mosque
The town art-flick house
Any girls or guys who don't look like the Baylor University powerlifting team in drag?

Every campus has at least two kinds of information sources: underground and overground. The overground sources are what you might expect. If you want a job, go to the placement office; if you want housing, go to the housing office; medical care, go to student health; advising, see the dean, one of the dean's assistants, the department chairman of your choice, or a friendly faculty member; for research materials, go to the reference librarian; for books, to the bookstore, etc. In the modern university, everything that you want to know has an office. In short, information processing has become institutionalized.

There are other sources, however, some of which are more reliable than the ones listed above. For example, sometime during the first week you are on campus, check out all the bulletin boards in the Student Union building. People who have things to sell to students usually advertise where students will see the ads. You can find some incredible bargains in stereos, musical instruments, furniture, apartments for rent, automobiles, etc., right there on largely neglected bulletin boards.

Another place to look is the bulletin boards at the local supermarket. These boards are also common sources of info on baby-sitters, auto mechanics, and all of the mer-

Sources of Information

chandise that you'll find on the Student Union boards. The closer to the school the supermarket is, the more likely it'll have stuff that students will find useful.

Don't be afraid to ask around the frat houses and dorms. Some frat houses keep files on everything from vindictive profs to bordellos. Some files are annotated by satisfied or burned customers. Most frats and dorms have bulletin boards, too.

Another place to check out for merchandise is the local laundromat. Most of them have bulletin boards, and some of them have places where you can enjoy a cup of coffee while your clothes are washing. You can pick up a lot of information at these places. It has something to do with "hanging out your dirty linen."

When you've decided on a major, get to know the departmental secretary. If she's honest and smart, she can save you a lot of trouble with bad profs, missed deadlines, and cantankerous chairmen. The same goes for the dean's secretary. She's got her hand on the pulse of the entire college. She knows things that the dean will never know (and doesn't officially want to know, if he's smart). Be careful here, however. If she's a real power-monger, she's not to be trusted. She'll use her influence for her own sake, and if she can help herself up the ladder by sending you into a course with a dud, she will. Again, ask the other students. They'll know the score.

The student newspapers are sometimes good sources of info about the school and other things you want to know. Be careful here, too, because editorial policies sometimes get in the way of objective reporting—even if it's reporting on where to go to get what you want.

Every campus has its "underground." Few of them are more than romantic conceptions of students and professors about how things work. The most powerful underground is the group of women who are the administrative secretaries. There isn't a revolutionary group on any campus that can hold a candle to these women. They know almost every secret there is to know, and the good ones provide grapevines that are almost always reliable. If you get a job on campus, you may have an opportunity to work directly with some of these people. Don't abuse the privilege, but do pay attention to their advice. Don't forget, they've seen different versions of you ever since they first went to work for Crawling Ivy.

Oddly enough, the faculty and the administration itself sometimes act as underground sources of information. Deans often step outside of official channels when they can do some good for somebody or when they can do some good for themselves. A good tip here and there can mean the difference between (for example) taking courses that you don't need and working out a program that will be of real benefit to you. If and when you do befriend a dean, a department chairman, or a faculty member, you should remember that he or she has probably been burned by loose-tongued students before, and will be reluctant to discuss anything with you other than generalities on the subject matter of a specific course. Be honest in your relationships with these people. Not only because they're in a position to do you a lot of damage, but also because they may be going out on a limb in giving you advice about things that are above and beyond the call of their duties. If the dean gets you out of jail, don't blab it all over the place.

Some schools still have the old custom of having a freshman orientation week—what used to be known as "Rat Week," or "hazing" or "initiation week"—when seminars, workshops, and other sessions are held especially for entering freshmen. This is an excellent time to learn about the organizations and support groups on campus.

It's sometimes considered "cool" (or "hot") to skip these and adopt an aloof attitude of being above such kid stuff. Our advice: don't do it! You may have been an expert in high school gamesmanship, but college is a different game and there's much to be learned. Attend all the sessions; listen to the advice on study habits, picking courses, and choosing a major. Pay attention to the dean's talk. Be attentive. Ask questions. Keep an open mind. Some of the things that seem obvious will prove helpful in the semesters to come. You may *think* you're above typical freshman mistakes, but midterm may find you in all the classic predicaments: five finals to study for, a term paper due, a string of broken campus romances, no money in your pocket, and a case of the flu. Listen to the orientation lectures on budgeting your time and money; they can help you avoid such embarrassing moments later on.

While you're looking around, here are a few tips on some kinds of information everybody needs at one time or another.

A good mechanic. Depends on what kind of car you have. The Yellow Pages are full of mechanics. But remember, the Yellow Pages are a form of advertising, and a listing there is no guarantee of competence. It's simply a guarantee that the joint has a business phone.

If you have an exotic foreign car, call the local chapter of the Sports Car Club of America. Or the local chapter of the Porsche/Jaguar/MG/Triumph Club. The next time you see a car like yours parked along the street, leave a note on the windshield telling the driver that you're new in town, have the same kind of car, and want to know where the best mechanic is. Leave your phone number and the person will probably give you a call. You could even post a note on the Student Union bulletin board asking for info on reliable mechanics for your Cyclops III.

If you have an American car, there'll be mechanics at every dealer. Some of them might even be good, you can never tell. Again, ask around.

Doctor, dentist, lawyer. For doctors and dentists, the student health office is a great source of reliable information. But it depends on whom you ask. Don't ask the people who work there unless you have a friend on the staff. Ask people who have already been sick. They'll know. We know some real horror stories about student health physicians, so don't let titles overimpress you. Ask around. Find somebody who is a student and who also works in the hospital. Ask him or her who's good and who's a joke around the campus.

For lawyers, take a quick look at the campus's law school (if it has one). Secretaries and clerks are good sources of information about lawyers, because they're operating behind the facade. If you can get them to open up, you'll get the straight poop on who's respected in the community and who's not. Don't, however, make the mistake of taking on one of the junior faculty of the law school as your own attorney. He probably will be long on theory but lethally short on the actual practice of law. Law professors are law professors, and lawyers are lawyers. Sometimes they fill both positions with competence or even expertise, but often as not they'll be on a faculty because they have no stomach for the rough-and-ready world of daily court battles.

But the law professors and their secretaries usually know which lawyers in town have a good record for defending their clients. Remember, it's not the titles but the pragmatic track record that you need. Get a lawyer who can win. Sometimes the law students themselves are hooked in with the village attorneys because they do brief-preparation work or other part-time jobs. Ask them. They'll know better than anybody who wins cases and who doesn't. Don't expect much help from the local bar association. It will tell you which lawyer handles which kinds of cases, but will not tell you which one is terrific and which one is merely competent.

Hi-fi, electronics, and other gear. Who knows? You really have to go out and dig for yourself. Dealers all have sales, and they all will give you some kind of bargain if you haggle with them enough. Whether a dealer is honest is often a function of who's working there at a particular time. Some people will do anything to sell you a hi-fi, and others genuinely want to help. Like any high-volume, mass-market business, hi-fi shops and record shops are out for all the bucks they can get. Shop around and ask around the campus. While you're looking, check out all of the dorm and frat house bulletin boards. There are almost *always* a few stereo items for sale. Also, don't forget the supermarket bulletin boards. If you've stumbled onto a friend who has a good setup, ask his or her advice. This is a type of merchandising operation that changes every day.

Baby-sitters or day-care centers. An easy one. Take a walk through the married students' housing neighborhood and knock on a few doors. You'll find out which sitters and centers are good and which are unreliable in a few minutes. The mothers who are already there will have the straight story. It's in their interests to know, and you can bet they'll know. Again, it's the underground, informal source that's to be trusted here.

A *good psychiatrist.* If you feel that you need to see a shrink, look in the Yellow Pages for one on the other side of town. Although psychiatrists are just as professional as any other person in the healing arts, the fewer people who know that you're in therapy the better off you are. Let us elaborate.

There was a time not too long ago when it was a black mark on your record if you were in therapy. Then times changed, and if you hadn't been in therapy, it was assumed that you weren't really interested in realizing your full potential to engage in meaningful relationships and all that jazz. Eventually, times changed again, and people who made a big thing of being in therapy were looked upon with suspicion: unstable, unreliable, too much into themselves.

In spite of the popularity of psychological subjects during the last two decades, most people are ignorant of the purpose or the implications of therapy. They do *not* classify a person in therapy as they would somebody who had a gallbladder operation, no matter what the Humanistic Psychology Association would like them to understand. So if you go into therapy, keep it to yourself for the time being. Make it something that you and your therapist are doing as a joint project. Don't give your classmates or your profs a chance to use it against you when decisions are made about fellowships or scholarships (and we're not being paranoid; we could tell you horror stories on this subject, too).

Keep your guard up. But remember also that there are many, many people who genuinely want to help you and *will* help you if you give them the chance. Such a person might be the campus chaplain, or a minister at one of the local churches. Whatever your religious feelings, never discount the genuine impulse to goodness that some people have. They're rare, and unfortunately they are as rare in the ministry as they are anywhere else, but you can find them if you look hard enough. Again, don't expect anything extra just because you have a problem. But if you need professional help, seek it out and take advantage of the large number of people in psychiatry, psychology, and other professional fields who still take their work seriously. You may find that you have more friends than you thought.

Cultural centers. Campus art-flick houses are a joy to behold. In Houston, for instance, the "old movie" house is the River Oaks Theater. It's not on campus, but it's where all the film buffs go. It's a fabulous old place, modest in structure, run by several people who really love film. In Chicago, the place to go is the Biograph. And every campus now has a film club, an art club, a music club, an opera club, and many other special-interest groups. One of the advantages of a large campus is that the school usually has the money to pay for fringe benefits such as these. On the other hand, some cities are large enough to support symphonies, operas, art-film houses, and scores of other cultural offerings that are simply not available in small college towns *unless* the campus itself provides them. If you're interested in this sort of thing, it's an argument against going to a small liberal arts college off somewhere in the sticks, regardless of how much you might miss the closeness of the small community. To find the cultural centers, consult the Yellow Pages or the student newspaper, or the faculty of the departments of music history, fine arts, film, theater, etc.

Cash. What's the first thing you should do when you arrive in town to begin your college career? Go to the nearest bank and open a checking account. And then go to a good shop and open a charge account if it's possible. Get right to work in establishing yourself in the community. Become a citizen, at least to the extent that you have credit and money in the bank, and are known at places other than the nearest off-campus bar. That way, if you do get into trouble with the local gendarmes, you aren't just a cipher from someplace else.

Voter registration and driver's license. If you're moving in for the duration and you plan to make your permanent home in the city in which the school is located, you may also want to go ahead and register to vote. There's one caveat here that should be checked out with either your parents or with the financial aid office. In some cases, voter registration determines place of residence for the purposes of grants-in-aid and state scholarships, loans, etc. Make sure that changing your voting registration doesn't foul up your residency requirements for your tuition funding. And make sure that you go ahead and take the test and get a driver's license in the state where you're going to go to school. It's a good, valid ID, and it will go a long way toward showing everybody that you intend to be on the up and up.

Which brings us to the question of meeting attractive members of the opposite sex.

Girls? Here you're on your own, friend. You can meet them at the cafeteria (where we met); you can meet them at church, at sorority or fraternity parties, at sports car club meetings, at gymkhanas, at picnics, at class, at the library, at the Student Union, on the tennis courts, and every other place that you normally find your kind of people.

If you run into trouble, write to the *Playboy* Advisor, or look into the library's collection of *Playboy* magazines. You'll find in the "Advisor" column one of the sanest, most enlighted collections of good advice about women to be found anywhere. I don't think there's any problem that you could have either finding girls or knowing what to do with them after you've found them that hasn't been covered in the column during the last twenty years. We're serious. Take a look and you'll see what we mean.

Sources of Information

In the meantime, you might try sitting on the library steps, wrapped in your Pierre Cardin scarf, pipe in hand, looking terribly existential. Or if you prefer, slide into your Dan Post lizard boots, put on your straw shit-kicker hat, and go the Levis and Gilley's jersey route. The girls will find you according to your plumage.

Last but not least, you should check out the annual college issue of *Playboy*. For years they have given beautiful and accurate insights into various campuses. As you might guess, they've got spies everywhere. Look for the man in the gabardine coat.

Women take note: the same sources for meeting men are available to you. The New Etiquette has taken hold, even on superconservative campuses, to the point where you *can* call him, invite him to a party, suggest a Dutch-treat dinner or movie or concert. Most campus "dating," thank heavens, is a lot more casual and less structured than it was five or ten years ago. Free films and concerts, after-study coffee breaks, lunches, dinners together in the cafeteria, informal meetings in the local pizza parlor or burger heaven—all are "dates" of a sort, without the formality that surrounds Big Evenings Out.

But even the best of women will occasionally hit a dry season when the only available males are, variously, married students, athletes who have eyes only for their sport, retired army officers and senior citizens, eggheads who live in the library stacks, nerds with bad breath and an inexhaustible supply of bad jokes, and people under five feet tall. If that happens to you, do not panic. Instead, launch an active search for some new material. Change your daily schedule so that you meet some new talent instead of the old faces you see each day in your biology lab or in the cafeteria. Change your eating and study times. Get to know the people in the gym or on the running track with you. Volunteer for some new clubs or activities. Get invited to a party with a new crowd. Try out the film society or the lecture circuit. And if all else fails, remember that you *can* go off-campus to meet Mr. Right. Wangle an invitation for a long weekend from a girlfriend at the university down-state, or better yet, one who attends a large urban campus. Find out where the graduate students and young singles-just-graduated congregate and put in a few evenings of intensive male-watching. Even if you don't meet your dream man the first weekend, you'll have a new network of friends and acquaintances you can call on for introductions. The more people you know, the more likely you are to meet the one who knows someone who knows someone who knows this toad who'll eventually turn into a prince. . . .

11

Planning a Program

NO MATTER how much you enjoy the campus social life, your new living quarters, the sports and other campus activities, hanging out at local stereo and camera shops, browsing the nearby bookstores and galleries, and generally soaking up all the Crawling Ivy ambience, it's good to remember that they're not why you came to college. They're fun, relaxing, and interesting, but they're not the real point of your college career. You're there primarily to learn, and only secondarily for these other things.

Which brings us to the whole question of primary and secondary goals. Ask any group of students chosen at random why they're in college and eight out of ten will tell you, "To get a degree." All right, that's certainly *a* goal, and an important one at that. But it's not *the* goal, any more than admission to the university is a goal in itself.

Imagine, if you will, a recent graduate with a liberal arts

degree or perhaps a degree in business. He's good-looking, poised, assured, articulate; he has everything going for him. He has a degree with a good record from a good university. Upon graduation, he gets a job with a prestigious firm and is quickly promoted to a junior vice-presidency. Three years from his graduation, he has all the earmarks of success: the sports car, the pretty dates, the posh city apartment, the five-figure salary supplemented by liberal perks and a generous expense account. Yet somehow something seems missing: he discovers that with all the success and affluence, he has no cultural sophistication, no taste, no interests outside of work and making money. He never reads a book, seldom picks up a magazine, feels strangely lost when his new friends talk of going to galleries and museums. He'd like to buy something for his walls, but he never took any art history courses and therefore doesn't trust his own taste. Art films? What's that? Movies are for entertainment, aren't they? When the girls he meets talk about social issues and politics, he feels lost at sea: he skipped over those courses in the university for one more accounting seminar that would help him get ahead on his job.

You in three years? We hope not. Of course, you want to get a decent job, make some money, earn a good living, get promotions. It's called "upward mobility" and it's a worthy educational goal. Without upward mobility, we would all be stuck in the same geographical region, same socioeconomic bracket, same career or job as our families, with no hope of advancement. All the old clichés about America's being the land of opportunity are true precisely because it *is* possible for people to advance so quickly and dramatically in their chosen careers. And education is one of the chief means to such career advancement.

No, we're not recommending that you become an impractical dreamer or reject the ideas of job security and social or economic mobility. Far from it. But we do recommend that you take a second look at some of the reasons why you are in college.

Let's try to set it all in historical perspective. Over the past decade, as the words "inflation" and "recession" have grown frighteningly familiar to us, we've become increasingly pragmatic in our orientation toward everything. Friendships are spurned for "business connections." We don't form close ties or look for intimacy anymore; we "network" or "trade support services." College isn't necessarily a place to gain a liberal education anymore, or, heaven help us, to become "cultured ladies and gentlemen." Rather, it's a place to gain a degree the quickest way possible in the shortest amount of time possible, acquire upward mobility, and use that as a springboard to the highest-paying job imaginable. Job satisfaction, career goals, dressing for success, winning through intimidation, and making it up the corporate ladder have become national obsessions —often to the point where we don't see much beyond these goals.

Yet with all this career orientation and tough eighties pragmatism, we're simultaneously rediscovering leisure. Sports, physical fitness activities, hobbies, books, records and stereo equipment, cameras, and craft materials are now big business—thus reaffirming our new respect for non-work activity. Along with this, look for the reemergence of "cultivated taste": people who at least know the difference between Biedermeier and Bauhaus, recognize Mission furniture and can spot a Mies van der Rohe building, know a Pouilly-Fuissé and Piesporter, listen to *both* Bach and the BeeGees, and don't think, after all, that James Joyce belongs in Woody Allen's "Category of the Overrated." In short, we're discovering not only leisure but also culture—with both a large and a small C—and as a result our attitudes toward education are also changing drastically. Suddenly, it is again important to speak and read a foreign language, know something about opera and symphony, read hardcover books, and decorate your walls with something other than portraits of the latest rock star.

So when you get to the point of actually planning your college program, don't consider it merely a series of hurdles standing between you and the all-powerful Degree. Instead, look on those one hundred and twenty hours of classwork as a means to introduce yourself to the best in civilization before you. It's the way in which you acknowledge your debt to your predecessors and at last claim your own place in history. Think of the classroom and your study hours as preparation for your *entire* life—the time spent not only on the job but also in leisure activities: the time you'll spend with your family and friends, enjoying art, music, books, playing sports, traveling, creating things, thinking, reflecting, appreciating, enjoying, savoring the universe that your education has opened to you. And if you think of it this way, you'll begin at last to understand what this mysterious process called education is all about.

ADVICE FOR FRESHMEN

On to the task of planning your program. Here are a few tips and pointers to get you started:

- Remember that most college programs are really quite simple in format. When you look past the complex combinations of courses required for particular degree programs or majors, they finally come down to three types of requirements: general education or core curriculum requirements, major courses and minor courses, and electives. Most college programs are generally structured so that you spend about thirty-six to forty-five hours (roughly your first two years) in general education requirements. You will probably spend thirty-six to fifty hours in a major area, and the remaining hours will be divided up among minor, related, and elective courses. Simple, isn't it? Your particular major may require forty hours instead of thirty-six, or your college may insist on forty-eight hours of core courses, but generally speaking the broad outlines will be much the same.

· Remember that there's a movement in contemporary colleges to simplify, and in some cases reduce, the general education requirements in favor of more time for the major and electives. Once-required areas such as foreign languages, higher math, and the "hard sciences" have been drastically reduced, even eliminated, in some colleges. At the same time, the practical nuts-and-bolts courses like freshman English, college algebra, "baby logic," and introductory statistics are finding their way back into the required curriculum (all this on the heels of a long hiatus in the sixties and early seventies, when it was fashionable to drop the gen. ed. requirements completely in favor of more socially and politically "relevant" courses). Now even some of the Ivy League schools are discovering to their dismay that their students, however glib about "issues" and "relevance," still can't read, write, or do elementary math and logic. Hence the reemphasis on the basic core curriculum. So don't be surprised when your school greets you with a hard-and-fast rule that all freshmen must take two semesters of composition, a semester of college math, (usually) one or two semesters of natural science, introductory logic, introductory statistics, and history of Western civilization. That's a sign that your school is right in tune with the current trends in curricular development: back to the basics again.

- Before you start to plan any program, do spend some time reading the college catalog in detail. It's the single handiest reference book you'll have in college and it's free to all students who attend. Pick up your copy in the admissions office, in the registrar's office, in various student activities offices, or at the information desk. Study the requirements for your degree program and major area carefully—that way you can ask more intelligent questions when you meet with your advisor or counselor for the first time. Over a period of several months, try to memorize as many of the requirements as possible. Become thoroughly familiar with the catalog and you'll save yourself many wasted hours in the next few years—plus the shock of having your cap and gown already in hand, only to receive a "We regret to inform you . . ." note from the registrar: you're still two hours short on the lab sciences requirement!

- As a beginning freshman, you'll probably receive your first counseling from either a representative of the admissions office or a faculty member picked at random from the faculty "pool" available at particular times during registration. This means that there's a good probability the faculty member isn't from your major area—probably not even from your college if you're at a university. This doesn't mean that this person will be your "permanent" adviser. It simply means that he or she will consult with you on planning a program for your initial semester. Many schools in fact have a rule that you must "declare a major"—that is, state your intention of majoring in a certain area—before you are assigned a permanent major faculty adviser.

Your beginning counselor will sit down with you, probably just prior to or during the registration period of

Planning a Program

freshman year, and work from a list of general education requirements and a list of currently offered courses (the semester's schedule) to put together a list of classes for that term. Typically, if you're just entering college, the courses will be such things as freshman composition, history of Western civilization, and several other basic core courses.

A few tips for working smoothly and easily with this initial adviser. Remember that he or she isn't familiar with your personal schedule, so the courses suggested may or may not fit the times that are convenient for you. If you have a part-time job, family commitments, extracurricular activities, commuting or travel complications, or anything else that limits your scheduling, speak up. Don't let yourself get scheduled for a full load of afternoon classes, only to discover to your dismay when you get home that they conflict with the times when you have to be at work. (This particular disaster has happened more often than you might think!)

In addition, try to schedule your heaviest load at times when your body and mind operate at their peak efficiency. If you're a morning person who's regularly up with the sun, jogs five miles around the park, eats a hearty breakfast, whistles operatic arias in the shower and speed-walks another mile to class, you'll thrive on an early-morning load that puts you in class at 8:00 or 9:00 A.M. and gets you away in time for lunch and an afternoon break. If, on the other hand, you're a slow waker and late riser, who drags out of bed at the last possible minute and gets going only with the aid of innumerable cups of black brew, give yourself a break: avoid the red-eye specials and schedule yourself for noontime, late-afternoon, and early evening classes. And if by chance you're a real night owl and plan to work/paint/talk/write/party all night and sleep in the daytime, consider an evenings-only schedule whereby you start class during the "twilight hour" (4:30–6:00 P.M.) and go until 10:00 or so. Remember, you're no longer on your family's or high school's schedule but on your own. Now is the perfect time to experiment with your internal "body clock" and find what kind of schedule really works for you. Unless your work or travel schedule demands it, don't put yourself under an additional burden by taking difficult classes at times when your body and mind aren't operating at peak efficiency.

Also, remember that your initial adviser may or may not know a great deal about the specific requirements of your major area. He or she is probably knowledgeable about degree requirements in general, but may teach and counsel in an area that's widely different from your own. If you're a journalism major, for example, you may even need to remind the adviser that Speech 101 is recommended in the first term for all freshmen students who are still technically undeclared majors, yet plan to enter the journalism program later. Here a little common sense and a close reading of the catalog are your best bets. If necessary, call or talk briefly with a student, professor, or department head in your major area to see if you're on the right track.

If you're undecided but want to go ahead and work out a schedule, seek counseling at the appropriate office. If the counseling and testing people leave you cold, go have a talk with your college dean. He sees little enough of the students, and he'll probably welcome the opportunity to chat. If he's too busy for you, he's too busy for his job.

As far as your first semester's course load goes, there are two general approaches to take. The first is to get all the requirements out of the way the first term: take only the required English, math, lab science, history of Western civilization, and physical education (if required).

The other route is to go with some requirements but also include some electives—probably a course or two related to the field you've tentatively chosen as your major. One or two "fun" courses, such as journalism, filmmaking, creative writing, a phys. ed. course introducing a new sport into your life, even a painting or crafts course, can add enjoyment and sparkle to a just-so roster of freshman courses. Courses that require some activity—crafts, theater, writing, sports, music composition, newscasting—often provide a welcome relief from hours of reading and memorizing facts or dates. Just be sure not to overload or overschedule yourself so that you have no uncommitted time to enjoy your first taste of campus life.

Many freshmen, once they get into college, get impatient with all the 100-level courses they must take and immediately start clamoring to take upper-level courses (200 and above in most places). Our advice is: proceed with caution. Most courses are numbered in sequence for a good reason; the 200-level course really does presuppose that you've had its prerequisites (101 and 102, or possibly both). Unless you have done a great deal of informal reading or research on your own, or have gone to an exceptionally good high school or prep school, you'll probably find yourself lost (sometimes hopelessly) sometime around the middle of the second week of class. The numbering system, you see, allows your instructor to assume you're already familiar with the elementary material of the previous course so that he or she can go on to deal with more advanced theories and concepts. So look before you leap. If you're really on fire to take sociology 201, go to the instructor and ask how much material from the 100-level course is included. Be honest. It won't benefit you at all to take a course that's so advanced you can't pass it!

If you really are qualified to take an upper-level course that interests you, but you don't have the prerequisites on your transcript, the best thing to do is to talk to the professor who is teaching the course. If he or she thinks you should be allowed to take it, a recommendation can be made to the department chairman. This is usually enough to do the trick. Sometimes the chairman will buck it on to the dean, who will probably rubberstamp the chairman's recommendation. Go through channels with something like this. If you don't, you may someday wind up in the chairman's or the dean's office anyway, asking for a waiver to allow you to get credit for the course.

While we're on that subject, how should you go about picking individual course sections and professors? Typically most freshmen courses are taught with a large number of individual sections listed in the catalog as "English 101, section A—Prof. X, section B—Prof. Y," and so on. How shall you choose among all these names and section numbers, which really mean little to an incoming student?

First of all, it helps to know that a great many sections will be listed as "staff." This means simply that at the time the schedule or bulletin was printed, it hadn't yet been decided which of a large pool of instructors would take that particular section. (No, Prof. "Staff" isn't teaching all thirty-nine sections of composition!) So your first step is to inquire in the departmental office or the college dean's office as to who is teaching which sections and at what times. Rather than ask who is teaching each section, narrow your choices down to two or three times which are possible

Planning a Program 213

for your schedule (say, MWF at 9:00, TTh at 10:00) and ask about those two sections.

Then start checking around. Ask the departmental secretary or work-study assistant. Inquire among any students who have had the course before. Check out student evaluation forms (often there's an annual or semestral booklet printed with this information). But be careful in relying entirely on the evaluations; often they reflect simply whether or not the prof is entertaining, an easy grader, a "good person," rather than whether or not he or she is really competent. You don't necessarily want Johnny Carson; you *do* want an intelligent, compassionate, rational, and well-informed person. So get a second or third opinion before you sign up on the strength of what's often merely a popularity contest.

A few last tips: most schools have a "late registration" period which serves as a sort of grace period for dropping and adding courses. Don't go wild with schedule changes, but do use the time for a little discreet shopping around. Visit a couple of alternate sections if you find yours is going badly. Sit in on a couple of lectures (with the instructor's permission, of course). Visit the class your roommate or cousin finds so exciting. Drop in on the section that the departmental secretary says is the best she's had. Then when the registration period is over, you can make your final choices based on experience rather than merely on catalog descriptions. Beware, however, of relying on late registration too heavily. Often a fee is charged for any schedule change or late registration.

· Once you're a "declared major"—usually at the end of your freshman year or at the beginning of your sophomore year—you will be assigned a major adviser. The assignments are generally made in the departmental office, although some schools will allow you to request a professor you know personally or by reputation.

The adviser-student relationship is one of the most important single connections you'll develop while you're in college. Good advising can save you countless hours of grief. It can even save you money by assuring that you don't waste courses and hence money in your progress toward the Big Sheepskin.

But how do you make sure you get good advising instead of bad—and how do you tell the difference between the two?

Let's state the obvious: not all faculty members are good advisers. That's no reflection on the quality of their intelligence, the value of their scholarship, or their intentions as human beings. It's just that advising students is a particular skill which some professors acquire and others don't. Many bright, well-intentioned, and highly educated men and women who are fine lecturers, respected scholars, and terrific human beings just can't advise students. They never take the trouble to read the catalog thoroughly or familiarize themselves with the changing requirements in their departments. Or they devote so much time to their reading and research that there's little time or energy left over for mastering each new piece of catalog copy when it comes out. Or whatever. Suffice it to say that some instructors will be great advisers, some will be mediocre, and some will be pretty sorry.

In working with an adviser, it helps to remember what he or she is supposed to do for you. He or she can't work miracles, give waivers for courses without the dean's or department chairman's approval, change graduation requirements, change the times when courses are offered, or juggle

Planning a Program

departmental or programmatic rules. He or she can, however, help you discover alternatives to classes that are scheduled at impossible times, plan programs that are both requirement-fulfilling and also interesting to you, point out possibilities for alternative and supplementary programs, even give advice about graduate school and future careers. (This latter item doesn't always apply: it all depends on how much your adviser follows the current graduate-school and job-market studies in a field. In general, you shouldn't expect your adviser to either "find you a job" or "get you into graduate school"—though they can be very helpful in writing recommendations when the time comes.) The university's placement or career service office is the place to go for the former kind of help; the graduate division or the departmental chairman or graduate adviser is more likely to give you good advice on the latter.

It goes without saying that the better your relationship with your adviser, the better off you'll be in planning your academic program. Remember that he or she is human, too, and will either like or dislike you, respect or not respect you, based on how much or how little initiative, *chutzpah*, determination, intelligence, and grace under pressure you display. So observe the common courtesies and amenities in dealing with this adviser. Make appointments well in advance (don't expect just to drop into the office at a moment's notice). Show up for appointments on time; call to say you'll be late or have to cancel; bring appropriate documents; act as if you've read the catalog and departmental bulletins in the last six months; and don't have a ready alibi out of every course suggested ("But Mr. Bumbershoots is too *hard*," "I don't *like* that course in Punch and Judy," "I can't take anything in spring term—I'm off to the Zonker Harris Tan-athon in Fort Lauderdale," or

"Psych. 101 conflicts with my disco roller-skating lesson."). Try at least to *sound* like a serious student and your academic adviser will have infinitely more patience with you. But don't expect to get through on mere "bull" or glibness. You also need to demonstrate some real interest in, and talent for, academic work. Nothing can substitute for that.

· If for some reason you have a bad semester (or even just a single bad course), you'll discover that honesty is the best policy. Tell your adviser about it in a straightforward way. No histrionics, please: this isn't *Othello;* it's just another routine case of academic probation. Maintain a sense of proportion (and humor) about your academic problems and failures and your adviser will probably respond more favorably. He or she will probably also have some ideas worth listening to as to how you can get off probation, raise your GPA, and generally redeem yourself.

· What to do if you get a real loser for an adviser? (Yes, unfortunately, there *are* such turkeys around every university, and you might just be lucky enough to draw one for yourself.) Here as in everything else, decency and fair play should prevail. Give him or her a chance. Make at least a few appointments each semester with the person in question. Be punctual, keep your appointments, and otherwise hold up your end of the deal. If your adviser consistently neglects you or is indifferent to you, fails to make appointments, doesn't keep office hours, gives wrong or incomplete advice, or in some other way materially damages your chances of having a good academic program, *then* approach the department chairman about switching advisers. Don't do this in the vehement spirit of a wronged consumer demanding his money's worth or a self-righteous Puritan who has just caught the village sinner in the act. Just ask for a

Planning a Program

change to someone more *simpatico* or more knowledgeable about the field. Chances are the chairman has had complaints about the turkey before and will make the switch with little or no comment.

· A word of warning: don't play the "I got through four years of college without ever seeing an adviser" game. Yes, we know: it's a popular game and is the height of macho in some colleges. It's cool, chic, In, and ever so laid-back to brag to your friends that you got the B.A. or B.S. or whatever without once visiting your friendly adviser. However, the colleges themselves are onto the game. (Valerie, who spent three years as associate dean of Roosevelt University's College of Continuing Education, psyched out the game her third day in office when she received four frantic calls from graduating seniors who claimed they'd been woefully misadvised on the English requirements and demanded a waiver of the University Writing Requirement. A quick check of her predecessor's files revealed they'd never even checked in at the college advising office.) Yes, there *are* ways of checking out your story that "Prof. X suggested I take this and then I found out it was the wrong course and I need a waiver so I can graduate because my company's paying for this course. . . ." But it's a risky game to play. Don't expect too much sympathy if you're one of these self-advisees and you turn up six hours short the week before graduation. Play the game by the rules and you'll find that the college will treat you accordingly.

· Keep your own advising files. You may think that an adviser ought to do all this for you, but many of them won't. Besides, faculty members do leave for better jobs (or because they don't get tenure). Or they go on sabbaticals to write, travel, do research, or take advantage of a grant. Or they change departments or areas, or get reassigned to administrative duties. So there's always a chance that some special dispensation or change in requirements which comes through for you is put in your files. Then your adviser goes away to Paris for a term on a fellowship, and horror of horrors, the slip of paper that frees you from Psych. 201, "Institutional Cruelty," may be lost forever. Your new adviser knows nothing of the deal you've made with your previous mentor, and doesn't care. So back you go to Psych. 201.

Solution: keep your own advising files. Whenever you get a memo, change of requirements, or other important materials from your adviser, make a Xerox or carbon for yourself. As Rolf Weil, citing Lyle Spencer's three laws for good administration, always says, "Be sure to get it in writing." That means everything! Verbal contracts may be binding in certain states by law, but the academic world has a penchant for honoring the written word exclusively. Get your adviser to put every waiver, every change in requirements, every special detail of your program in a memo. And keep a copy for yourself.

TRANSFER STUDENTS

So far, so good, you're thinking, if you go to the same school for four years. But I'm a transfer student, and all of this is just ten times more complicated for me. Help!

Fortunately, transferring from one college to another isn't nearly so rare as it once was. There was a time when people started school in one place and typically finished there. And the transfer student was always the oddball, the loner, the one who didn't quite fit into old Crawling Ivy.

Planning a Program

But now times have changed and so have attitudes about transferring. People change schools with the nonchalance and aplomb of someone trading a car or buying a new fall wardrobe. Often a student will change schools not once, but twice, even three times or more in a college career.

Why transfer? It's hard to generalize. There seem in fact to be almost as many reasons as students. Some are purely personal: difficulties with transportation or travel, a sudden decision to live away from home or to move back home, a change in financial status (you need to find a cheaper school or decide you can afford a more expensive one). Or you want or need to be closer to friends, family, or a special girl/boy. Or you marry, divorce, move in with someone, or move out of someone else's apartment or life. And so on.

But often the reasons are academic. You may find that your present school is too hard/too easy/too demanding/not demanding enough/poorly rated in comparison to others/an inadequate preparation for graduate school/not strong enough in your chosen field. Or you decide to change fields and want to seek out a really distinguished program or faculty in that area. In many cases, too, it's a simple matter of finishing a two-year or junior college and making the logical move into a senior institution.

Whatever the reasons, the hassle and trauma of transferring can be minimized if you follow these suggestions for college-hopping:

- Make sure your motives for transferring are sound and merit making the switch. A transfer because of the strength or reputation of the program you plan to enter is sensible and rational. A transfer to Tangled Ivy from Crawling Ivy because TI has more liberal dorm rules and later curfews, serves beer in the lunchroom, and has foxier coeds (or better-looking men) is *not* a legitimate transfer. Examine the reasons why you've chosen to change *before* you make the move, not after.

- In general, expect to lose some credits in the process of transferring. Unless the school you're leaving is a prestigious Ivy League or Big Ten school, very few colleges will accept *all* of your previous alma mater's courses. We'll give you more info later on about how you can minimize the credit loss; just be prepared for some courses to be dropped in the shuffle.

- Before you transfer, spend some time studying the new school's catalogs and familiarizing yourself with its rules. Write to the department or program you'll be entering for additional information. Don't assume that the rules of your old school apply. Chances are that they don't. Be prepared to spend some late nights learning a new set of gen. ed. requirements, major requirements, and academic procedures.

- Particularly if you're going from a junior college to a four-year college or a university—or from a smaller school to a larger one, a less difficult to a more difficult or prestigious one—be prepared to go through some reentry pains. You may experience an immediate (and unsettling) drop in grades as you adjust to the more rigorous standards of the new school. Each fall, scores of unhappy junior college transfers from city and community colleges all across the country sweat out English 101, not understanding why the same types of essays that yielded A's and B's last year now bring C's at best, D's at worst. So be prepared to have to adjust to newer, more demanding standards. But also be assured that it's well worth it. The bachelor's degree that you're working toward now will mean infinitely more than

Planning a Program

an associate of arts degree or a B.A. from a smaller, less notable school.

· As for the credit loss: a certain amount is inevitable. Not every school can be expected to accept every other school's courses straight across the board. However, if and when you transfer, you can minimize the mess and trauma as follows.

Decide early on in the semester when you expect to transfer. For example, if you expect to transfer to a new school starting in winter term, the beginning of fall semester is the time to begin your preparations. First, write to the new university for an application for admission (yes, you *do* have to go through all that paperwork again). But be sure to state on the application that you're a transfer—then you at least may be spared the freshman essay and much of the testing that first-time applicants must go through. At the same time, request a catalog and other materials such as brochures, lists of course requirements and programs from your major department, and so on.

At the same time that you make the application for admission, notify the registrar's office of your present university that you need a transcript sent. Costs vary, but usually the first one is free and a charge of anywhere from $2 to $5 for the other copies is standard. *Don't* try to squeeze pennies by failing to pay to get the transcripts sent. This is not a time to cut corners. Go ahead and pay the fee to make sure the transcript arrives on time. If your records aren't there, your application for admission can't be processed and will eventually end up in a big in-out box marked "incompleted admissions." Eventually you'll be relegated to the circular file under the desk. So get that transcript sent—the sooner the better.

When you're notified that you are accepted, call or write your new college's admissions office and ask that a credit evaluation be done. Often this is standard operating procedure for all transfer students, but sometimes you have to request it. This means, simply, that the courses from your old college will be evaluated in terms of the new school's course requirements and a total number of transfer hours granted you. Often the number is discouragingly low—especially if you took the easy route and specialized in "The World of Pottery," "Cosmic Tennis," "Myths and Legends of the Third World," and "Relating as Persons." Better you should take the hard-core stuff. When in doubt, remember that hard-core usually transfers. Soft-core stuff is often marginal and often is not transferable. Therefore, if you want to minimize the pain and shock of the pink slip that comes back from the registrar, go for the tougher courses. If you've planned your transfer intelligently over the long haul, you should cut your losses to a minimum.

Once you've got the credit evaluation and your permit to register in hand, check on registration dates and procedures. Ask about advising for transfer students. If the school has a sizeable number of transfers each term, there's probably some standard procedure for dealing with your situation. If not, you may find yourself wandering around *sans* adviser, wondering what on earth you're supposed to do. In this case run, do not walk, to your departmental office or to the dean's office if necessary and request an adviser. If you haven't yet declared a major, the dean's office is the best place to start. He or she may have an assistant who advises undeclared majors full-time. But *don't* —we repeat, *don't*—try to advise yourself. You may be taking just exactly the wrong subjects and will pay dearly for it later, both time-wise and money-wise. That extra semester isn't a freebie, you know.

When you sit down with your adviser, make sure you have your credit evaluation in hand. The transcript or list of courses from the old school might help, but that alone isn't enough. The adviser doesn't know what was covered in "Latter-Day Writings of Beat, Hip, and Punk Poetasters." It may well be the equivalent of his course, "Classics of the Avant-Garde," but unless the credit evaluation says so, no one will take the trouble of going through your syllabi and term papers to find out.

Another thing it's useful to remember: your new adviser isn't in the business of granting credit. That's a very strict and somewhat technical process which is a product of institutional, formal or informal agreements between colleges, or regulations within particular universities. There are manuals, rules, strict procedures, and educated guesses which apply to the process of credit evalution. It's somewhat like the Blue Book prices for used cars. There's a maximum and a minimum limit on how much credit you can receive for your semester and a half at Crawling Ivy. Remember that courses you dropped or took Incompletes in don't count. Neither do half-semesters, although you may have dropped out because of mono, illness in the family, or some other completely legitimate excuse. Credit is figured in terms of semester hours, and that's that. So spare the registrar and your new adviser the long, tedious arguments about whether or not you've "already had" X or Y or Z course. If it's on the credit evaluation, you've satisfied the requirement; otherwise, you haven't.

· As we've said before, expect a bit of readjustment before you feel completely comfortable in your new environment. Procedures are different, people are different, and schools themselves are different. If you're moving from a denim-and-sweatsuits casual junior college in the suburbs where everyone is fresh out of high school and goes home to Mom and Dad at night, it will be a real culture shock to move into a downtown commuter college where half the student body is over thirty and comes to class in three-piece suits sporting attaché cases. The same goes for moving from small, friendly, informal Staghorn Fern College to snobbish Big Ten-ish Crawling Ivy, where everyone is tweedy, preppie, blue-blooded, and moneyed, and talks yachts, sports cars, and country clubs. Or for a different but equal culture shock, try avant-garde, artsy-craftsy Tangled Ivy, where everyone is *beyond* abstract expressionism, experimental film, and electronic music. Or imagine big, sprawling Barrel Cactus State U., where everyone parties, jogs, swills beer, and cheers the home team with inexhaustible fervor. No two campuses are alike, and the best present you can give yourself is a little time for reentry. Don't swing right into a staggering eighteen-hour course load the first term. Give yourself time to adjust to the new atmosphere, course work, colleagues, and instructors. In the end, you'll be better for it.

CHOOSING COURSES

One of the most frequent and loudest complaints among college students is that they can't take the courses *they* want to take because they have to take the courses the university wants them to take. It's the requirements-versus-electives controversy, and it's been around for a long time. Students feel hemmed in by requirements; they feel their creativity is stifled by those seemingly endless lists of courses, workshops, seminars, reading lists, and tests that are required of every major in every field. The subject matter changes, but the "thou shalts" and "shalt nots" keep right on coming.

Let's face it: there are a great many requirements in college—any college. They're not just hurdles to get past or hoops to jump through on your way to the Colossal Job that the degree will get for you. Colleges, remember, are in the business of "credentialing"—granting credentials that certify you're a competent journalist/political scientist/ computer programmer/social worker/philosopher/teacher. Even at the undergraduate level, this is serious business. At the graduate and professional levels, it's even more serious. If inept students are given credentials, the school's reputation for excellence is endangered, and both its image and its programs can be damaged.

So while it's true that among the numbers of undergraduates that graduate from colleges and universities each year will be some incompetents, still we have to say that the credentialing process is pretty valid. At least no one has found a better substitute. Implicit in the notion of credentials in the liberal arts, at least, is the assumption that certain types of learning make the educated man or woman. The old concept of liberal education is still around, and despite the radical sixties and the pragmatic, job-oriented seventies, it hasn't been replaced. Scholars such as Wayne Booth (in a fine little essay entitled "Is There Any Knowledge That a Man Must Have?") argue persuasively that the liberal education is still relevant to contemporary universities; that men and women still need to know things that are not strictly necessary for bare survival. Booth claims that "the knowledge that a man must have" is the capacity or power to act freely as a man. He classifies "liberal knowledge" into three broad categories: knowledge of man's own nature and his place in a larger Nature; the capacity to respond to art made by our fellow human beings; and "practical wisdom" that allows us to make the proper choices in government, education, politics, and economics.

"Fine," you say, "but where does that leave me? My major has so many prerequisites, it will take me two years to fill them." Or: "I transferred in from little Staghorn Fern College, lost fifteen credits in the transfer, and am struggling to make up for lost time. I've now got another twenty-four hours in general education to complete, plus another thirty in my major, and only a limited choice of electives because of the hours my job and commuting arrangements impose on me. How can I take what I really enjoy and still get in all those requirements?" Again, there's no hard-and-fast answer, but try these ideas to get yourself started:

· Remember that any well-planned undergraduate program is going to have space for *some* electives. Some of these will come up in your major area and some in your minor, and some will be "free" electives. Count on anywhere from twenty to thirty hours of these various electives, depending on the requirements and complexity of your program (one course generally yields three hours' credit in a semester system). These twenty to thirty hours are not totally "free" choices, of course; but they can give you a chance to sample, explore, sip, taste, and dabble in areas that fascinate you but lie beyond the bounds of your major.

Here, a little judicious window-shopping pays off. Listen to lunchroom and coffeehouse gossip. Read class evaluations (but be wary: often the highest scores go to the courses that provide the least amount of challenge. *Caveat emptor!*). Look through the catalog, but also skim the schedule book that appears at the beginning of each new term. Sometimes fascinating courses are one-shot deals scheduled because of the availability of a certain lecturer, professor, or writer. Some even center around a special facility such as a museum or a historical archive. Others are topical and revolve around current interests, such as a hot new best-seller, a controversial scientific discovery, an election, an architectural project, a film, or an opera or theatrical performance in your city. Be ready to spring for one of these when the time is right. Often it's a once-in-a-lifetime chance to experience a first-rate performer, lecturer, or writer in action.

· Remember that all courses don't have to be full-semester three-hour courses. Explore the adult education and noncredit divisions of your university, which often offer fine mini-courses, workshops, seminars, and weekend/evening/lunch-hour classes. You can often find classes in resumé writing, workshops on a currently produced opera, short courses in fiction, exercise classes, or weekend walking tours. Many of the courses will be short, and as an added bonus, most require little or no out-of-class preparation. They're relaxing, mind-stretching, inexpensive, and often just the right antidote to the mid-semester doldrums.

· Short on cash but long on curiosity? Then explore some off-campus course options. The local library, YMCA or YWCA, high school, bookstore, art-film theater, museum, symphony, or opera company may sponsor short courses that are sometimes free or are available at a very modest cost. You'll also want to watch the campus newspaper, bulletin board, and student activities information sheets for things of interest in the city that are free to students or offer sizeable student discounts. In addition, watch local newspapers, both dailies and weeklies, for things that sound interesting. Remember that learning doesn't have to take place in a classroom; it can take place during a guided tour of a museum, an architectural walking tour, or a pre-concert lecture.

· Even if you're the type who is very intent on your own field of study, try to branch out a little. Nothing is duller than the narrowly defined specialist who is tops in his field but lost when he gets outside of it. Use your elective hours and leisure time to try out some new activities and subjects. If you're in a field that's almost strictly math and physics, try pottery, jewelry making, ceramics, watercolors, or weaving for a change of pace. Go to the physical education department and sign up to learn a new sport. Learn a foreign language or explore gourmet cooking. Do something totally unrelated to your own field of study and you may surprise yourself. It's enjoyable and a welcome change of pace from yet another course in differential equations or atomic theory.

· Even within your major, you may have some choice of electives. Often departments are surprisingly flexible about what they consider "related topics." If you're an English, theater, or journalism major, for example, you may be able to get permission to take courses in film, psychology, history, political science, foreign languages, sociology, anthropology, or even advertising and marketing. If you have some choice, pick things that genuinely interest you. Don't choose solely on the basis of convenient time. The best course isn't always the one that allows you to sleep an extra half-hour on Tuesdays and Thursdays.

· Some schools have the option of "interdisciplinary" or "cross-disciplinary" programs that student and faculty adviser design together. Some of these can result in incredibly interesting and varied combinations of courses that

Planning a Program

allow for both specialization and "fun" electives. But make sure that you have proper guidance in putting together such a program; otherwise you can leave with a hodgepodge of unrelated courses that will make your graduate dean or employer shudder in horror. The program has to be intelligently planned and conceived; otherwise you will lack the specialization that the liberal arts major is intended to provide.

CHOOSING A MAJOR

The major is often misunderstood in terms of what it's supposed to provide. It does give you specialization, yes, but of a certain kind. The major, or "area of concentration," as some schools call it, is supposed to give you a strong background in one particular subject in which you're interested or especially talented. You get "subprofessional" competence in many areas that require further study for full credentialing—for example, law, medicine, education, or accounting. But in many areas, the bachelor's degree from a good university is quite sufficient training for whatever you'll be doing once you're out of school. With this introduction, let's explore some ideas on the whole process of choosing and using a major area to your best advantage.

· First, remember that the major really is supposed to represent the field you'll stay in, if not for the rest of your life, at least for the foreseeable future. It's supposed to represent your best, most educated guess as to what you'll be concerned with for the next several years. If you intend to go on to graduate or professional school, it should prepare you to do that. If you intend to enter the job market, it should give you the credentials—and knowledge and skills

—that you need to get the job you want. If you plan to freelance or to go into business for yourself, it should give you the skills you need to survive on your own. And if you intend to enter a creative or performing field such as art, music, theater, creative writing, or filmmaking, your major should give you the theoretical and practical skills you need to become a respected performer or creative artist.

The major certainly isn't going to provide *all* the career training you'll need. It would be impossible to do all that in thirty-six to forty hours' worth of courses. Much of what you will need in your career will be hands-on experience that you acquire on the job itself. But what the major will and should do is to give you real in-depth knowledge of a particular area. It gives you the chance to focus, to zero in on a particular area and learn all that you can reasonably learn about it in the allotted time. And that in itself is valuable. Never mind if each course you take isn't specifically career-oriented. There's plenty of time to acquire actual job skills once you're out there in the working world. Right now, savor the time and opportunity to learn so much about an area which interests and excites you. Whatever your level of expertise or training when you finish the major, your life will be enriched by the concentration of courses it provides—and you'll have a strong foundation for whatever further knowledge you acquire in the form of practical skills.

· Which neatly brings us to the next point: just how should you go about choosing a major anyway? There are many considerations that should enter into the decision: your personal interests and inclinations and tastes; the areas where you perform best and are most comfortable; the availability of jobs and/or further training in an area. There are some factors that should not influence—or at least, should not control—your decision: for example, your family's opinion or tradition ("but all the Smythe men have been lawyers" isn't a valid argument if you're flunking out of the pre-law program and bored to tears by the thought of law school). Nor should you base your choice of major on your friends and what they're majoring in; current fads in popular culture are usually short-lived and vanish as quickly as they came. Ecology or Afro-American art may be In topics today, but what about two or three years from now?

Also forget considerations such as your personal like or dislike of certain faculty members in the area; the convenience of the courses; the difficulty of the qualifying exams; or the length of the reading list. If you belong in the field and are good at it, the hurdles will be jumped somehow.

· How do you know if you should be in a certain field? Well, for starters, take a quiet weekend or evening and reflect on your life. What subjects did you do best with in high school or in the early part of your college career? Which subjects genuinely interested you and which bored you? What things did you like or dislike about your high school courses? What are your interests outside the classroom? Is there any way that you could make those interests compatible with the major? Most important of all, could you imagine yourself with a job in your major subject, working enthusiastically and well and still being content with your choice ten years from now? If so, you've probably found your niche.

· Remember that today, more than ever before, there's a growing tendency to have not just one but several careers. So as you pick a major area, pick one that's multifaceted and versatile enough to allow you to move in several directions. Far better to major, say, in a concentration that combines English, theater, speech, journalism, marketing, and advertising than to take a strict English lit. major, which equips you only to teach, do research, write, or possibly work with an educational foundation or consulting firm. The more broadly defined field, by contrast, could take you in many different directions and allow you to go into media work, free-lance journalism, editing, writing, public relations, advertising, and employee relations or training. Then if you become one of those "statistics" who want a second or even a third career, you have the groundwork already laid.

· Want to sample and experiment before you settle down to the choice of a major? Then register for courses in several different subject areas in your freshman year so that you can learn what different fields are like.

· You don't want to pick as a major an area in which you're especially weak. But don't limit yourself strictly to the "safe" fields you think you'd do best in, either. Don't rely entirely on standardized test scores or high school grades for indications about how you might do in a field. Just because you've always done well with "numbers" doesn't automatically mean you should go into accounting or engineering. Logic or computer programming might be more your style. Grades are only one indicator of your interest in, and aptitude for, a subject.

Do consider taking some vocational preference tests (one widely used test is called the Strong Interest Inventory Test). But keep in mind that the tests measure interest, *not* ability. They also compare your interests to those of people already working in a field in an attempt to construct a sort of total personality profile for such people. And so they're not definitive answers; their real strength is that they can start you off in a train of thought that will eventually lead to the right major for you.

- Think you've found the right field? Take another look at the program. Sit in on some upper-level courses (most department chairpersons will be delighted to let you do so). Go to some lectures, workshops, or seminars. Talk to some majors and some professors—also to the graduate students and teaching assistants.
- Don't base your choice of majors on the current job market. Everything will have changed drastically by the year you graduate, and it's *that* job market, not the present one, that you'll enter. Given the current flexibility in careers, business and data programming aren't the only employable areas. And don't shy away from liberal arts majors if that's what you really want to do. Take those literature and philosophy courses, all right—but supplement with some business or "numbers" courses to give depth and versatility to your background.
- If you're a business, data processing, or economics major, or if you're in a technical area such as engineering, take some business writing, some communications, some English, some psychology—in other words, the courses that teach you to get along with other people, speak and write effectively, communicate clearly. These are the general skills that you'll need to become a first-rate manager, administrator, or supervisor. And they'll set you apart from the people who have merely the technical skills and knowledge and nothing more.
- Finally, don't be afraid to switch majors if you find you really are unhappy with the one you've chosen. It's often simpler than you think. There's a tendency to look on the time and money you've put into the major as an "investment"; to see a switch as something you can't "afford." But can you really afford to spend a lifetime in the wrong field? It's rather like spending a lifetime married to the

wrong person! Unless you're close to graduation or planning to enter a highly technical area, the switch is worth consideration. Far better than to spend the next ten years yearning for the field you didn't enter!

12

Learning How to Study Effectively

EARLIER, we mentioned the work and study schedule of our friend Joe Garble. Let's visit Joe again, and see how he studied, how he prepared for exams, how he budgeted his time between the demands of school, job, and family. We'll also go over some writing tricks that professional writers use to save time and energy.

Whether you are a doctor, a lawyer, or the proverbial Indian chief, your life is full of schedules. The more complex your life, the more you will have to learn how to make out schedules that you can live with. It doesn't mean that you have to be a slave to a schedule. Instead, it means that if you have a lot of things to do and you want to do well at all of them, a carefully planned schedule can actually give you a little freedom that you didn't know you had.

Many things enter into the schedule equation. The variables are:

Class schedule.
Job hours.
Reading requirements.
Writing requirements.
Taking class notes that will save time later.
Friends and social life.
Family life.
Some time to think things over.

There are other things, of course, but these are the main ones. Add to them the constant worry about being able to survive economically and you've got the average middle-class married student. In order to fit all of these things into your schedule, you're going to have to learn how to handle each element as efficiently as possible.

Let's go over the categories, and see where we can find a fudge factor.

SCHEDULED CLASSES

This one is an absolute. If you have to go to class at 9:00 A.M., that's when you have to go to class. You have leeway if you're doing independent study, but if it's a class, you have to go. Don't try to cheat on this one. You'll only cheat yourself. Even if you're not getting everything that's being said in class, your presence there will assure you of learning more than you would if you skipped. Some students are dumb enough to take two classes at the same hour, going to one of them one day and the other the next. That road leads to madness.

JOB HOURS

This is also an absolute. If you want to keep your job, go to work when the boss says go to work. We assume that you need the job, else you wouldn't be there. If you can work out flexible hours, all to the good. But don't jeopardize your livelihood by absenteeism. Some jobs are ideal for a student, such as Joe's ambulance driver's position. As long as there were no emergencies he could get some studying done, and the boss didn't care as long as he was at the ambulance company ready to go.

Other jobs such as health club instructor, salesman, or work that involves irregular hours can fill the bill. The thing to do is have an understanding with your employer from the beginning about your hours. Also, you'll have to make sure that you won't lose the job if your schedule of classes changes next semester.

READING

This item is the support work for the classes. Especially in courses such as history, philosophy, languages, literature, or some of the social sciences, there will be a great deal of reading. More than you would ever have believed! If you've got a tight schedule, make sure that you can keep up. If you once fall behind, you may find it hard if not impossible to catch up again.

Learn to read for content, not merely for pleasure. It takes some doing, but a little work will stand you in good stead and save you a lot of time in the future. If you have trouble with your reading, many colleges offer reading lab work that will help you to identify the problem and correct it.

When Ralph started to college, he had been reading four or five science fiction novels a week. The reading assignments seemed paltry to him until he realized that studying troop movements in Xenophon's *Anabasis* was not necessarily as much fun as reading Ray Bradbury's *Martian Chronicles*. He had to shift gears to keep rolling.

We have a copy of selections from Aristotle's works that contains the following message to the future: "Hello, up there. I'm tired as usual, and it's 3:35 A.M. I've got 123 pages left, and I'll be ready for the exam at 10:00 A.M." Along with the note we found a yellowed schedule of reading times that included three hours that afternoon, four hours after dinner, and the rest of the night to catch up on what needed to be covered.

You might consider the following guidelines as you read your text and reference materials:

· Don't procrastinate. This is usually a sign that you're afraid you won't understand the material. Far better to try to learn it now than the night before the exam.

· *Underline the relevant passages.* Don't worry about marking up your books. They're learning tools. Use them that way. Love them, handle them well, but remember that they're fundamentally practical resources. When you underline or highlight the passages, make sure you're highlighting the right ones. Which means that you've got to read for content and coherence, not just look for the good parts.

· Stop periodically and think about what you've read so far. Think about the individual passages as they relate to the whole. What's the point of the passage? What's the point of the whole work? What is the author saying with his words?

• Don't waste time trying to psychoanalyze the author through his works unless that's the assignment. Otherwise, it's extraneous, irrelevant, and a waste of time. Such analysis was so popular during the sixties that many students went all the way through advanced degree programs without ever coming to grips with the works themselves. Who cares what Milton thought about his daughters? It's *Paradise Lost* that counts!

• Read steadily. Don't read in spurts, unless you are falling asleep. If you do start to fall asleep, get up and walk around for a while, then get back to it. A good tip: if you're burning the midnight and wee-hours-of-the-morning oil, be careful of hot coffee. The heat will make you drowsy, and by the time you have slogged sleepily through the reading, the caffeine will finally take effect and keep you awake. This is not original with us. American philosopher Charles Hartshorne pointed it out in one of his seminars. Seems everybody had the jitters that morning.

• If you read in spurts, try to summarize in your mind what you've just read before getting up to go to the stove or the fridge. It will help you to hang onto what you've read.

• Stay away from the drug route. Ritalin may keep you awake, but it will sometimes affect your judgment. Caffeine can seriously affect your ability to do problems based on the application of simple principles, such as you would encounter in doing logic tests. Grass will convince you that you know more than you actually know—something that will become painfully evident when you get your test back. Bennies and other stimulants will jack you up only to throw you down at the crucial time. There's no substitute for clarity of thought and simply knowing the material. Don't fall for the euphoric tales about expanding your mind for exams with drugs. The only thing that gets expanded is your expectations.

· In addition to underlining and highlighting, you should make notes to yourself in the margins. Annotate the text as much as it takes to help you get the material.

· Make notes on what you've read. Discuss your readings with yourself as well as others. Ask yourself questions about what you've read. Try to figure out what's most important, what's next to the most important, and on down the line.

· Don't be afraid or ashamed to ask about reading laboratories. This is a relatively new thing in colleges, and it's one of the best things ever to happen. Many people have reading problems that have nothing to do with native intelligence, but are physiological, psychological, or a result of poor reading habits. If you have trouble reading, whether the problem is in understanding, remembering, or simple slowness in the act of reading, take advantage of the help that's available. You won't regret it.

· All of the tips given here work equally well for reading in the sciences. Reading for comprehension is reading for comprehension, regardless of the subject matter. There are, however, fundamental differences between reading, for example, a text on astrophysics and a copy of *Madame Bovary*. The astrophysics text will proceed logically from page to page, with various pieces of factual material juxtaposed with theoretical considerations. *Madame Bovary* is a novel, and works not according to the laws of logic but according to the "world of the work."

We have a mathematician friend who feels great if he

can slog through a page a day in some of the journal articles he reads. Because we sometimes read several novels in a week's time, our friend has decided that there is nothing to the novel. According to him, if there were, the things wouldn't be so easy to read.

The difference between novels and science is vastly overrated. They are both models of the world around us. In the sciences, the models lend themselves to mathematical or logical explication. In the humanities, the models lend themselves to experiential explication: to a greater understanding on the part of the reader of what it is to be a human being.

You certainly must read with care when you read a physics text or a math or logic text. You should read with no less care when you read in the humanities. Whichever you read, the same advice for reading holds for both kinds of material.

WRITING

A disturbing number of people not only can't read well but can't write well, either. This problem is not confined to college students. Few college graduates can write clear, simple prose, as engineering specs amply demonstrate. Seminars in plain writing abound in corporations all across the country.

Part of the problem is the very way in which writing is usually taught in secondary schools. More attention is paid to form than to clarity, and the average high school English teacher, while appreciative of good writing, is little better at actual writing than the students.

The situation is much the same in college. More than likely, few of your teachers, whatever their field, could write clean, clear prose if their lives (or tenure) depended on it. For productive college professors, writing usually means scholarly articles, research books, or texts. Universities are full of professors whose powers of discrimination enable them to tell the difference between bad writing and finely wrought prose. But few of them could write a simple declarative sentence without entangling themselves in lethal clutches of "that which," "it appears that," "we are led to," and "the evidence indicates."

That's the kind of stuff that scholarly articles are made of, and any professor worth his or her salt will quickly develop such a writing style if he or she expects to climb up the ladder to a full professorship and a committee chairmanship in a scholarly society.

It's all a matter of audience, and you should make up your mind soon which path you want to tread. The best way to learn to write scholarly prose is to read reams of the stuff. You'll pick up the style with no trouble if you have any talent for writing at all.

Besides, you should remember that the act of writing is different in important respects from the exercise of scholarly judgment. Many hack comic book writers are superb plotters and dialoguists. Many scholarly geniuses have great difficulty in making themselves understood by anybody except other scholars who are working on the same problem.

If you are trying to learn to write clean, clear, plain English, don't expect your average college professor to be able to give you much advice. Freshman composition is usually considered an odious teaching task, relegated to graduate students and low-prestige faculty members.

Occasionally, you'll find an exception to the rule. Professor J. Carleton Nunan was one of these exceptions. When Ralph was a freshman at Emory University, he was scheduled for one of Mr. Nunan's classes. Everybody warned him against the good prof, and it was with no little trepidation that he took a seat in the class.

Nunan was the best writing teacher we've ever seen. His trick was to make the students learn to write. He did this by assigning them short themes. Each time a grammatical or syntactical mistake was made, it was noted in the margin. If you ever made that mistake again, not only did you lose points for the repeat of the mistake, you lost points for the first time, too. A hard system, but it paid off. After a quarter in Nunan's class, Ralph never had to worry about writing again. He could always count on being able to pull a term paper out of an afternoon's hat.

The class with Mr. Nunan polished the rough-and-ready ability Ralph had to focus his thoughts and translate them into the written word. S. T. Capps, his high school English teacher, had instilled sensitivity and curiosity. Nunan showed Ralph how to use it. Both of the men had a bag of tricks.

Here are some of the tricks. Use them. They'll make things immensely easier for you, and you'll use them for the rest of your life.

- Whether it's a 500-word theme, a term paper, a thesis, or a dissertation, the first thing you should do is make an outline. And don't tell us that that's kid stuff. It's not. It's the easiest, quickest, most foolproof way to turn out *consistently* good stuff. If you become a professional writer (read: somebody who makes his living at it), you'll discover that the prospectus that is necessary to make a sale is nothing more than a good solid outline.

- Don't stop at one outline. Make several. Try out combinations of ideas. Shuffle the order. Try to crystallize exactly what it is that you are trying to say.

- With each section of the outline, put the important

things first, and trail the rest of it out according to a descending order of importance.
- Stay away from technical jargon and overblown diction.
- Don't tangle yourself in overly complex sentences.
- Be sure to make each paragraph an exposition of its topic sentence.
- Proceed with the most important material first, and don't jump around in the subject.
- Strive for clarity.
- Write for the person who is going to read the paper. Don't assume that your English professor is familiar with electronics or that your physics professor knows anything about Restoration Comedy.

TAKING NOTES

As you learn to write well, you will also learn to take class notes well. If you do it right, the notes will save you a tremendous amount of time when you study for exams. If some of what follows sounds simpleminded, it's because it's really a simple process. Unfortunately, few students ever learn to take notes in class, much less learn to take the kind of notes that will make studying easier.

We've always been amazed at students who do not take notes. They sit passively day after day, just listening to the lectures and discussions. Then, when exam time comes, they have to start from scratch with the text, without benefit of the guidelines that the classes provide. It's next to impossible to remember class discussions weeks after they are held, and you are flirting needlessly with failure when you don't note what's being said.

There is an art to taking notes, of course, and you won't be able to take good notes unless you have some idea of what the subject matter is about. That comes from careful reading and from discussions outside of class with others who are taking the course. With proper preparation, you can turn class time into profitable time. Remember, you don't have a minute to waste in activities that don't yield results. If you don't think along these lines yet, you'd better get into the habit. That's how the world outside of the university works, and the sooner you find it out and learn to develop skills that will make you competitive, the sooner you'll get what you want out of life. Here are a few pointers on how to take class notes.

- Learn to think analytically. Even if the prof doesn't lecture coherently from topic to topic, you should learn to separate the wheat from the chaff. Write down the wheat.
- Many professors will drone on and on about their own personal anxieties. Some do this because they are compelled to use class time for their own therapy. Others, however, use examples from their own experience to bring immediacy to the topics under discussion. Don't dismiss an example just because it's something that happened to the prof. You may miss the point of the class. Write the examples down in abbreviated form. For practice, try taking notes on some of the jokes you hear in TV comedy routines. It'll train your mind to focus on the important parts that lead up to the punch line. And don't forget the punch line.
- Learn to write notes in the same form that you use to develop outlines for papers. It sounds hard, but it really isn't. Here's an example. Let's say that the prof is lecturing on the pre-Socratic philosophers, and you're trying to distill the important points of the lecture so you can use your notes as a study guide. Here's the lecture.

Greek philosophy began on the island of Miletus with a man named Thales. Thales was a political leader on the island, and also was somewhat of a proto-scientist. Through travels in Egypt, he learned to predict eclipses, and is said to have predicted an eclipse during his lifetime. As founder of Western philosophy, Thales is also exemplary of the contribution that the early Greeks made to philosophy: his was a philosophy of what is called *physis*, from which we derive our word "physics" or "physical." For Thales, as for all the pre-Socratics, philosophy was the search for *physis*, or the substratum that underlay all things. Thales thought that this basic substance was water, and that everything was made of water. Perhaps it is no accident that he thought this. It is said that he once fell into a well while observing an eclipse.

OK, what's the substance of this passage? Here it is in a nutshell:

I. Pre-Socratic Philosophers
   A. Thales
      1. Founder of Western & Greek philosophy.
      2. One of the contributors to concept of *physis*, substance that underlies all matter.
      3. Also politician, scientist.
      4. Traveled in Egypt, once predicted eclipse.
      5. Thought the basic substance was water.
      6. (Prof's joke to make you associate Thales with water/*physis* theory) "Maybe he thought everything was made of water because he once fell into a well while looking at an eclipse."

If we were to continue outlining the professor's lecture,

section B would be Anaximander, Thales' philosophical successor, who thought *physis* was "the infinite." He was followed (section C) by Anaximenes, who thought it was air. Each of the philosophers would be noted as they were discussed, following the analytical outline form.

No matter how entertaining and edifying a professor's lectures might be, you can neither remember nor write down all the details. The analytical note form will train your mind to do the sorting before your pencil moves. With a little practice, the sorting process will become automatic and you will crank out précis of the lectures as quickly as you can write.

In fact, you will surprise yourself. You'll find that your note taking will vastly improve your ability to assimilate material, no matter whether you are reading, listening to lectures, watching films, or whatever. What you are really doing is developing a personal analysis and classification procedure, which will improve your powers of memory and judgment. It's like weight training: the more you lift, the more you will be able to lift.

· Use a different notebook for each class. Fill it up not only with your analytical summaries of the lectures or discussions but with notes to yourself about things you thought of during the lectures, things you need to find out about before the next class, schedules of class events such as exams, etc.

· Read over your text and your notes frequently. Don't wait until the night before the exam before you go over them. By that time, they'll be as unfamiliar as they were when you first encountered them. Learn to live with your notes. Learn to love them. Sometimes, they're the only thing you'll be able to trust.

· As you read over your notes, and as you use them to

help you understand difficult portions of the assigned reading in textbooks or primary reference sources, you may find that you can abbreviate them even more. Do it, as long as you don't reduce too far. Don't do what one legendary student is supposed to have done: reduced his notes down to four sentences, each of which was supposed to trigger a whole chain of memories, only to forget the four sentences.

· In the same way that you underline or highlight your text, underline and highlight your notes. As you progress in the course, you will also grow more and more aware of what is central and what is peripheral to the course. You'll be able to use this knowledge in refining your notes.

· You'll run into people who'll tell you not to memorize your notes. Ignore them. If you don't memorize your notes, learn them pretty damn well. Surround the subject. Become a mini-expert in it. Use the notes as your guide.

· What about taping the lectures? Unless you plan to sleep during the class, it's a waste of time. Why? Because you'll still have to make the translation, still have to transfer the substance of what's said from the tape into your mind. Since the tape runs in "real time"—that is, you have to listen to the whole thing in order to hear it all—you're wasting the amount of time that you already spent in class. Why listen to the lecture twice? You'll still be getting the whole thing. What you need is the *substance* of the lecture. Bite the bullet. Learn to take notes. Take them properly. They'll help you study, and taking them will train you to distill, to separate, to discern—in short, to think. And that's what it's all about, isn't it?

· Begin to study your notes intensively about a week before the exam. By the time the exam rolls around, you'll be thoroughly familiar with them. After the exam, study them again. We know that this is the last time that you will want to be looking at your notes, but you'll find that the intensity of the exam will help you to remember the material. Every little bit counts, and until the final you're never off the hook for the material that's in your notes.

FRIENDS AND SOCIAL LIFE

When you make out your schedule, you also have to allow some time for friends and social life. This seems perfectly obvious, but it is not as easy as it seems.

In the first place, you probably will not be around the friends you had in high school. This is especially true if you've left home for a campus school in another city or town. Your friends will be the new ones you make at college. They'll likely be interested in the same things you are, and they will probably be taking the same courses that you are taking. They can be a source of comfort when academic problems arise, and they can be a source of information when you need it.

Don't forget, however, that your newfound friends probably share the same fears and anxieties that you have about making it in school and the world beyond graduation. Long ago, social psychologist R. G. Schacter documented the tendency of anxious people to seek out other anxious people. "Misery loves company" is more than an old adage. Don't allow yourself to be swept up into your friends' anxieties. Don't allow them to take over your spare time to the point that you aren't doing what you came to college to do: learn what you don't know and make use of it.

There is a fine line between constructive and destructive socializing. You cross from one to the other when your friends and the time you spend with them take you away from your work to the detriment of that work. College society is incredibly complex. There is a seniority class structure (literally) with a meritocracy embedded in it. Your friends can be the best or the worst thing that could happen to you. You can have friends for emotional release and friends for intellectual exchanges. You'll find friends who will be just good friends.

But don't forget why you're in college in the first place. We're not saying that you should approach every potential friendship with a selfish motive. We're simply saying that you should choose your friends wisely. The best friends are the ones who help you. The worst are those who waste your precious time.

FAMILY

Your schedule should include some time for the family. If you have a spouse and children, you're going to have to set some time aside for them. They aren't going to school, so you can't really expect them to intuit what your situation is. Further, the kids are probably too young to understand things, even if you told them.

On the other hand, don't make the mistake that most parents make when they're in school: feeling a guilty obligation to drop everything for the kids. Children have capitalized on parental guilt feelings for about twenty years. Maybe it's time for a change. No household should be reduced to the four-year-old's wishes, no matter how cute and cuddly the little darling is. Adult concerns are important: they're the concerns that make up the world around us. If you're in college, you have adult concerns. This is no time for the kids to take over the household.

Right now, the most important thing in your life is to use your college education as an opportunity to learn how to live the life you want to live. With a college education, you'll be in a better position to help your kids both financially and intellectually. They'll benefit from it in the long run and so will your spouse and you.

So don't let anybody lay a guilt trip on you about the amount of time you're spending with your studies. That's what you're in college for, and as long as you're there you've got to do what's required. Do a good job of it, and don't let sentimentality and guilt stand in your way.

Let us give you a few case histories, and you'll see what we mean. In each case, the people are real. Taking the worst one first, we'll pay another visit to Joe Garble and Beverly.

When Joe and Beverly met, neither of them had any idea that Joe would someday go to college. When he started his freshman year, they both looked on it as a grand adventure. The children were the first problem. Bev wanted to have them while she was young. Joe wanted to wait until he finished college and had a good job. It became a contest: if Joe really loved Bev, he would help her start the family now. If Bev really loved Joe, she would wait until he finished school.

Beverly won. She also quit work as soon as the first child came. She worked sporadically for the next year or so, until the second child was born. Then came a third.

By this time, Joe was working full-time and going to school full-time. Since he had no money saved, he had no other choice. This meant that he and Bev saw less and less of each other. Joe's world continued to expand with every new course he took. Beverly's world, on the other hand, began to shrink. By the time Joe decided to go on to graduate school, he and Beverly were living in different worlds.

By the time he finished graduate school, there was nothing but bitterness between them.

What happened? Whose fault was it? The fault of both. Joe's fault for not realizing how far he had drifted away from Bev and the family. Beverly's fault for requiring children as proof of love, and in doing so setting up a situation in which Joe was left with the choice of quitting school or drifting away from her.

There are only so many hours in a day.

Another example: Bill and Gloria. Same situation, except that the feeling of the grand adventure never left them. Gloria was as interested in learning as Bill was, and she took every opportunity she could find for cultural enrichment on the campus. Money was just as tight, but they both worked part-time instead of one of them working full-time and going to school full-time the way Joe did. They remained close through it all, and their children were enriched by their parents' education. What made the difference? Both Bill and Gloria—working together—kept up with each other and each other's interests. The children were not weapons, but products of their love for each other. By each of them working part-time (instead of putting the onus on Bill alone), they avoided the separation that was inevitable in Joe and Beverly's marriage.

Then there was Jeff and Dawn. For them, school was of secondary importance, anyway. Jeff came from a moneyed family, and Dawn had never had to wait very long for anything she wanted. School was a lark. Jeff got his "gentleman's C's" and Dawn picked up a degree in art history along the way. There were no children, and there were no complications. They went to all the dances in their 280SL, and were the darlings of the campus.

The moral of the story is this: the more complicated your

family life, the more creative you have to be in solving your problems, whether they be financial or psychological. If you've got the cash on both sides of the family, and if there are no children, then the odds are on your side for coming out of college with either less or a different kind of trauma than the one that almost did Joe Garble in.

For Jeff and Dawn, I doubt that higher education really made any difference, either in the way they thought or the way they looked at the world around them. If you and your spouse are like these two, your problem is going to be discovering the point of education itself.

It's Joe Garble who needs the help. If you're in his shoes, let us give you some practical advice on how to avoid repeating his and Beverly's mistakes. It's not very palatable, but it's good advice. Here goes.

Arrange your schedule in such a way as to spend time with your kids, but be sure that such time is productive of more than just tossing a ball or watching TV. Bring the kids into the adventure you're embarking on. Tell them bedtime stories about the Homeric heroes, or about the mysteries of the world around them. Bring them up to your level instead of letting them drag you down to theirs. They'll thank you for it someday as their own adult lives are enriched by what you taught them when they were kids.

If you deal with your children this way, you can be a joy to each other, and you can all have a lot of fun along the road to your college education. Make them a part of it, and make them a part of you.

Your wife, especially if she does not have a college education, is in for a rough time. Your interests will be changing almost daily as you pile up class after class, book after book, while her life may not be changing so rapidly. It's not her fault, and you should be aware of the deadening effect that staying at home can have on her. If she has a job, it can be even worse: she works all day on the job, and works all evening with the kids while you go to classes with good-looking coeds (all of whom are ravishingly young and juicy-looking —at least, that's what she'll think), exploring new worlds and new civilizations just like an academic version of Captain Kirk.

From her point of view, when you come home at night, you stalk off into another part of the house to read exciting stories and complain about the noise, while she is stuck with wiping runny noses and bottoms, feeding and caring for the kids, and doing the housework by herself.

As the years go by, you will drift farther and farther apart unless you make her a part of your college education, too. If you can swing it financially, get her out of the house. Arrange your schedule so that you can have some time together that is not interrupted by the kids and the books. If you don't, she will eventually hate your books, your courses, and you.

If you love her, this is the last thing you want. If you want her to keep on loving you, you'd better find some time to keep the home fires burning. Take her to campus functions, introduce her to the people you're meeting every day, and make her feel a part of what you're doing. She'll eventually have to make a decision of her own: whether to live at home with the kids or get out into the world. Maybe this will help her to decide what she wants to do.

On the other hand, you may run into a situation like Joe Garble's. The more education he got, the farther away from Beverly he moved. By the time he got his Ph.D., there was an infinite gulf between them. He had thrown his entire being into his work and his studies. Beverly had little interest in Joe's work from the beginning, and feelings of inadequacy made her retreat farther and farther away from it.

In the end, the marriage broke up, with the expected traumas on everybody's part. Better that both Joe and Beverly had realized the truth earlier, and had parted before bringing children into the world. Also, it would have been better if they had broken up sooner, so that each would have had more time to make a new life. As it was, both of them (and the kids) spent years picking up pieces.

Let's get right down to the point. The girl you married may or may not be the girl for you after you get a college education. There's a risk involved when one member of a marriage pursues a course that will take him or her into a different world than the one both of them lived in when they met. By the time you finish your education, especially if you go on to a graduate degree (which you should, if you expect to be competitive), your wife may or may not be able to cope with the new world.

It's the oldest story in academe, especially among faculty wives who traditionally despise the young female Ph.D.'s who surround their husbands at work. It's a bad trip in every way possible.

So try to take her along with you. If she's got potential for growth, she'll welcome the chance and she'll respond by running along with you, helping you along the way. If she has little or no potential for growth, she will either drag you down or lay such a heavy guilt trip on you it will affect everything you do. If you're lucky, she'll leave you. If you're unlucky, she'll stay or she'll leave you and put an economic burden on your head that will slow your progress for the next twenty years.

This is mean stuff we're talking about, but it can spell the difference between getting a college education or not getting one. It can mean the difference between going through life with someone who can help joyfully or someone who will destroy you, not out of malice, but out of an inability to cope with the world you've discovered.

Think about it when you develop your schedule. Think about your long-range goals, both for yourself and for your family. Seek help in making your decisions, but do decide, and decide early in the game.

Unlike Joe and Beverly, Bill and Gloria were a good match to begin with. But they had problems, just as Joe and Bev did. The difference is that they were both sufficiently aware of what was going on to try to solve the problems in the ways we've described above.

It wasn't that Gloria became a patient drudge around the house, sacrificing her life for Bill like some Wagnerian heroine. To the contrary, she had her own life to live, which included not only her children and Bill but her work as well. In the end, Bill and Gloria were closer than they had been when Bill started to school.

But wait! Men aren't the only ones with problems doing a balancing act between marriage, children, job and school. Women have those same problems, often multiplied tenfold because so much of the responsibility of running a home falls on the woman's shoulders.

Consider these three "case histories" of working women who went back to school:

Jane rushed home from work one afternoon and delivered an ultimatum to Jim: "I'm through with all this demeaning housework. I'm nothing but a servant to you and the kids. And I'm sick and tired of my job. I can't be a secretary the rest of my life. I'm going back to school!"

Jim did everything he could to be supportive—he'd secretly wished Jane would finish her degree for years. He did some quick calculations and found they could scrape by on his salary. They moved to a cheaper apartment and cut expenses to the bone so that they could pay for Jane's tuition. The two-year-old got sent to Mom's—that is, until Mom, who wasn't physically up to taking care of a toddler, had a heart attack. Then he was packed off to stay with Jim's sister, then sent to a couple of friends, and finally parked at a just-average day-care center.

By now, tuition wasn't Jane's only expense. She was seeing a therapist twice weekly, had joined several women's groups with dues of about $25 a month, and had to shell out for books, plus a total new wardrobe as she "discovered her potential." The apartment was always full of Jane's friends from the university—Jim had to stay at the office to work at night. The house fell apart and meals were catch-as-catch-can, but Jane didn't notice. She had latched onto a higher consciousness.

Things went from bad to worse. Jim Junior was bounced back and forth like a rubber ball among a succession of sitters and day-care centers. Jim Senior seldom saw Jane except when she was going out the door on her way to class, meetings, or rap sessions with her new friends. Finally one day, Jane, having seen *Kramer vs. Kramer* one time too many, did the ultimate "liberated" thing (or so she thought): she packed up and left. End of scenario. Sad thing was, she didn't finish school either. She's still a secretary in another city. The custody case is still in court, and the lawyers' fees are eating up what little the family had left. To this day Jim still wonders where it all went wrong.

Kathy, having observed Jane's mistakes, decided that when she went back to school things would turn out differently for *her* family. She interviewed every single day-care center for Tommy and finally settled on one that had excellent credentials and a topflight staff—but was thirty miles from home. She found a good sitter to stay with Tommy and small Deena from 2:00 to 4:00 P.M., when her classes were over. Every day she made the thirty-mile drive twice in order to make sure that Tommy had the very best care available; somehow it eased her guilt over leaving him in anyone else's care. Deena was in a private school, too; they had to cut corners to afford it, but after all, the kids shouldn't be deprived of anything just because Mom was in school.

Kathy wanted to get through as fast as she could, so she took a full load each term. But she continued to play Supermom at home. Every evening she cooked a full meal for the family. Weekends were spent in a mad whirl of grocery shopping, laundry and dry cleaning, shopping for the kids' clothes, entertaining business associates of Don's. In between, there was the washing, waxing, polishing, shining, dusting, mopping, and sweeping. The house was spotless, the food was five-star, the kids were model children—but Kathy was a nervous wreck. From the beginning, Don offered to help around the house, but Kathy felt duty-bound to do it all herself.

And she kept up her schoolwork, too. Kathy stayed up every night long past the family's bedtime. Don fell asleep listening to the sound of her typewriter, which ran well past 2:00 A.M. every weekday night. By the weekends, even if she managed to finish the household chores she was "too tired" to go out—and besides, there were the term papers to do. She graduated *summa cum laude* and then spent her "vacation" in the hospital, where she'd been taken after she collapsed from exhaustion. Kathy's now about to apply for master's candidacy, and Don still can't convince her that he really prefers her to Wonder Woman. Too much of her ego is tied up in being the perfect wife, homemaker, mother, community leader, PTA officer, Boy Scout den mother, charity worker, and student. Kathy just can't say no to Christmas Eve with the in-laws, requests for a "little" holiday buffet dinner for eighteen, the spring charity fund-raiser, the neighborhood block party, or the PTA Halloween auction. She'll still be waxing floors, making homemade bread from scratch (mixes are cheating), polishing the silver tea service weekly, sending handwritten invitations, and sewing Deena's ballet costumes by hand when she's a top executive in her field—*if* she survives this self-inflicted torture until then.

Carol took a long time to decide whether or not she'd return to school. First she talked it over with Ted and the kids. "We'll all have to work a little harder and make some sacrifices," she said, "but in the end it'll be worth it; I can double my salary if I can just complete these last thirty-six hours of residence." Together she and Ted worked out a schedule. He would cook dinner, assisted by Lisa, age nine, and Kevin, age eleven, on Tuesday and Thursday nights when she had class. As a tradeoff, she'd make sure he had Friday mornings free for breakfast meetings with an important client each week. A big master schedule of shopping, meal plans, and cleaning chores for the week was posted by the phone on the kitchen wall. Everyone had a job to do, and somehow, it all got done.

Carol started slowly at first with a half-time load. She also cut back on her work schedule by four hours a week so that she had more flexible hours. Her boss grew enthusiastic about her education, and the company offered reimbursement for half of her tuition expenses. Eventually a special scholarship for women returning to school picked up the rest of the bill.

True, the house wasn't about to win any model-home

awards. But it was always reasonably clean, thanks to the fact that the whole family spent Sunday evening picking up odds and ends and making sure the next week's chores were evenly divided. They saved Thursdays after Carol's class for "family night," when everyone relaxed over a pizza or fried chicken. Although they cut back on entertainment, the kids didn't mind; they enjoyed the university children's library, gym, film center, puppet theater, and annual Christmas party. Carol and Ted enjoyed the free art films and concerts and used her student pass to get into museums and exhibitions at half-price. When emergencies came up, Kevin and Lisa even sat in on Mom's classes, and they claim they understood the lectures!

When Carol graduated, it was a family event. Ted and the kids were there, as were her parents, his parents, his brother, and her two sisters. Carol's handshake from the university president was greeted with whoops and cheers. Everyone felt they'd earned a bit of that degree!

There is a marvelous scene at the end of Truffaut's film of Bradbury's *Fahrenheit 451*. The "book people" live in an abandoned railyard at the end of the tracks. Each of them has memorized a book, so that the beauty and wisdom of the books can survive the massive destruction of the written word by a totalitarian government. A man and a woman walk side by side in the snow, both reciting their respective books, committing them to memory. They belong to each other, but they also belong to themselves and to their books. They each respect the other's work as much as they love their own. And they both operate on the same level, on an equal footing.

If you can discover a partner like that, your dreams are safe. We know. We did.

ATHLETES

If you're a high school athlete, you already know how hard it is to play a full season and keep up with your studies at the same time. And you have probably worked out some kind of schedule that makes it possible for you to do both. All of the scheduling and studying procedures outlined in this chapter can be used by the athlete as well as by any other student.

As an athlete, you're a special case. There are demands on your time that don't exist for the ordinary student. Scholarships are granted in a more complex way than for other students: you've got to have superb athletic skills as well as the grade-point average to be considered for a scholarship. You have to work with your high school coach, and you have to get to the coach at the college of your choice. The college coaches themselves usually control the scholarships given in their departments. Rest assured that the decision will be made on the basis of your potential contribution to the team, not your potential to be an intellectual luminary. Don't sweat it. Take the money and run.

The college coach is under considerable pressure himself, from alumni, the college president, and the fund raisers. While the rest of the faculty either has tenure or is on a tenure track, coaches rarely get tenure, and their jobs are on the line at the end of each season. The National Collegiate Athletic Association has guidelines on how many players in colleges in certain divisions can be on athletic scholarships. Your coach is not going to waste his scholarships on people who will not be an asset to the team.

The Byzantine politics of college athletic recruitment

has long been a national scandal. Many players see college as a stepping-stone to the pro ranks. Many administrators see the players as a means to fill grandstands and put alumni fund-raising drives over the top. Many coaches see the whole process as a rat race, with themselves caught in the middle in a dead run. The coach has to recruit players who can win for him, but he also has to make sure that the players he recruits can do well enough in the classroom to remain eligible to play.

That's what the coach is up against. What you're up against is (1) competition with other high school players for scholarships; (2) competition (once you've gotten in) with other players on the team for continued scholarships (in this, you're in exactly the same position as a person in graduate school: you're in competition with your classmates for the fellowship that will let you come back next year); (3) the need to do well enough in your classes not only to remain eligible to play, but also to get the education that you ought to be seeking while you're in college.

"Eligibility" is a flexible term. It usually means that the student is making reasonable progress toward a degree in whatever program he's enrolled in. Unfortunately, it is up to the individual schools to decide what "reasonable progress" is in their case. This is one of the places where the fudge factor comes in. As a consequence, the pressure is on the coach to get the guys through their courses. The faculty, on the other hand, feels determined to uphold academic standards. The administration is also caught in the middle: it needs the publicity that a winning team gives the school, but it also has to stand behind the faculty in its efforts to uphold the standards of higher education.

In the end, it is the athlete who suffers. Every time a course such as "The Philosophy of Football" or "Women's

Track and Field Events" is substituted for a solid course in the humanities, the social sciences, or the sciences, the student is put that much farther from the preparation he needs to survive in the world after graduation. This is no joking matter, since only about 2 percent of all college players make it to the pro ranks.

So unless you are one mean dude in football, or one tough woman basketball player, or if you excel in one of the other top team sports that has a pro counterpart, you should do everything you can to make sure that you get a genuine education while you're in school. Don't let them exploit you. Don't let them get away with it.

This may sound strange coming from a former philosophy professor and literary criticism professor. But don't forget that Ralph founded and taught the University of North Dakota's karate team for three years, and has been lifting weights since 1948. Valerie has been into women's bodybuilding for seven years, and squats 235 at a bodyweight of 108. We're into sports, and have been for years.

Because we're into athletics, we can testify to the shortsightedness of most liberal arts faculty when it comes to athletes. Many of them can't conceive that an athlete can be just as intelligent, just as sensitive as the other people in class. What most of them also don't realize is that the athlete, as a member of the team, is in a position similar to that of anyone who is going to school full-time and also working full-time. The demands on an athlete's time are tremendous. The discipline required of a top-notch athlete to stay in shape and improve skills is beyond most professors' comprehension. Don't make the mistake of thinking that this is strictly a men's problem. As women become more and more involved in collegiate athletics, they too become victims of the same kinds of prejudice. It shouldn't be this way, because athletes have to have the same kind of discipline, at least in thinking, in order to get through a good Ph.D. program. But the professors don't make the extrapolation. Further, it's part of the academic orthodoxy to think that athletes are dummies, overgrown boys and girls, and are useful only to provide entertainment on Sunday afternoon TV shows.

Well, don't let this kind of thing get you down. If you have special physical talent, use it and be happy that you have it. Don't let people put you down because you're an athlete. But don't let the coaches exploit you, either. This may be your only chance to get an education. Get it while you can. Learn everything that you can. Pack as many substantive courses into your schedule as you can stand. Don't jeopardize your athletic eligibility by overloading yourself with hard courses. But, at the same time, don't jeopardize your future by missing the opportunity to take the courses that will make you employable and make your life enjoyable after you graduate.

We work with high school, college, and pro athletes every day at the Sports Fitness Institute. We know who you are, what you're like, and what you can do when you set your mind and heart on it. We're on your side.

So get in there and win! We know you can do it. Apply the same determination that you use on the field to getting an education. If you go into it with that attitude, nobody can stop you.

TIME TO THINK

College is not merely a matter of classes, books, papers, and assignments. Nor is it a matter of bull sessions, rotgut wine,

Learning How to Study Effectively

and Existentialism, or staying up all night listening to old George Carlin records. You need to ruminate—literally, to *chew*—on what you're learning and on the ways in which what you're learning is changing you. You will change, irrevocably, and you must prepare for the life that is waiting for you outside the doors of old Crawling Ivy.

As you change, you'll find yourself more and more receptive to new ideas, new ways of looking at things. This is the real joy of getting an education. We both remember coming home night after night, full of new knowledge, thinking about how we'd have to sift everything we'd believed before through the new sieve we'd just discovered.

If your higher education works—if it changes you into a person who learns, analyzes, reflects, appreciates, synthesizes, creates—you'll continue to experience the euphoria of discovery for the rest of your life. This will happen in direct proportion to the amount of effort and thought you put into your college years. They aren't years of "deferred adulthood," as the revolutionaries of the sixties called them. They are the glorious years of exponential growth that will cause you to metamorphose into a fully sentient being.

Wow! Almost got carried away there for a minute. But its true. People who hated college never got the point. Our friend and mentor, Professor Harry Dobson, once said that every subject has a secret, which it is the duty of each student to discover. The secret is that magic thing that causes grown persons to devote their entire lives to its study. There must be something truly fascinating about the subject matter of a field to make rational human beings devote their entire lives to it. The student must try to discover what that thing, that object of fascination, is. Whoever does this will have discovered part of the secret of higher education.

13

A Few Political Considerations

IN ADDITION to being a fermenting vat for learning and creativity, a university can also be a cesspool of political intrigue, back-stabbings, departmental feuds, catty sniping, character assassinations, broken careers, petty bickering, territorial imperatives, and downright rottenness. Or it can be a proving ground for liberalism in thought and deed, a gathering place for scholars and humanitarians alike.

In short, universities are in some respects just like the rest of the world.

In this chapter, we'd like to talk about the way that universities really work. You don't begin to learn about it until you become a faculty member, and you don't really lose your virginity until you become a dean. Let us hasten to assure you that the faculty and administrative types described here are not real personages. They are, instead, composites of many, many people we've known, loved, hated, liked, and despised down through the years. We knew some of them when we were students, others as faculty colleagues, and still others when we were deans.

They are universal faculty and administrative types. You'll find them wherever you go to school. We present them to you so that you may know both friend and enemy, fish and fowl. It's a sort of academic bestiary, so that you can recognize the different kinds of plumage. As always, it pays to know your bird!

First, let's go through the organizational structure of the average university. Few beginning students know anything about it, and you really must know the territory if you're going to do battle. Here goes.

Universities are owned by states or by private corporations. If they are private universities, they usually have a president who answers to a Board of Trustees. State institutions often have chancellors, who answer to the State Board of Higher Education or the Board of Regents. Once you get to the presidential level, the internal structure is pretty standard.

The president, almost always the possessor of academic credentials (a Ph.D., D.Litt., or an Ed.D.), is the chief officer of the university. Under him or her, on the business side, will be the controller and all the clerical, financial, secretarial, maintenance, and other departments necessary to keep the place running.

The faculty usually considers these people to be enemies, who neither understand nor care about such faculty ideals as carrying the torch of knowledge to successive generations.

The three most important people on this side of the university are the director of development (who raises funds), the controller (who administers the budget), and the head of the maintenance department (who feels that it is he who really runs the university. Sometimes, he's right).

On the other side of the coin is the academic part of the university. The next down the line from the president is the dean of faculties or vice-president for academic affairs, who usually has impeccable academic credentials, but is almost never respected by the faculty, who feels that he or she has "sold out" to the administration.

Under this dean come the deans of the various colleges, all of whom must likewise have impeccable academic credentials; they, also, are no longer respected academically by the faculty because they, too, presumably sold out to the administration. The theory here is that if they were *really* intellectuals and scholars they would never have joined the administration. Deans who don't understand this simple principle usually don't last very long.

In every university, there are several colleges. For example, you will always have a College of Arts and Sciences. This is the main college of the university, and it services not only the other college programs in the university but the graduate program as well. It is the fountainhead of all university activities. Most of the university scholars come from this college, and the faculty usually takes itself more seriously than the faculties in the other colleges.

Colleges of Arts and Sciences generally have less status nowadays because enrollments in the arts and sciences have been dropping since the mid-sixties. Dropping enrollments means less money for faculty salaries, which in turn means smaller departments, which means less political clout. Get the picture?

While the faculty (especially the Arts and Sciences faculty) considers a College of Arts and Sciences absolutely necessary if you are going to call the place a university, the other side of the university—the financial side—considers the College of Arts and Sciences a necessary evil.

Other colleges may be a College of Education, where professional teachers teach people to be professional teachers. This is usually a low-status college except in state universities, where the professional educators have a stranglehold on the State Board of Higher Education.

Then, you might have a musical college, such as the superb Chicago Musical College, which is a part of Roosevelt University. The dean here will be a musician as well as an academic, but will be suspect as far as the faculty is concerned, no matter how well he plays piano, because he has sold out to the administration.

The big guns are often found in the business colleges, since accounting and M.B.A.'s have brought more students into the universities during the last few years than all the Arts and Sciences courses combined.

There is a dean at the head of each of these colleges. Each dean must fight the other deans for his or her slice of the budget. The battleground for this fight is varied: in the Faculty Senate, in the Arts and Sciences Council, in the hallways, the byways, the smoke-filled offices of the campus politicos, and in the Budget Committee.

Sometimes you will run into a dean who has read all of those obnoxious success books and has the dull wit to take them seriously as paradigms for successful behavior in the dean's office. Watch out for these people. They'll gut you before you know it. They have no respect for the faculty, for the students, for the ideals of the university, much less for you. They'll shoot the college right out from under you if they get the chance. If you're a student, stay out of the crossfire. It could be fatal not only to your college career but to your career after you graduate (*if* you graduate).

Each dean may have one or several associate and/or assistant deans. These people will help you with your schedule, go over your requirements, grant waivers, etc. They're good people to get to know, because they have a pipeline to the dean himself, who is usually bogged down with important things such as finding office space for Professor Gobbledygook, who absolutely cannot stand sharing the office with the Greek History professor, Dr. Souvlakis Avgolemono, because he comes to school reeking of feta cheese. This will be a knotty problem, since Professor Gobbledygook is also the Chairman of the Committee to Eliminate Racial and Ethnic Prejudice from the university.

Deans have to do this sort of thing all the time. And the faculty thinks they enjoy it. They really do it for the money. The money and the power and the prestige. There is a lot of prestige involved in playing nursemaid to a bunch of prima donnas who have neither knowledge of, nor sympathy for, the dean's job.

It is good for you to know what the dean does, because a good dean is one of the best friends you can ever have in college. He or she writes the waivers that will get you out of freshman composition, administers the budget that will make your department the one that has the best faculty, and eventually will shake your hand when you graduate. The dean's the one who makes the recommendation to the president that you receive your diploma. Know your dean.

Faculty members never know what deans do. Jokes abound, which only serve to underline the faculty's ignorance not only of what deans do but of what the other administrators do as well.

A Few Political Considerations

Here's what a dean does.

Secures and develops his power (or her power, as the case may be).

Prepares the annual budget for his college, department by department, and defends the budget before the dean of faculties, the president, and the Budget Committee.

Acts as chief personnel officer for his college, initiating searches for new faculty members, making recommendations to the dean of faculties and the president for appointments to the faculty, promotions, raises, tenure, etc.

Mediates all squabbles within his college.

Uses every means at his disposal to get as much money for his college as he can, since it is only through cold cash that he can maintain the quality of the faculty and thus the quality of the programs in which the faculty members teach.

Maintains a network of people who can supply him with the information he needs to keep his college at the top of the heap.

Pretty much follows Thrasymachus' version of justice: he rewards his friends and punishes his enemies. If he conducted himself otherwise, he would be squashed, quickly.

Keeps track of everybody in his college, without letting it appear obvious that he is doing so, so that he can anticipate problems before they appear.

Maintains *very* cordial relations with the dean of faculties.

Maintains *very, very* cordial relations with the president.

At least appears to maintain cordial relations with the controller, although they are natural enemies.

Keeps his finger on the student pulse, not only through the

dean of students (with whom he maintains a cordial relationship) but through students scattered throughout the university.

Tries to leave the internal workings of the different departments to the departmental chairmen.

Tries to handle individual faculty or student problems through departmental chairmen or the dean of students (that way, if it turns out all right, it's because he was wise enough to let the department chairmen have the freedom necessary to do the job; if it turns out wrong, the chairmen get the blame).

Maintains a pipeline to the underground information channels. This is called the DEW line, or Dean's Early Warning System.

Knows every faculty member's name and face, and, regardless of how grotesquely petty or snide that faculty member might be, must be prepared to defend the little bastard from attacks by faculty members or deans from other colleges.

Keeps in touch with both the faculty and the department chairmen through a round of regular and informal meetings.

Acts as a locus of forces both within his college and from the outside.

Serves as an authority figure so that wrath may be dissipated on him without going outside of the college, where it could cause him problems with the other deans.

Maintains a wary, watchful eye for any dean who purports to be interested in helping his college.

Trusts no one and keeps his own counsel.

Follows Lyle Spencer's laws of administration: (1) never lets himself be caught by surprise; (2) always gets it in writing; (3) makes it come out right.

Finally, he never pleads his case before the faculty. That is, he must accept the burden of his office and not complain about the silliness and childishness of some of the faculty; he does his job well because that's what a pro does. Above all, he must never expect any praise or understanding from the faculty.

To put it bluntly, he must maintain his fiefdom for the sake of the people in it, protect it from other barons, and stay in the good graces of the viceroy and the king. If he doesn't, he's had it. If he does a good job—that is, if he both builds his fiefdom with productive people and has enough political savvy to keep his job—he may someday be king himself. Yes, it's all very feudal.

Under the deans are the departmental chairmen (or chairpersons, or—praise God—"chairs"). The departmental chairman must hold impeccable credentials in his field, but will not be respected by the faculty because he has sold out to the administration, etc.

The chairman's job will vary, according to the size and nature of the department, but usually consists of the same things done by the dean, only at a lower level and on a more personal basis with the faculty and students.

Usually, when the dean is requested to waive a requirement for graduation, it is a department chairman who makes the request. Waivers of requirements for the major, however, are usually done by the department chairman himself, in consultation with appropriate faculty members.

Some department chairmen, the good ones that is, run their departments as a taut ship. Faculty members keep the office hours they post, secretaries are polite to students, requirements and schedules are always posted, job opportunities and graduate fellowship information is always passed along to the people who need it. Rotten profs are not recommended for tenure, and good profs are given the time they need to do their work.

The best department chairmen are members of the Enlightened Nobility (see page 284). They are often former deans, or at least they understand what the dean has to do. They have the best interests of both their faculty and their students at heart, and are not impressed by power-mongers.

The worst department chairmen are Corrupt Cardinals (see page 282). They are interested only in their own political advantage, and they'll stop at nothing to gain power and keep it.

All of which brings us to the faculty, the people with whom you will have the most immediate contact. They come in all shapes and sizes, temperaments and tendencies, parameters and perversities.

We had professors when we were students who changed our lives irrevocably for the good. They inspired us, they motivated us toward self-improvement, they introduced us to a world that we never knew existed. They cajoled us, berated us, embarrassed us with our own ignorance, pushed us, led us, and helped us become what we are. The greatest and most noble of all these people was our beloved friend and colleague Harry Dobson, whom we met after we finished our doctorates and became faculty members ourselves. Nobody ever taught us as much as Papa Dobson did.

We want to tell you about Papa. He died eight years ago at the age of seventy-seven. But maybe you'll run into him someday, walking about the campus smoking his cigar, following the smoke—as he told Ralph one day—to see which way the wind is blowing. Maybe you'll see a man who died eight years ago? If you knew Papa, you wouldn't dismiss the idea at all.

But Papa's the best. Let's talk about the ones you will assuredly see before we talk about Papa. Then you'll be able to appreciate him more.

At the top of the faculty status heap is the tenured full professor, or TFP, pronounced "tpfap!" The TFP can lose his job only through moral turpitude or financial exigency. That means he has to be caught with his hands either in his students' panties or in the university till, or the university has to eliminate him and his department because of financial problems that can't be solved by other means.

In short, he's got it made.

At the other end of the spectrum is the lowest denizen of the faculty status heap, the teaching assistant. He's still a graduate student, has no status at all, has all the troubles of a junior faculty member (large classes, poor students, etc.) and none of the rewards. If he keeps his nose clean, is "hard but fair" with the students, and keeps plugging along on his graduate degree, he will someday become a faculty member—at which point he will no longer be respected by his fellow students because he has—you guessed it—sold out to the faculty.

The faculty member he will become is an untenured instructor, or UTI, and UTIs have practically no status at all. UTIs begin on a six-year road to (they hope) tenure. Along the way, they will be promoted to the rank of UAP, or untenured assistant professor. This will give them a little more status, but they will still be wary of the TFPs who roam around on the upper floors of the college.

If UTIs survive the six years in one piece, and if they either perform "significant university service" or publish their asses off, they will be given a tenure vote. The faculty in their department will hold (usually) a secret ballot, and some will write letters either recommending tenure or recommending boiling oil, and the department chairman will make a recommendation to the dean of the college. The college dean will in turn make recommendations to the dean of faculties, the president, the Tenure Review Committee, and whatever other pressure group must be consulted before the poor candidate is given a permanent job.

If it's go all the way, the bloke is made a TAP, or tenured associate professor. Now he's legit.

Of course, nobody ever uses the word "tenured" when talking about these people. It's the Unspoken Thing. Everybody knows. And when you get tenure, you can relax a little and decide how you really want to live your life as an academic. You don't really have to publish as much now, nor do you have to keep your nose quite as clean. You may not get substantial raises with this attitude, but you will keep a steady job with a three-to-four-day week and three months' vacation a year.

We said earlier that colleges are much like feudal fiefdoms, with the deans playing the role of barons. Let's take the analogy a bit further. Colleges resemble feudal political systems because their present internal structure is a holdover from medieval times. The master's thesis and doctoral dissertation, especially in the liberal arts, are fair models of the scholastic method, straight out of the twelfth and thirteenth centuries.

Moreover, many colleges, even if they have no overt ties to the Church, at least emulate the atmosphere of the medieval Church. Full professors are like cardinals, instructors are like acolytes, and so on. The students are the flock. The purpose of college is to save the intellectual souls of the students. This conceptualization is not contrived. Most of America's first universities were directly linked with the

Church, which has influenced the development of colleges and universities down through the years.

Scratch a professor and you will find someone with a sense of mission. Scratch him hard enough and you may find a true believer. Rub him the wrong way and you will be banished from the fold. Rub him the right way and you can become one of the elect.

Because faculty roles are so well defined (however covert), there are certain easily recognizable faculty types. Following our handy (if imperfect) analogy, here's what you will probably find on any campus of any first-rate university.

THE SAINTS

These are the true intellectual giants. They are always tenured full professors, and they are the front-runners in their fields. They are internationally known scholars, they contribute regularly to their respective journals, and they usually hold endowed chairs (which means that a special endowment fund has been set up to protect their jobs from economic fluctuations).

Not only do they contribute to their fields, but in a real sense they define their fields. They are the Major Figures whose works students will study twenty years from now as required reading in the subject. Such people are also prizewinners: Pulitzer, Nobel, and so on. They are the *crème de la crème*.

They also teach, but they rarely teach large lecture sessions for freshmen unless they happen to like teaching large lecture sessions. They hold chiefly graduate seminars in the field for which they are known. One seminar with one of these people is like an entire college education from anybody else. If you're lucky enough to be able to listen and talk to one of these people, your intellectual life will be incredibly enriched.

Don't confuse these people with the Scholastics, Pseudoscholastics, and Defenders of the Faith (who come next). The Saints are at the forefront of their field. They are usually extraordinary teachers. Tenure means nothing to them. They could get it anywhere they went, as a condition that they set for accepting a position. Don't expect entertainment from these people (although some are extremely talented entertainers). Listen to what they say. Then think about what you've heard. Ten years later, you'll stumble across your old notes and be astounded to find that some of your most cherished ideas—ideas that you thought sprang fullblown from your own creativity—came from these people.

Some names? Charles Hartshorne, Paul Weiss, Merritt Hughes, Willard Van Orman Quine, R. P. Blackmur, Bertrand Russell, John Crowe Ransom, Alfred North Whitehead, Edward Sapir, Milton Friedman, and the first one (and founder of the first university), Plato. Some of these people are dead, you say? Guess again. These people never die. They live as long as human beings are willing to try to solve the mysteries of the cosmos and its inhabitants.

One word of caution. These giants tend to be overwhelming. Let yourself be overwhelmed for a while, but then pull yourself out of it and synthesize what you have heard with what you know yourself to be true. Develop your own unique way of looking at the world. Don't pass anything up along the way, but be sure that you accept nothing "whole cloth"; sift everything through your own perspective. Maybe someday you, too, will become one of the Saints.

SCHOLASTICS, PSEUDOSCHOLASTICS, AND DEFENDERS OF THE FAITH

The Scholastics are the emulators of the Saints. These are the people who grind out a few lines each year, get them published in whatever journal will take them, and then stalk up and down the halls of Academe as if they were True Intellectual Giants.

Actually, universities abound with such people. They are often sad cases, because they are obviously far more intelligent than the run-of-the-mill faculty member but don't have the spark of true genius.

Thus, at the top of the scholastic scale, you'll find people who contribute to the best journals, who collect definitive anthologies, who know more than anybody in the world about some small segment of their field, and who give papers at their professional association conferences every year: standard, legitimate scholars.

At the bottom are the Pseudoscholastics, who never write at all (they don't want to sully themselves by getting into the vulgar fray of the scholarly journals), but instead often establish for themselves the reputation of being Defenders of the Faith. Which means that they are the ones self-elected to Uphold the Standards of the University. Any suggestion of change in the curriculum is looked upon as the work of the Devil. People who want to update courses, create new programs, review existing programs, change admissions standards, review the grading system, or change the wording on the diploma are all viewed as False Prophets, to be stopped, smashed, banished. There is nothing more frightening to see or hear than a Defender of the Faith in action.

Defenders of the Faith usually developed their notion of what a genuine university is during their graduate school years. Many of them attended real universities, but unfortunately did not continue to develop when they were thrust out on their own after graduation. This is probably because of two things: (1) they never had much intellectual curiosity anyway; (2) having no genuine perspective on the nature of their field, they were overly impressed with the single version they got in graduate school.

Further, they rarely if ever are good enough to get a job on the faculty in the school from which they graduated (much less a better one), and they assure themselves of their own legitimacy by sticking to the version of higher education they learned at Crawling Ivy.

The Pseudoscholastic will usually find a sinecure, a place where his or her word is law, not to be questioned by people of lower rank such as assistant professors or teaching assistants. Pseudoscholastics often wind up directing freshman composition programs or "Introduction to Philosophy" programs, although they would never teach such courses themselves.

There are several reasons why they like this arrangement. It gives them the title "Director," but this does not mean that they have sold out to the administration. It gives them power over other people, without carrying the onus of being a chairman or a dean. *They* are in charge of Intellectual Matters, while the chairmen and the deans are merely in charge of money and people.

Thus, they can have their cake and eat it too. They can have power—which is real, because they are usually politically powerful and can cut a young faculty member out of the tenure track with a flip of the wrist—and not have to pay the price for it that is paid by the chairman or the dean. Further, by assuming the role of Defender of the Faith—Defender of Academic Standards—they put themselves in a morally unassailable position. Which is what this is all about: they want to be morally unassailable so that they can dictate the way that other people think without having to defend their reasons.

The reason is always the preservation of Academic Standards. Or the defense of Sacred Doctrine. Or the infallibility of the Full Professor. (Notice how the student gets lost in the shuffle here: none of this has much to do with him except insofar as he is looked upon as a vessel to be filled with Sacred Doctrine.)

Don't dismiss the value of the Scholastics and Pseudoscholastics (Defenders of the Faith) too quickly. They constitute the conservative faction that tends to hold the university together. They lend stability to the whole affair. They constitute the Establishment, with all its bureaucratic ills, but they also provide continuity between one generation of students and another. What you have to watch out for is the temptation to emulate them. Slogging out bibliographies and "Replies to Professor So-and-So's Article on the Use of the Comma in *Beowulf*" is the easy route to follow to academic security. If you plan to go into the university life, you will find that a steady flow of two or three articles a year will assure you of a secure place on the faculty, unless times get so tough that mass layoffs occur.

THE CORRUPT CARDINALS

Every campus has its professional politicians. Some are good and some are superb. The bad ones don't last.

These are the people who love to tell other people what to do. They are unlike the Defenders of the Faith, because as a rule they couldn't care less about academic standards. What they are interested in is power. Getting it, keeping it, wielding it. To the extent that a politician is also a Defender of the Faith, he is vulnerable, because he believes in some absolute.

This does not mean that he will not occasionally defend the Faith. It means that when he defends it, it is not for the sake of the Faith. Nor is it for the sake of swaying people's ideas, except insofar as those ideas will keep him in office. The Corrupt Cardinal uses pious professions of the Faith as a tool to rally the Young Priests around him when he is fighting the dean. The younger and more naïve the Young Priest, the better chance the Corrupt Cardinal has of using him for his own political ends.

We remember vividly an archetypal instance of a Corrupt Cardinal in action. The dean was trying to put a cooperative education program through the Arts and Sciences Council. If he was successful, hundreds of students otherwise not able to go to school would have a chance. Unfortunately, the history department and the philosophy department, both suffering from dropping enrollments, were seeking to reinstitute their freshman courses as requirements for graduation. This maneuver had nothing to do with academic standards, broadening the students' horizons, or any other altruistic purpose. It had simply to do with the desire of the members of those departments to hang onto their faculty members, thus hanging onto their budgets, thus hanging onto their clout.

Unfortunately, the co-op program, which integrated school and work, became an easy scapegoat for the Defenders of the Faith. To give people credit for what they were learning *off* campus was clearly a case of corrupting the standards of the university, while insisting that every student take a history and a philosophy course was clearly a case of upholding the standards of the university.

In the midst of the arguments and counterarguments, a faculty member stood up to speak. He was the single most powerful political figure in the college. Never, except for political ends, had he evinced the slightest interest in either the intellectual welfare of the students or the economic welfare of departments other than the one he was chairman of. This man stood up and made an impassioned plea on behalf of the students' minds, academic freedom, the role of the liberal arts in higher education, and the necessity of history and philosophy in a well-rounded curriculum.

Obviously, a deal had been made!

Unbeknownst to the faculty, the dean already knew about the deal. In fact, he was in on it. And after many arguments and just as many pious statements, the chairman "reluctantly" threw his support to the dean and the new program. When he shifted his vote, his followers shifted theirs. As a payoff, he was made chairman of the committee that would determine the role of the College of Arts and Sciences in the new program.

The results:

The students got a new program that would open new opportunities for them.
The chairman was hailed as a Defender of the Faith.

The dean was identified as the Devil.

The faculty, while disappointed with the final result, felt that they had vigorously and rigorously defended the Faith.

Consequently, everybody was more or less happy in the end: the dean, because he got the program through; the Corrupt Cardinal, because he had once again ingratiated himself with both the administration and the faculty by Defending the Faith while at the same time working a deal with the dean; and the faculty, because they had once again identified the Devil (if not his minions), and had once again acquitted themselves admirably in the face of overwhelming evil.

If it is to his political advantage, the Corrupt Cardinal can be your best friend. Remember, whether you are a student or a prospective faculty member, that his motives are self-interest. Don't hitch your wagon to his star unless you are ready for a rough ride.

THE ENLIGHTENED NOBILITY

These people are sometimes former deans. They are almost always department chairmen or former department chairmen, and they sometimes are recognized scholars in their fields. They have a flair for management as well as academics, and they are in some ways the bedrock of the university. Many are accomplished politicians, but have no real desire for power. They appreciate both the academic and the administrative mentality, and they have little sympathy with the rabid Defenders of the Faith. This is because they know it's mostly a sham, perpetuated either for psychological or political reasons.

They can help the dean and the president push through legislation that the Senate must approve. They can sway the faculty with a few well-chosen words. Their influence is weightier than that of the Corrupt Cardinal or the Defender of the Faith because they are not slaves to self-interest.

When the university is under fire from outside forces, it is these people who are the most valuable. The Defenders of the Faith have little stomach for actual combat, and the Corrupt Cardinals run for cover when the barricades are actually manned.

The Enlightened Nobility usually have a heightened sense of irony about the entire intellectual/political game. They can be devastatingly effective politicians when they need to be, and when the Faith really needs to be defended you can rely on them to separate the important issues from the false ones generated by various pressure groups. Any dean worth his salt will thank the powers of the universe for the presence of such people. They will be painfully honest with the administration as well as with fellow faculty members. They will also face the political realities with considerably more élan than their lesser colleagues.

THE YOUNG PRIESTS

Of course, this is the personnel pool from which come all the people mentioned above. The Defenders of the Faith, the Corrupt Cardinals, the Enlightened Nobility, even the Saints, all got their start in the ranks of the Young Priests.

As you look around you, try to spot the tendencies that will lead your prof into one or more of these paths. Remember, he will eventually work his way up the ladder (if he survives the various tests of his faith). The roles are already laid out for him.

The political climbers will make peace either with the administration or with the Corrupt Cardinals. If they plan to enter the administration themselves, they would do well to be from the faculty but not *of* it. Deans rarely live down being stout Defenders of the Faith in their dealings with other administrators. On the other hand, an administrator will have more influence with the faculty if at least *they* believe he is one of them.

The whole trick here is in orientation. The president will always see the dean as the representative and implementer of the administration's policies. The faculty will also see the dean as their representative to the president, as the person who protects them from the ravages of the administration.

The good dean must learn to ride this fence effectively, for the good of the university as a whole and for the good of his college in particular. It's not an easy job.

The Young Priests must therefore decide early in the game which side of the fence they are going to be on. Once you have crossed over the line and into the administration, there is no turning back. You're forever tainted. You have become a servant of the Devil.

Consequently, some Young Priests, especially those who are neither politically nor intellectually aggressive, will become Defenders of the Faith. Other Young Priests, more aggressive but less intellectual, will become Corrupt Cardinals. Still others will become members of the Enlightened Nobility, being politically astute but not ambitious, intellectually superior but not driven by the peculiar monomaniacal quest that leads to the Sainthood of the True Intellectual.

Some Young Priests will become Saints. Watch them on their way up. Sparks will fly off their heads, and everybody will be jealous of them until they see that they have no political ambitions. Then they will be left alone, being no threat to anybody but other scholars in their field. Universities can't stand many of these people at a time, and there should never be more than one in a single department.

HERETICS, FALSE PROPHETS, AND OTHER SINNERS

These are the faculty members who don't fit. They may be brilliant in their field, but they are usually naive politically (except for a few, who are absolutely stellar politically, and have taken on the persona of Heretic *because* it is the politically astute thing to do).

There are many types, for these people, like Satan's minions, come in all sizes, shapes, and persuasions. Many of them are thought to be illegitimate because what they're doing has not yet become a department. Others are considered illegitimate because they are radical revisionists in fields that have been stable for a long time. Still others are known as Heretics, False Prophets, or Other Sinners because they violate one or more of the overt and covert Commandments of Behavior that are a part of the taboo system of academic life. Here are the Commandments:

Thou shalt not consort with the dean or any other member of the administration.
Thou shalt not commit adultery with thy students, either male or female.

Thou shalt not consort with students any more than is absolutely necessary, lest it appear that you identify with them and not with faculty.

Thou shalt not preach unpopular doctrines (defined here as any interpretation of a field that is not held by politically powerful members of a department).

Thou shalt not betray faculty secrets to either the administration or the students.

Thou shalt not give easy grades.

Thou shalt not contest the opinions of full professors, especially if they are also Defenders of the Faith or Corrupt Cardinals.

Thou shalt be a vassal to thy department chairman and to all thy colleagues until thou hast been given tenure (then you're on your own).

Thou shalt serve on many committees, cheerfully.

Thou shalt publish or perish.

Thou shalt rack up excellent course evaluations (but only if you grade hard and do not consort with your students).

Thou shalt not place any political cause over the interests of the faculty.

Thou shalt never *ask* for a raise or a promotion.

Thou shalt *never* initiate thine own tenure-vote process.

As you try to spot all of these faculty and administrative types, keep in mind that few of the faculty members have any knowledge whatever of the economics of running a university. They consider themselves above the mundane task of attracting students to anything other than their own discipline.

If class enrollments are low, they feel no obligation to look for more students. Instead, they hold the administration responsible for providing them with students. Neither do they take responsibility for making the departmental budget balance; and the relationship between class size and break-even figures is an equation that escapes even some of the most brilliant math professors.

Most faculty members consider it their sole duty to teach their classes and write in their field. Everything else is somebody else's job. This, of course, is a fool's paradise. Few of them realize that if the university collapsed financially, tenure wouldn't mean a thing. They are far removed from the fiscal firing line, and given their lack of talent with money matters, it's probably just as well.

So don't expect much economic realism from your profs, even if they are economics professors (*especially* if they are economics professors!). This is true of almost all of them except for the business profs, and some of them have never made a payroll, although they teach courses on payroll.

The Corrupt Cardinals are another matter altogether. They understand power and finances all too well. That's why they are so successful. They combine genuine shrewdness with an ability to appear to the idealistic elements of the faculty as Defenders of the Faith. It's a winning combination.

To them, the Heretics, False Prophets, and Other Sinners are tools to be used for their own ends. They are masters at fence straddling, and, when the occasion calls for it, will support unstructured classes and traditional classes, hard grades and no grades, tenure and dismissal, curriculum change and the petrification of the curriculum, all for the same reasons.

You shouldn't condemn the faculty either for being naïve or for being so politically corrupt. It's no different from any other group of people, only a little bit smarter in some ways (dumber in others). And you shouldn't feel sorry for the dean. He knows what he has to do, and if he doesn't want to be the dean, there are a dozen others (staunch Defenders of the Faith, Corrupt Cardinals, and Young Priests) who will gladly and quickly reverse their previous position on the administration and take the job. Especially if it means a $7,000 per annum raise and an expense account.

In some ways, it's the Heretics, False Prophets, and Other Sinners who are the saddest cases. Most of them are basically Evangelists, and they spend their lifetimes trying to convert people who are neither interested nor talented in the field under discussion. The politicized film critics, the revisionist historians, the amateur proponents of "touchy-feely" group therapy, and the deeply sincere defenders-of-the-rights-of-students are all basically dead-enders, and you should think twice and examine your own motives before you join their causes.

Many of these people are great showmen, and are terribly entertaining teachers. Don't be misled. An easy manner and an entertaining teaching method has little to do with the truth. It's just window dressing. Everybody should take several classes from the departmental radicals, if for no other reason than to hear all sides of whatever question is being examined. But don't get sucked into their trip just because they have an engaging way of presenting it. You should approach them in exactly the same way that you approach their opposite numbers, the Defenders of the Faith: with caution, an open mind, and a healthy measure of cynicism.

If it's allowed, go to the meetings of the Faculty Senate. Look around you and record all the types. They'll be there, all of them. What most of them don't realize is that their behavior is predictable. Most of them have allowed themselves to become stereotypes of different versions of the Great American College Professor.

None of this has a great deal to do with improving your mind, but it is good insurance for survival. The horror stories we mentioned in the opening pages of this book occurred at least in part because we weren't aware of the forces in motion in the halls and offices of ole Crawling Ivy U.

We thought people went to college to get a higher education. And we thought that faculty members lived the Life of the Mind. We were simply naïve. Many students go to college with no intention of learning any more than they need to get by. Few faculty members are intellectuals. They spend their spare time watching the tube, reading pulp literature, and taking their kids for rides in the family car. Perhaps they watch only the Public Broadcasting Service station (doubtful, since so much of it is so dull), and perhaps they read only top-grade science fiction and detective stories (instead of stock disaster or romantic novels), and their family car is probably an energy-saving foreign compact (twenty years ago it was the VW bus, now it's the Toyota stationwagon). But they aren't particularly intellectual. As our friend Tucson Arthur Jacobson once put it, "They're just people who like to read books, that's all."

This is not to say that the world is not full of good-natured, well-intentioned faculty members, who will work with you and spend an inordinate amount of their time trying to help you make up your mind, find yourself, find a suitable major program, succeed, and do the things you want to do.

Most faculty members, after all, are no Intellectual Giants (Saints), nor are they Corrupt Cardinals, Defenders of the Faith or the other more familiar types. Most are people who like to read books, like to discuss topics of interest in rational ways, like to think about events and ideas. Whether or not they make an original contribution to their field is beside the point.

We've had courses from all of the faculty types listed above. Some of the worst courses we've ever taken were from the Intellectual Giants. Some of the best were from young, earnest assistant professors who hadn't yet had time to become cynical.

Most faculty members do not write at all, nor do they do anything that could meaningfully be called research. Most faculty members teach courses in their respective fields, at either lower or higher levels. In universities with graduate schools, the percentage of research and writing faculty will be higher. But the main activity of faculty members is teaching.

There are good teachers, bad teachers, superb lecturers, abysmal discussion leaders, teachers who teach courses primarily about their hangups, and profs who don't deviate from the text enough to be more than organic recording machines.

As you make your way through college, you will be astonished at how many of your professors fall into one or more of the categories described above. Rarely do you find a pure type, but occasionally you will run across an unreconstructed Defender of the Faith or Young Priest. Sometimes you will run across a member of the Enlightened Nobility, and sometimes you'll bag a rare Saint. Most of your professors will be Pseudoscholastics and Scholastics. The heady spice of the Heretics, False Prophets, and Other Sinners is fading from academe. Fewer jobs and less money on campus have sent them into more lucrative ways of making a living.

You will also find that the plumage of these birds remains pretty much the same as the years go by. Although a particular Young Priest may start out with turtlenecks and corduroy coats, he may well metamorphose into a dark-suited, watch-chain-toting Defender of the Faith. Or he may become a cigar-chewing, conservatively dressed Corrupt Cardinal. It's the type that's important, not the person who fills the type at the moment.

Now, the engaging young sophist will want to know how all this can be used to his or her advantage. If you do not by now know the relevance of all this, you probably should not try to use it to your advantage. There are no hard and fast rules that will tell you how to tread successfully through this minefield. There is no list of do's and don'ts that will make it possible for you to deal with all these people in a way that will assure success for you in the classroom and in the world beyond graduation. The best that can be offered is a few observations that are quite hoary.

The more closely a person approximates a particular type of human being, the more his or her behavior will be predictable. People who wear Brooks Brothers tweeds don't usually act the same way as people who wear Levi's and lumberjack shirts. There's a lesson to be learned from this, since it applies everywhere, not just in the academic world.

What you will see in the university is a vast array of academic types. There will be people who hate their students, and people who love them. There will be professors who exult in their students' hatred of them, and others who will do anything to get the students to love them. The university is a microcosm of the world around you. Read this section thoroughly, and then go sit on the library steps and look out over the quadrangle. What do you see? You see all the people we've described, of course.

Professors often feel that they have a mission. The simpleminded ones will feel that that mission is to convince every student that there is no road to the truth except the one represented by their discipline. These are the Evangelists, and they are found among Young Priests as well as Defenders of the Faith.

The better ones will know that their field is only one road, and they will prod their students into finding their own personal roads. Look around you. Take it all in. Catalog the types. Sift all of it through your own sieve. Most importantly, try to learn which category you yourself belong to. Then, try to figure out if you really think that way, really want to live that life.

Which is what all this is really all about: learning to find yourself (not in the mushy, sixties sense, but in a carefully calculated, constructive, intellectual sense), learning to know who you are. One of the best ways to do this is to learn what other people are, what they do, what they think, what they believe. Which one of them are you? Do you really want to be on that particular road?

In Woody Allen's movie *Stardust Memories*, Woody is on a train. It is cold, bleak, and full of people who stare without smiling. Across the railyard is another train, full of people who are laughing and having a good time, drinking and joking and occasionally looking over at his train. Woody tries to get off the train, so that he can board the other one, but it is too late. He is on the Bergman train, he wants to be on the Fellini train, but it's already leaving the station.

Which train are you on? College is the best place in the

world to look over all the destinations, all the tracks. While you're in college, take a ride with them all. It's not for life, yet. By riding them all, you'll be able to decide which train you really want to take.

While you're riding, don't get sidetracked by university power games. They aren't worth playing, and they'll simply waste your time. One kind of power game that purports to be a way to learn which professors are good and which are bad is known as "course evaluations." Don't trust them. They aren't necessarily what they purport to be.

A brief digression is appropriate here, because one of the best ways to understand the limitations of an accepted practice is to learn the origins of it. The field of history is grounded on this principle.

During the sixties, partially in an attempt to separate the good profs from the bad, students began to evaluate courses. Such evaluations are now standard practice in most universities. Many students, instead of riding all the trains, use the course evaluations to decide which courses are good ones and which ones are a waste of time.

Actually, they are used not to evaluate courses, but to evaluate the professors who teach them. The push for course evaluations began when students involved in the Revolution (as we all called it way back then) tried to purge the Professoriat of people who refused to bend the subject matter of their courses to fit into current revolutionary interests.

That's a nasty statement, but it happens to be true. We know that there was a lot of rhetoric about "improving the teaching standards of the university" (see how quickly even a revolutionary can begin to sound like a Defender of the Faith?), but the truth is that it was an attempt to strip the faculty of its power to make judgments about whether or not particular students could or would meet the requirements of their courses.

Legal, moral, political "rights" were collapsed into a catchall "human rights," and then applied willy-nilly to anything in sight. Among those affected by the new philosophy of rights was the faculty member. It was thought by many students that "student rights" included escaping the grading process. Jerry Rubin's shrill "Yippie Manifesto" was only one of many articles that called the protection of academic freedom inimical to student rights.

The universities became battlegrounds not for ideas, but for the power to get rid of faculty members who would not alter their courses and their grading systems to accommodate the demands of the students.

The classroom changed into a free-for-all, with politics and power plays, muddled logic and downright hostility replacing the opportunity to learn. If all this seems alien, it is because the pendulum is swinging back now to where it was during the fifties. This is neither good nor bad. The horror stories listed in the Introduction are all from the late fifties and early sixties.

Course evaluations had diverse origins:

The honest desire of good students to make sure that they got in class what they had come to college to learn.
The desire of politicized students to politicize the classroom, in an attempt to gain power over not only the faculty but the curriculum as well.
A desire on the part of university administrators to control the faculty and rid themselves of troublemakers.
The desire of conscientious administrators to upgrade the faculty.

The results were:

Many a good man and woman saw years of work and preparation go down the drain because they refused to be compromised by pressure groups.
Many rotten teachers were driven from the universities.
Many administrators used the evaluations as a way to get rid of dead wood and replace it with genuinely talented faculty.
Many rotten administrators used the evaluations for the same political ends as the students.

So, when you read the course evaluations at your school, ask yourself the following questions:

What are the crieteria for the judgments made?
Do you agree with the criteria or not?
If so, why? If not, why?
Have the course evaluations resulted in more knowledge being gained by students, or are the courses simply more exciting or popular?
Whatever happened to the sense of intellectual adventure?

The last question gets us back on the track. College is about learning, about broadening your horizons and also giving depth to your understanding. If it doesn't, then you've wasted your time. You'll never have another chance like this one to learn all the things you should learn. Don't waste it by getting swept up in somebody's else's trip, whatever their sales pitch may be.

Be your own judge. Remember, this is simply another instance in which you're going to have to take responsibility for the creation of your own life. Use as your prime criterion for course selection the rule that you must gain in knowledge and insight. That's what you're in college for. Nothing else is as important as this is.

If you want to get the best, then seek out those professors who are well known in their fields. They may be dull sometimes, and at other times they may be brilliant. Dull or bright, they're the leaders. They'll give you the straight dope.

Seek out the hard profs. Don't fool with the ones who make a show of being easy. They're probably more interested in having you like them than they are in having you learn from them.

Steer clear of people who always turn their classes into current events sessions, whether they are teaching Restoration comedy or Xenophon's *Anabasis*. The relevancy of these works will be self-evident. It doesn't have to be forced.

If you do run into a rotten prof, talk to the department chairman about him. If you don't get any satisfaction there, go see the dean. Don't fool with the assistant deans. They're flak catchers. See the dean. He'll put the screws to the department chairman and get to the bottom of things. He'll do this because it's in his own interests to find out about rotten spots in his fiefdom.

Pay more attention to long-term reputations than to semester-by-semester course evaluations. It's the long-term record that counts, not what a particular group of students say about Professor X during a given semester.

If you're really interested in a field, seek out the Saints, the True Intellectual Giants. They may appear dull on the surface, and they may be monomaniacal about their discipline, but these are the people who know all there is to know about their fields. Don't accept substitutes! And don't expect to be entertained, either. The entertainment here is purely intellectual. If this isn't your cup of tea, don't waste your time and the professor's. Forget sparkling lectures. Any good standup comedian can give sparkling lectures, without knowing anything about what his script says. The Saint writes his own script.

This is not to say that the Young Priests, Heretics, Other Sinners, Corrupt Cardinals, and Enlightened Nobility have nothing to offer. Some of the Young Priests will be Saints someday, and you can get in on the ground floor of their intellectual triumphs as you watch them grow. The really good ones will send sparks flying wherever they go.

Don't pass up the Heretics. They, too, may be tomorrow's Saints. Most of the True Intellectual Giants were once Heretics. That, unfortunately, is how progress is made. Famous Heretics? Oh, there's Wagner, Pasteur, Lister, Einstein, Wittgenstein, to name a few. The problem is that you can't tell the real ones from the phonies, because whatever level they're on, it's probably higher than the one you're on, if for no other reason than the fact that they've been exposed to more than you have. You'll have to trust to luck and common sense. Go ahead. Embrace a few wild ideas. They probably won't kill you. In fact, they'll probably be tomorrow's orthodoxy, stoutly defended by Scholastics and Pseudoscholastics.

Forget about good teaching. "Good teaching" has become a shibboleth, fueled by power games on the part of the students, the administration, and the faculty themselves. There is only one definition of a "good teacher." A good teacher is someone who can inspire in students the same feeling of awe and mystery about a field that he (or she) feels personally.

This is not a one-sided thing. While a stammering professor may try the patience of a classroom of excellent students, the most brilliant lecture in the world will go unappreciated in a classroom of students who have other things on their mind. The classroom is not a talent contest for the professor. It is a place where people share the knowledge they have and try to make contributions of their own. The same pitfalls are present in the classroom that are present anywhere else when two or more people congregate to listen, exchange ideas, and express themselves. Power games, insecurities, egotism, superciliousness, pettiness, and, sometimes, a magical, soaring achievement—all of these things are possible in each classroom. But most of all, you get out of it what you put into it. In this last respect, the classroom is exactly like the rest of the world.

Now that you're familiar with all the faculty types, we can introduce you to a real faculty member, someone we both knew and loved. We promised to tell you more about Professor Harry Dobson. Well, now is the time. And in telling you about Papa (which is what all of us called him, students and faculty alike), we want to tell you not only about what he did in the classroom, but what he did on the way to becoming a professor. No professor bursts suddenly full-blown from the head of Zeus, to take up chalk and pointer before a class of students. Professors are people, just like you, who have lived, suffered, enjoyed themselves, and committed minor (and sometimes major) sins, and who have been caught up in the world of books and thoughts.

The orthodoxy presently is that none of this counts. This is silly, since a professor is not merely his voice or his words, but is himself as well. What he says and does is a projection of what he is, where he came from, where he is going. If you're really to understand a person's thoughts, you must understand what it is to be that person and have those thoughts. You can't dismiss the importance of the human aspect of being a professor by some behavioristic sleight of hand.

So we want to tell you not only about Papa the brilliant teacher (for there were none more brilliant than he), but about Papa the man, Papa the human being, Papa the nineteenth-century gentleman scholar, who gave us and all of his students a priceless gift: himself.

Harry M. Dobson was born a millionaire. His father was in railroads. His mother was a personal friend of Mrs. Potter Palmer. He knew Sibelius and Roger Fry, lived in the Plaza Hotel in a multi-room suite, and saw Gallicurci's and Igna Manski's debuts at the Metropolitan Opera. He never attended public schools. He never matriculated in any university in a degree program, although he studied at the University of London, at Heidelberg, and at many other universities across the European continent.

He spent four years at Bayreuth, studying Wagner. At the time of his death, he was one of the greatest Wagnerian scholars in the world.

Nobody ever heard of him. Nobody except the thousands of students who took his courses at Oglethorpe University in Atlanta, Georgia. He left reams of written materials when he died, all of which are in a special section of the Oglethorpe library. Time and time again in his classes, he offered interpretations of musical passages and portions of libretti which would be hailed by scholars years later as signal contributions to the field. Papa never published. He was fearful of the shark-infested waters, for he had no credentials. Not even a high school diploma.

Besides, and more importantly, Papa genuinely was not the slightest bit interested in publishing in the fields of musicology or music history. He was interested in preserving the great works of musical geniuses, and in creating a situation in which others could learn to appreciate their works. He did this year after year in the music room in Hearst Hall, on the campus of a tiny university in the northern suburbs of Atlanta.

Each day, he would arrive at the door precisely three minutes before class was to begin. At the stroke of the hour, everybody would be seated, and Papa would be standing behind the little desk from which he lectured. He would smile, nod to us as we sat in our seats in the front row by the window (permanently reserved for us, in case we were in town and had the chance to drop by), place his Elgin railroad watch (which had belonged to his father) on the desk, sit down, wave his hands as if signaling an invisible orchestra to begin, and then weave a spell over his audience as magical as any *Tarnhelm* that ever draped across Siegfried's shoulders.

After leading us into the events of the opera, capturing our imagination as fully as if we were actually in those mythical times and places, he would silently rise and start the music system (a present to him from his students for his seventieth birthday). We would be instantly swept away into the music and the world of the work to which we were listening.

We don't mean that we were simply enjoying the music. That's not it at all. We were there, in the music, in the opera, in the mythical world that the opera was about. When the leitmotivs weaved their ironic counterpart to the actions of the players, it was as if we had become immortal, omniscient beings, looking and listening, experiencing the emotions and thoughts of the characters.

Carried away? Absolutely! It was a magical time in our lives, a time that has never left us, which lives with us and reasserts itself each fall when the leaves begin to turn and the chill winds brush the smoke and clouds from the sky. Those classes are as vivid and as immediate in our minds as if they happened yesterday! We could take the final today and make an A in the course.

What happened? What did Papa do? Well, he did something that was truly magic. He drew us into the works themselves. Not critical articles about the works. Not debates about the works. Not anecdotes about Wagner's life, and his many affairs. Not any of these. He drew us into the works themselves, showed us the door in our minds which opened into the world of the works. It was an electrifying experience, a pure communion with art. It was the ecstasy of the aesthetic experience that Plato feared because of its power over the rational mind.

But with Papa, it was emotion transcendentalized by understanding, not the other way around. Which is why it's still with us after seventeen years. It was truly a total experience, in which the impossible became actual. What we heard and felt became as much a part of us as our eyes and ears, our feelings and thoughts. That's why it's still there.

If you live in Atlanta, you might take a trip out to the Oglethorpe campus sometime. Papa lived in a little faculty home at the time of his death, but he lived many years in the tower over the building at the far end of the campus. He had a little apartment there which he shared with his cats and his books. The music room is in Hearst Hall, across the quadrangle from the administration building. There is a huge tree by the building that turns golden every fall.

And there is a hawthorne tree in front of the music room windows that has been known to bloom in the winter, and that is reputed at one time to have harbored a witch, who cast a spell on a junior faculty member that was broken only by Papa's direct intervention.

If you're lucky, you may run into somebody who knew Papa. Don't expect much from the faculty in this regard. Few of them who were there then are there now. Few of the ones who were there then had the remotest idea of who was in their midst. Look in the library for the literary magazine that was dedicated to him, and look also for the special collection.

Late at night, in the early fall, you might stand under the hawthorne tree as the evening winds curl around the buildings. We will guarantee that you will see no witches. We will not guarantee that you will not see Papa. There are those who claim that they have.

So, which one was Papa? Saint? Enlightened Nobility? He was both of the above. When investors lost the millions for him in 1929, he fell back on his musical training and his native intelligence to make it through the Depression. He played with the New York City Symphony under Walter Damrosch, but was injured in a taxicab accident. The broken fingers ended his career as a bass violinist.

He taught either at the University of Florida or at Florida State. His records are unclear. Between the Symphony and the teaching position, nine years are missing. Rumor had it that he had spent the time on Skid Row, but he would neither affirm nor deny it.

He was given an honorary doctorate by Oglethorpe University in an attempt to retire him. The ovation he received from the hundreds of students, past and present, who turned out on honors night assured him of a place on the faculty until his death.

He had a talent, nay, a genius, for opening minds to the world of the aesthetic experience and to the world of understanding. Nobody we have ever met, no matter how distinguished in his or her field, has had that gift as he had it. No person we've ever met in the years that have followed his death has even come close to him. He was a unique individual, one of a kind, in a league that had only one member.

We've hit you with these mundane facts about him here at the end because it was his idea. That is, years ago when we talked with him and laughed with him and listened with him to the great musical works he loved so dearly, he used to say that it was not a good idea to leave people up in the air or down in the dumps. Take them there, but don't leave them there. The world itself is mundane. Some experiences are not. But you must learn to accept the irony of experiencing the truly electrifying and the truly banal. It's part of the way the world works. And it'll help you to appreciate the other kind of experience even more.

We must say that it seems somehow wrong to talk about politics after thinking about Papa. But it was Papa himself who taught us that the real key to the experience of what's valuable in life is to develop the ability to be both politically astute and aesthetically sensitive at the same time, without letting either of the two talents wipe out the other.

Papa was no published Saint, for he was not known in his field. He was a member of the Enlightened Nobility, and nothing went on either on or off campus that he didn't know about. He was as worldly as they come, and given to frequent binges and sometimes drunken sprees. The best one happened a couple of years before he died. He had become acquainted (finally) with a retired grande dame of the opera, whose debut he had seen as a child. She was in her eighties and he was in his seventies. They went out on the town, to Henry Hamburger's delicatessen, then to the Top of the Mart, where they drank, sang duets, and drew everyone around them into their fantasy.

All of higher education is fantasy, in a certain sense. It's vicarious experience—experience through books and paintings and music and sculpture, philosophy, poetry, history, and the sciences. But the truly valuable thing about higher education is that it makes worlds available to you that would never have been available to you otherwise. When you read and listen, and, as Carlos Casteneda's Yaqui Indian sorceror put it, really *see* those worlds, then you will change your mind very quickly about which world is real and which one is not. The unreal world is the one that you plow through every day.

As the ad says, "Try them and compare."

Use our analysis and descriptions of the university and its denizens to help yourself survive. But don't forget: you're missing the whole point unless you are surviving in order to try to find that door in your mind that Papa opened for us. Nothing else is more important to you. Don't get trapped into thinking that the sophistry of politicking your way through college will give you the true philosophy of higher education. That comes from the changes you make inside yourself. Look for that door. Look for the secret that lies behind every class.

Look for Papa.

Sources and Resources

THE FOLLOWING BOOKS will give you basic information about colleges across the nation, with specific data and advice on applying for admissions, getting through interviews, filling out all the papers, and all the other details of getting into college.

PRE-ADMISSIONS READINGS

Barron's Guide to the Two-Year Colleges. New York: Barron's Educational Series, 6th ed., 1978.
Barron's Profiles of American Colleges, 2 vols. New York: Barron's Educational Series, 11th ed., 1979.
Lovejoy, Clarence E. *Lovejoy's College Guide.* New York: Simon and Schuster, 1979.
Mitchell, Joyce Slayton. *What's Where: The Official Guide to College Majors.* New York: Avon Books, 1979.
Moll, Richard. *Playing the Private College Admissions Game.* New York: Times Books, 1979.
Peterson's Annual Guide to Undergraduate Study, 1980. New York: Peterson's Guides, 1980.
Wickendon, James W. *The Admissions Process at Selective Colleges.* New York: Peterson's Guides, 1979. (Wickendon is director of admissions at Princeton University and knows whereof he speaks!)

TEST-PREPARATION GUIDES

These guides will help you make sense out of the tests that you will probably have to take to get into college. They give you not only general information about the tests but specific advice on how to take them, how to prepare for them, and how to do well on them.

ARCO GUIDES

Scoring High on College Entrance Tests. New York: Arco Test Tutor Series, 1978.
Scholastic Aptitude Test. New York: Arco New Editions, 1980.
The College Board Examinations. New York: Arco Test Tutor Series, 3rd printing, 1978.
The ACT. New York: Arco Books, 6th ed., 1980.

BARRON GUIDES

Math Workbook for College Entrance Examinations. New York: Barron's Educational Series, 1976.
How to Prepare for the College Entrance Examination (SAT). New York: Barron's Educational Series, 10th ed., 1980.
Verbal Aptitude Workbook for the SAT. New York: Barron's Educational Series, 1979.

CLIFF'S NOTES

ACT Preparation Guide. Lincoln, Nebraska: Cliff's, 1979.
PSAT and NMSQT Preparation Guide. Lincoln, Nebraska: Cliff's, 1979.
SAT Preparation Guide (including Test of Standard Written English). Lincoln, Nebraska: Cliff's, 1979.

CONTEMPORARY BOOKS GUIDES

Preparation for the SAT. Chicago, Illinois: Contemporary Books, 1978.

MCGRAW-HILL GUIDES

How to Prepare for the American College Testing Program. New York: McGraw-Hill, 1980.
How to Prepare for the SAT. New York: McGraw-Hill, 1980.

MONARCH GUIDES

SAT for College Entrance. New York: Monarch Books, 1976.

Standard Written English Test (SAT). New York: Monarch Books, 1975.

GED (HIGH SCHOOL EQUIVALENCY TEST) PREPARATION GUIDES
Preliminary Practice for the High School Equivalency Diploma Tests. New York: Arco Books, 1975. (A guide in Spanish is also available through Arco.)
How to Prepare for the New High School Equivalency Examination (GED). New York: Barron's Educational Series, 1979.
Other guides available are by Contemporary Books, McGraw-Hill, and Monarch.

GENERAL BIBLIOGRAPHY ON COLLEGE AND CAREERS

There are many books that give general information about how to go to college, how to study, how to make the transition between the university and the world outside, how to make sure that your college career prepares you for your postgraduate career. These books are the best of the lot. You won't need to read all of them, of course, but if there are specific things that we haven't mentioned, you'll find them here.

Armstrong, William H. *Study Tips.* New York: Barron's Educational Series, 1975.
Bear, John. *The Alternative Guide to College Degrees and Nontraditional Higher Education.* New York: Stonesong Press, 1980.
Bestor, Dorothy. *Aside from Teaching English, What in the World Can You Do?* Seattle: University of Washington Press, 1977.
Cass, James, and Birnbaum, Max. *Comparative Guide to American Colleges.* New York: Harper and Row, 1979 (9th ed.).
The College Blue Book. New York: Macmillan Information Publishing, 1974. (This book is published in a number of "regional" editions, most of which cover ten to twelve states in a geographical area.)

College Placement Council, eds. *Four-Year Liberal Arts Graduates: Their Utilization in Business, Industry, and Government.* (Order direct from College Placement Council, Inc., Box 2263, Bethlehem, Pa. 18001.)

Douglas, Martha. *How to Get Your First Good Job: Go for It!* San Francisco: Chronicle Books, 1977.

Figler, Howard E. *PATH: A Career Workbook for Liberal Arts Students.* Boston: The Carroll Press, 1975.

Fox, Marcia R. *Put Your Degree to Work: A Career Planning and Job Hunting Guide for the New Professional.* New York: W. W. Norton, 1979.

Gale, Barry and Linda. *The National Directory for Occupational Information.* New York: Arco Books, 1978. (A sourcebook of books, articles, free pamphlets, and send-away materials on every career imaginable.)

Green, Kenneth A. *Better Grades in College with Less Effort.* New York: Barron's Educational Series, 1971.

Hanau, Laia. *The Study Game: How to Play and Win.* New York: Barnes and Noble, 1979.

Holland, John L. *Making Vocational Choices: A Theory of Careers.* Englewood Cliffs, N.J.: Prentice-Hall, 1979.

Hutchinson, Marilyn A., and Spooner, Sue E. *Job Search Barometer.* (Order direct from The College Placement Council, Inc., Box 2263, Bethlehem, Pa. 18001.)

Kocher, Eric. *International Jobs: Where They Are, How to Get Them.* Addison-Wesley Publishers, 1979.

Kohl, Kenneth and Irene. *Financing College Education.* New York: Harper and Row, 1980.

Malnig, Lawrence R., and Marrow, Sandra L. *What Can I Do with a Major in . . . ?* Jersey City, N.J.: St. Peter's College Press, 1975.

Millman, Jason, and Pauk, Walter. *How to Take Tests.* New York: McGraw-Hill, 1969.

Mitchell, Joyce Slayton. *STOPOUT: Working Ways to Learn.* New York: Avon Books, 1978. (Also published by Garrett Park, Maryland: Garrett Park Press paperback, 1978.)

National College Databank. New York: Peterson's Guides, 1979. (2,400 colleges indexed according to 200 characteristics.)

Nyquist, Ewald B.; Arbolino, Jack N.; and Hawes, Gene R. *College Learning Anytime, Anywhere*. New York: Harcourt Brace, 1977.

Peterson's Annual Guide to Careers and Employment, ed. Sandra Grundfest. New York: Peterson's Guides, 1980.

Shingleton, John, and Bao, Robert. *College to Career: Finding Yourself in the Job Market*. New York: McGraw-Hill, 1977.

Suchar, Elizabeth W. *Financial Aid Guide for College*. New York: Monarch Books, 1978.

Vargas, William. *Career Development Handbook*. Grayslake, Ill.: Office of Continuing Education, College of Lake County, 1978. (Order direct from the above at 19351 West Washington St., Grayslake, Ill., 60030.)

Wynne, Edward A. *Looking at Schools: Good, Bad and Indifferent*. New York: Lexington Books, 1980.

Yeomans, William N. *Jobs '80–81, College Edition*. New York: Paragon Books, 1979.

You Can Do Just About Anything: A Chronicle of First and Current Jobs and What Helped Most in Getting Them for College of Arts and Sciences Graduates of 1971, 1973, 1975. Bloomington, Illinois: The Career Center, Indiana University, 1976.

SOURCES, REFERENCES, AND ADDRESSES FOR FINANCIAL AID

The lowdown on financial aid is one of the most valuable kinds of information you can get. The following books and information sources will tell you where to go to get the money you need, and how to get it when you get there. If your situation isn't covered in the chapter on financial aid in our book, it'll probably be covered in one of these. You can also write to the various services listed and get information directly about your eligibility for funds. Don't be afraid to write or call the various offices.

Two excellent sourcebooks (in addition to those listed below):
Proia, Nicholas C., and Di Gaspari, Vincent. *Barron's Handbook*

of American College Financial Aid. New York: Barron's Educational Series, 1978.

Leider, Robert. *Your Own Fnancial Aid Factory.* Alexandria, Va.: Octameron Publishers, 1980.

Tuition Plan, Inc., 1 Park Ave., New York, N.Y. 10016, or 400 N. Michigan Ave., Chicago, Ill. 60611.

Tuition Plan of New Hampshire, Inc., 18 School St., Concord, N.H. 03301.

Funds for Education, Inc., 319 Lincoln St., Manchester, N.H. 03102.

The Scholarship Search Company, 1775 Broadway, New York, N.Y. 10019.

United Student Aid Funds, 6610 North Shadeland Ave., Box 50827, Indianapolis, Ind. 46250.

BEOG, Basic Grant Program, Box A, Iowa City, Iowa 52240.

SEOG forms available through BEOG address or through the U.S. Office of Education, Washington, D.C. 20202.

Financial aid forms: available through College Scholarship Service, Box 176, Princeton, N.J. 08540.

Family financial statements: available through American College Testing Program, P.O. Box 767, Iowa City, Iowa 55420.

The College Board's Early Financial Aid Planning Service offers information on how much financial aid is available, differing costs of various colleges, etc. To qualify, complete the form (available through high school counselors) and send $3.50 to College Scholarship Service (address above) before June 30 of each academic year. Remember, these are forms for the *coming* academic year, so start early!

More financial aid materials: send $7 for the *Catalog of Federal Domestic Assistance* to Superintendent of Documents, U.S. Government Printing Office, Washington, D.C. 20402.

OTHER LOW-COST MATERIALS YOU CAN ORDER DIRECT

The A's and B's of Merit Scholarships and *Don't Miss Out* (available from Octameron Associates, P.O. Box 3437, Alexandria, Va. 22302, at $1.50 each).

Sources and Resources   313

Need a Lift? Order direct from The American Legion, attn. Need a Lift, P.O. Box 1055, Indianapolis, Ind. 46206, for 50¢).
How to Obtain Money for College by William E. Lever (order from Arco Publishing Co., 219 Park Ave. South, New York, N.Y. 10003, for $5 plus 75¢ postage).
Selected List of Postsecondary Opportunities for Minorities (write: U.S. Office of Education, Bureau of Postsecondary Education, Washington, D.C. 20202, for this free booklet).
Student Information Booklet. Free booklet published by National Scholarship Service and Fund for Negro Students (NSSFNS), 1510 Broadway, Suite 610, New York, N.Y. 10036.
America's Lowest Cost Colleges, by Nick Roes, Jr., contains a list of 500 fully accredited colleges with annual tuition costs of $350 or less. Write direct to Education Guild, 15 W. Church Road, Saddle River, N.J. 07458. It's $4.95 in paper, but check price and availability before ordering.

INDEPENDENT STUDY, HOME STUDY, AND EXTERNAL DEGREES

Many colleges and universities now have external home study and independent study degree programs. If your home or work situation makes it impossible for you to attend college during regular class hours, you might try one of these avenues to a college degree. Write or call the offices listed, and ask for the latest update on opportunities.

CLEP (COLLEGE LEVEL EXAMINATION PROGRAM)
The CLEP exams are administered by the College Entrance Examination Board (CEEB) and find acceptance in about 17,000 colleges and universities in all 50 states, some of which grant up to two years of college credit for high scores on the tests. CLEP itself awards no credit; it merely offers the testing vehicle so that the scores can be sent to your school, which in turn evaluates them as college credit.

There are five general areas: English composition, humanities, natural Science, math, and social science/history. Each test is 90 minutes long. In addition, there are 47 subject areas, each also 90 minutes. All are multiple-choice, but some also have an essay portion which can be given at the discretion of your school. The areas include Afro-American history, American literature, English composition, money and banking, and tests and measurements. For further information about available tests, write the CEEB, 888 7th Ave., New York, N.Y. 10019. This is a good way to get a head start on your college education if you've been out of high school for a while but have considerable vocational, technical, or on-the-job training.

COLLEGE PROFICIENCY EXAMINATION PROGRAM

Write State Educational Department, 99 Washington Ave., Albany, N.Y. 12230.

Outside New York State write: ACT Proficiency Examination Program, American College Testing Program, Box 168, Iowa City, Iowa 52240.

This program, similar to CLEP, is called CPEP in New York and PEP (the Proficiency Exam Program) elsewhere. The exams are three hours in length and are given nationwide by the American College Testing Program. CPEP/PEP exams are offered at testing centers throughout the country during a two-day testing period four times a year (Feb., May, Aug., and Nov.). Fees are $20–$50.

Areas include arts and sciences (11 exams, including applied music and Shakespeare), criminal justice (2 exams), business (6 exams), Education, health education, foreign languages (French, German, Italian, Russian and Spanish), and nursing.

INDEPENDENT STUDY PROGRAMS

Board for State Academic Awards, 340 Capitol Ave., Hartford, Conn. 06115.

Regents External Degree Program of the University of the State of New York, 99 Washington Ave., Albany, N.Y. 12230.

Thomas A. Edison College, Forrestal Road, Princeton, N.J. 08540.

Empire State College of the State University of New York, Saratoga Springs, N.Y. 12866.

Sources and Resources

External Degree Program of the California State Universities and Colleges, 5670 Wilshire Blvd., Los Angeles, Calif. 90036.

University Without Walls, Union for Experimental Colleges and Universities, Antioch College, Yellow Springs, Ohio 45387 (write for list of participating schools and colleges).

External Degree Program (c/o Bachelor of General Studies Degree Program, College of Continuing Education), Roosevelt University, 430 S. Michigan Ave., Chicago, Ill. 60605.

Independent Study Division, National University Extension Association, 1 Dupont Circle, Suite 360, Washington, D.C. 20036, will furnish a nationwide list of correspondence courses and external degree resources upon request.

CLEP Study Guides are published by Arco Books, Barron's, McGraw-Hill, and Monarch Books.

On-Campus/Off-Campus Degree Programs for Part-time Students, ed. Linda Gordon and Judy Schub (available through the National University Extension Association, 1 Dupont Circle, Suite 360, Washington, D.C. 20036, for $4).

The Weekend Education Source Book by Wilbur Cross. New York: Harper and Row, $6.95 in paper.

Guide to Independent Study Through Correspondence Instruction, published by the National University Extension Association (order from Peterson's Guides, 228 Alexander St., Princeton, N.J. 08540, at $2 plus $1 for postage and handling).

Directory of Accredited Private Home Study Schools (available from the National Home Study Council, 1601 18th St. N.W., Washington, D.C. 20009).

For a comprehensive guide get the 1980–81 *Guide to Independent Study Through Correspondence Instruction* for $2 prepaid (order from the National University Extension Book Order Department, P.O. Box 2123, Princeton, N.J. 08540).

College on Your Own by Gail Thain Parker and Gene R. Hawes. New York: Bantam Books, 1978 (at $6.95 gives a reading list in 22 different subjects; it's a useful guide to a completely independent education or as a brush-up for reentering college).

Two freebies: *The External Degree as a Credential* and *Guide to Undergraduate External Degree Programs in the United States* (both by Carol P. Sosdian and Laure M. Sharp) are available (with a self-addressed gummed label) through Mr. Noel Vivaldi, Publications Management Division, National Institute of Education, 1200 19th Street N.W., Washington, D.C. 20208.

Two more sourcebooks: *College Degrees for Adults* by Wayne Blaze and John Nero (Boston: Beacon Press, 1978, paper) and *National Directory of External Degree Programs* by Alfred Munzert (New York: Hawthorn Books, paper, 1976).

COLLEGE FAIRS AND EXHIBITIONS

For a list of fairs and exhibitions to be held in your area during the academic year write: National Association of College Admission Counselors, 9933 Lawler Ave., Suite 500, Skokie, Ill. 60077.

NATIONAL STUDENT EXCHANGE PROGRAM

It may be more expensive to travel overseas than it used to be, but there are still some excellent exchange student opportunities available for qualified people. Check out these sources of information about taking part in an exciting alternative path to a college degree.

Sophomores and juniors participating in this program can study for up to two semesters at another school and still pay their original school's tuition. Get your school to participate by writing: Bette Worley, Executive Director, National Student Exchange, Indiana University–Purdue University (Fort Wayne), 2101 Coliseum, Ft. Wayne, Ind. 46805.

SUMMER TRAVEL, JOBS, AND STUDENT EXCHANGE PROGRAMS

The 1980 Directory of Overseas Summer Jobs (available through Writers Digest Books, 9933 Alliance Road, Cincinnati, Ohio 45212, for $8.20 including postage and handling).

TESOL (Teaching English as a Second Language), School of Languages and Linguistics, Georgetown University, Washington, D.C. 20057.

American Youth Hostels, Inc., National Headquarters, Delaplane, Va. 22025.

The 1981 Whole World Handbook ($3.95, paper) is available through the Council on International Education Exchange, 777 United Nations Plaza, New York, N.Y. 10017.

Overseas Summer Study Programs (available for $1 through the National Association of Secondary School Principals, 1904 Association Dr., Reston, Va. 22901).

Summer Study Abroad, ed. Gail A. Cohen (available for $6 from the Institute of International Education, 809 United Nations Plaza, New York, N.Y. 10017—new editions are available yearly, usually in mid-February).

Summer jobs in government can be located through The Summer Job Bulletin (Announcement #414), U.S. Civil Service Commission, Washington, D.C. 20415.

A good sourcebook: *International Education: A Directory of Resource Materials on Comparative Education and Study in Another Country* by Lily von Klemperer (Garrett Park Press, Garrett Park, Md. 20766, at $5.95).

For aspiring Anglophiles, try: *Junior Year in Britain* by Barbara H. Pierce (Peterson's Guides, 1979, paper).

Outward Bound training: write Outward Bound, Inc., 384 Field Point Rd., Greenwich, Conn. 06830, or call (800) 243–8520.

INTERNSHIPS, SUMMER AND OTHERWISE

In addition to exchange student opportunities, there are a vast number of internships available for qualified students. The internships forge the links between school and the career you've chosen to follow. They are extremely beneficial if they are done correctly. If your career is covered by the intern concept, you may want to make your summers doubly profitable by getting a head start on your career while you're still in school.

The 1980 National Directory of Summer Internships (available through the Career Planning Office, Haverford College, Haverford, Pa. 19401).

The 1978–80 Directory of Washington Internships and *The 1980–81 Directory of Undergraduate Internship Programs* (each available at $7 through the National Society for Internships and Experimental Education, 1735 1st St. N.W., Suite 601, Washington, D.C. 20006).

For information on student internships available all over the country, write: Washington Center for Learning Alternatives, 1705 DeSales St., N.W., Washington, D.C. 20036.

Also check out: *The International Directory for Youth Internships* (available at $2 from United Nations Headquarters, NGO Youth Caucus, c/o Center for Social Development and Humanitarian Affairs, Room DC–976, United Nations, New York, N.Y. 10017).

STUDENT FILM AWARDS PROGRAMS

The film industry is one of many kinds of businesses that now offer fellowships and award programs that give students a chance to "try out" in a career while they're still enrolled in a degree program. If you're interested in a career in any of the many aspects of the film, don't pass up this opportunity.

Awards of $500 and $1,000 are made annually to students at accredited colleges and universities by the Academy of Motion Picture Arts and Sciences and the Academy Foundation. Categories include animation, documentary, dramatic, and experimental filmmaking. Deadline is typically around April 1. For information write to Director, Educational and Cultural Programs, Academy Foundation, 8949 Wilshire Blvd., Beverly Hills, Calif. 90211.

GENERAL INFORMATION

For general information on educational opportunities, you should write to: The National Center for Educational Brokering, 405 Oak St., Syracuse, N.Y. 13203.